WITHDRAWN

D1300475

OCKHAM'S THEORY OF PROPOSITIONS

160
W670c

Ockham's Theory of Propositions

PART II OF THE SUMMA LOGICAE

*Translated by Alfred J. Freddoso
and Henry Schuurman*

*Introduction
by Alfred J. Freddoso*

UNIVERSITY OF NOTRE DAME PRESS

NOTRE DAME   LONDON

Copyright © 1980 by
University of Notre Dame Press
Notre Dame, Indiana 46556

Library of Congress Cataloging in Publication Data

Ockham, William, d. ca. 1349.
 Ockham's theory of propositions.

 Includes bibliographical references.
 1. Logic—Early works to 1800. 2. Proposition
(Logic) I. Title.
BC60.025213   160   79-18383
ISBN 0-268-01495-7
ISBN 0-268-01496-5 pbk.

Printed in the United States of America

Contents

CAT Jul 19 '82

6-08-82 ABS 18.00

81-6734

ALLEGHENY COLLEGE LIBRARY

Preface

It is something of a philosophical scandal that most of the major works of William of Ockham, himself an Englishman, have yet to be translated into English. The *Summa Logicae*, which contains Ockham's most extensive treatment of logic and philosophy of language, is a case in point. Even given the translation of Part II found here and Michael Loux's recent translation of Part I, more than half of the *Summa Logicae* remains untranslated. We view the present volume, then, as merely a small step in what is, we hope, a continuing movement to make Ockham's writings generally available to readers of English.

But even this small step would have been impossible without the diligent work of the Franciscan Institute, which has already published five volumes of the proposed critical edition of Ockham's philosophical and theological works. Our translation is based on the critical edition of the *Summa Logicae* prepared by Philotheus Boehner, Gedeon Gál, and Stephen Brown and published in 1974 as volume I of Ockham's *Opera Philosophica*. This critical edition also provided many of the references which appear in the notes accompanying our translation.

Our aim has been to make the translation as accurate as possible. Luckily, Ockham's generally lucid prose lends itself to a translation which is both accurate and at least as readable as most logic texts written in English. Occasionally, an example used by Ockham to illustrate a given point does not remain an illustration of that point when translated into English. In such cases we have retained the Latin in the text of the translation and added an explanatory footnote.

The essay preceding the translation focuses on Ockham's semantic account of the truth conditions of various types of propositions. Although it is meant primarily as an introduction to Ockham's semantic theory, it also raises certain systematic issues which that theory might suggest to those interested in contemporary philosophical logic and philosophy of language. Ockham's account of truth conditions will undoubtedly strike many as surprisingly contemporary, though perhaps it is fairer to say that contemporary theories should strike the reader of Ockham as surprisingly medieval.

We wish to thank, first of all, Michael Loux, who first suggested this project to us. He introduced us to Ockham's philosophy and helped us to appreciate its importance, both historical and systematic. We also extend our gratitude to Paul Vincent Spade, who carefully read the entire manuscript and made many helpful suggestions that improved both the translation and the introductory essay, and to Marilyn McCord Adams, who provided several useful comments on the introductory essay.

In addition, Freddoso wishes to thank the Mellon Foundation and the Philosophy Department of Brown University for the opportunity to spend two years as a postdoctoral fellow in a philosophical environment that Ockham himself would have envied. It is only because of this opportunity that the present volume has something other than the status, if any, of a merely possible being. Special thanks are due to Philip Quinn for his typically incisive comments on the introductory essay, and to the members of the Fall 1978 seminar on Ockham's philosophy, whose questions and criticisms led to several improvements in that essay.

Ockham's Theory of Truth Conditions

by Alfred J. Freddoso

1. In Part II of his *Summa Logicae* Ockham's main task is to present a fairly comprehensive account of the truth conditions of propositions, i.e. indicative sentences. Starting with the semantically most simple kinds of propositions and gradually wending his way through more complex and troublesome cases, he hopes to put the reader in a position to determine what is necessary and sufficient for the truth of any proposition and on that basis to discern which inferences are valid and which are not.

This account of truth conditions is in part motivated by ontological concerns. Ockham has already argued in several places that there are no extramental universals or even Scotistic common natures.[1] He contends, rather, that terms like 'universal', 'genus', 'species', etc., are terms of second intention which signify certain mental qualities that are themselves individual in nature and universal or common only in signification. In chapter 2 of Part II he presents us, accordingly, with a theory of predication which presupposes the existence only of individual substances and qualities. In this way he attempts to counter the realist's claim that we cannot account for the truth of even the simplest predication, e.g. 'Socrates is a man', without presupposing the existence of shared entities which are really (or at least formally) distinct from the individuals that possess them or are partially constituted by them. Ockham then in chapters 3 through 6 extends this account of predication to present-tense non-modal universal and particular propositions, thus insuring that none of these propositions involve a commitment to the existence of non-

1

individuals. Finally, in chapters 7 through 10 he explicates the truth conditions of past-tense, future-tense, and modal propositions in terms of the past truth, future truth, and modal status, respectively, of present-tense non-modal propositions. Hence, the role of general terms in these semantically more complex propositions is seen to be no more problematic from an ontological point of view than their role in simpler kinds of propositions.

However, Ockham's reasons for proposing his theory of truth conditions do not all stem from ontological considerations. For he is convinced that ignorance of logic in general—and of propositions and their properties in particular—leads to errors and confusions in theology and the other disciplines. This theme is repeatedly emphasized in Part II, with "modern" theologians bearing the brunt of Ockham's criticism.

Consonant with this pragmatic motive is Ockham's interest as a logician in clarifying the sense and logical structure of semantically more complicated propositions in terms of their relations to simpler propositions. He takes present-tense non-modal categorical propositions as his starting point and explicates their truth conditions directly in terms of the notion of supposition. In each case the truth of such a proposition depends on what its subject and predicate supposit for and how the suppositions of the subject and predicate are related to one another. Hence, the notion of supposition plays a role in Ockham's account which is roughly analogous to the role played by the notion of satisfaction in contemporary semantic theory. More complicated propositions are then explicated, as noted above, in terms of certain semantic properties of present-tense non-modal propositions. Ockham's project in Part II, then, is as much an expression of a general theory of language, including tense and modality, as it is an outgrowth of his theory of universals.

In his treatment of exponible propositions (chapters 11 through 20) we find Ockham engaging in a type of analysis which, as will become clear, is similar to the type of analysis exemplified by Russell's theory of descriptions. Here Ockham deals with propositions containing connotative terms, verbs such as 'begin' and 'cease', or syncategorematic terms like 'except', 'only', and 'insofar as'. In each case he tries to show that such propositions are

reducible to conjunctions or disjunctions of the sorts of propositions already treated in earlier chapters.

The next section of Part II (chapters 21 through 29) is devoted
to a discussion of conversions, i.e. inferences involving propositions related in such a way that the subject of one is the predicate of the other and the predicate of one is the subject of the
other. This tract on conversions is a necessary prelude to the
treatment of syllogistic inference found in Part III–1 of the *Summa Logicae*. However, in what follows I will allude to this section of Part II mainly in order to shed light on certain remarks
that Ockham makes about truth conditions.

The last section of Part II (chapters 30 through 37) deals with
the truth conditions of hypothetical propositions, i.e. conditional,
conjunctive, disjunctive, causal, temporal, and local propositions.
I will briefly try to show how this part of Ockham's account of
truth conditions can best be understood as related to his earlier
treatment of non-hypothetical, i.e. categorical, propositions.

In what follows, then, I will lay out and discuss the most important features of Ockham's account of truth conditions, noting
along the way certain questions and problems that it engenders.
The reader is assumed to have some familiarity with the following features of Ockham's theory of terms explicated in Part I of
the *Summa Logicae*: the relation of the mental language to spoken and written language, the distinction between categorematic
and syncategorematic terms, and the distinction between absolute and connotative terms.[2]

2.   In order to understand Ockham's account of predication
we must first understand the notions of signification and supposition as he employs them. Signification in its origin is a psycho-
logical notion. A sign signifies a thing just in case it brings that
thing to mind or, in Boethius' words, "constitutes an understanding of it." According to Ockham a mental categorematic term
naturally signifies whatever it brings to mind, while its spoken or
written counterpart conventionally signifies the same thing or
things in virtue of being subordinated to the mental term in
question. But what is signified by a categorematic term—especially a general or common term like 'man'? Since Ockham

repudiates the postulation of both extramental universals and
common natures, he rejects both the view that a general term
signifies a universal that can be shared by many individuals and
the view that a general term signifies a common nature. He
claims, rather, that general terms—no less than singular terms
like proper names—bring to mind only individual substances and
qualities. For example, the term 'man' brings to mind all individual men in a "confused" manner, i.e. in such a way that it
brings one to mind no more and no less than it brings any other
to mind. In what follows I will take this generic notion of signification as primitive.

When the concept of signification is transferred to semantic
theory, a categorematic term 'T' is said to signify each entity
of which it is true to say "This is possibly (a) T." (Since 'T'
is used here and below as a schematic letter, my use of quotes
in the principles which follow is not, strictly speaking, correct.
It is, however, more convenient and should not lead to any mis-
understanding.) This, at least, is the primary sense of signification, which can be captured somewhat redundantly by the following principle:

(P1) A term 'T' primarily signifies a thing x if and only if (i) 'T' signifies x and (ii) at least one of the following propositions is true,
where 'this' indicates x: 'This is (a) T', 'This was (a) T', 'This
will be (a) T', 'This is possibly (a) T'.

The term 'man', to put it somewhat indelicately, primarily signifies all present, past, future, and merely possible men. (Later I
will argue that Ockham's semantic theory need not presuppose
that there are merely past, merely future, or merely possible
beings. If that is so, then (P1) would have to be restated more
carefully.)[3]

An absolute term, e.g. 'man', 'animal', 'Socrates', is such that
it primarily signifies whatever it signifies. However, connotative
terms, e.g. 'white', 'chimera', 'non-man', bring to mind things of
which they are not truly predicable by means of any sort of
verb—present-tense, past-tense, future-tense, or modal. Just which
things are brought to mind in this way is, according to Ockham,
revealed by a close examination of the nominal definition of the
connotative term in question. (Only connotative terms have

nominal definitions in the strict sense, i.e. definitions which are altogether synonymous with their definienda.)[4] For example, 'white' signifies individual whitenesses, even though it is impossible that a whiteness be white. For one who understands the term 'white' knows that a white thing is something which has whiteness, or something in which whiteness inheres. That is, one who understands the term 'white' and can use it correctly knows, at least implicitly, that its nominal definition is 'something having whiteness'. Again, even though it is impossible, according to Ockham, that a chimera exist, still the figment term 'chimera' brings to mind goats and cows, since its nominal definition is 'an animal composed of a goat and a cow', where the terms 'goat' and 'cow' occur in oblique cases rather than in the nominative case. Similar considerations apply to infinite terms (e.g. 'non-man'), privative terms (e.g. 'blind'), relational terms (e.g. 'father'), and transcendental terms other than 'being' (e.g. 'one'). Hence, (P1) does not capture all the ways in which a categorematic term can stand in the basic semantic relation of signification to a given individual substance or quality. So Ockham recognizes a second type of signification, which he sometimes calls 'secondary signification'. Unfortunately, he never gives a precise characterization of this notion, i.e. one which marks off all and only those terms which he claims at one time or another to have secondary signification. The following, somewhat inelegant, characterization is tantamount to that suggested by Paul Spade after a lengthy discussion of the difficulties surrounding this issue:[5]

> (P2) A term 'T' secondarily signifies a thing x if and only if (i) 'T' has a nominal definition in the strict sense and (ii) either (a) there is a term 'T*', distinct from 'T', such that 'T*' occurs in an oblique case in the fully expanded nominal definition of 'T', and 'T*' primarily signifies x; or (b) 'T' signifies x but does not primarily signify x.

Thus, while an absolute term primarily signifies whatever it signifies, a connotative term is such that it signifies something secondarily.

It is important, I think, not to take (P1) and (P2) as expressing definitions in any standard sense. For one can have all the concepts needed to understand (P1) and (P2) without accepting them. In fact, since many of Ockham's contemporaries rejected his account of primary and secondary signification, it would have been foolhardy for him to assert that principles like (P1) and (P2) are true in virtue of the meanings of their terms in the way in which, say, 'If Socrates is a man, then Socrates is rational' might be construed as true in virtue of the meanings of the terms 'man' and 'rational'. Neither are (P1) and (P2) merely stipulative definitions, since Ockham undoubtedly takes them to reflect a correct understanding of the notion of signification used by his predecessors and contemporaries. It is best, I think, to regard (P1) and (P2) as proposals which emanate in part from Ockham's theory of universals and whose adequacy cannot be judged apart from that of the theory of predication that is built upon them.

Whereas signification is a characteristic which a categorematic term has independently of its use in any given proposition, supposition is a characteristic which it has only as a part of a proposition. The notion of supposition is sometimes equated with the contemporary notion of reference or, perhaps better, denotation. However, as we shall see, this equation holds only if (a) a predicate term may be said to have reference or denotation and (b) a term may be said to have reference or denotation even when it has no referent or denotatum.

A term has supposition when by means of the proposition in which it occurs it is asserted to stand for something. The notion of supposition plays a central role in Ockham's account of the truth conditions of simple predications. The three types of proper supposition are personal, simple, and material. Of these personal supposition is the most important. For on Ockham's view, in any proposition in which a categorematic term constitutes an extreme, i.e. the whole subject or the whole predicate, that term may have personal supposition.[6] That is, there is a reading of that proposition on which the term in question is asserted to supposit for whatever, if anything, it primarily signifies. The following principle seems to accord with what Ockham says:

(P3) There is a reading of proposition 'P' on which term 'T' has personal supposition if and only if (i) 'T' is an extreme in 'P' and (ii) either (a) there is something which 'T' primarily signifies or

(b) there is something which 'T' secondarily signifies or (c) 'T' is a demonstrative pronoun.[7]

Hence, in 'A man is an animal' both 'man' and 'animal' have personal supposition. In this case 'man' supposits personally for all men and 'animal' supposits personally for all animals. Moreover, in 'A chimera is a man', the term 'chimera' has personal supposition, even though, if we follow Ockham, it is impossible that there be anything for which 'chimera' supposits. However, in 'And is a conjunction', only the term 'conjunction' has personal supposition, since the term 'and' does not fulfill any of the three conditions listed under (ii) of (P3). In short, only categorematic terms and demonstrative pronouns may have personal supposition. Further, just which things a term with personal supposition supposits for in a given proposition is a function of two factors, namely (a) which things, if any, it primarily signifies, and (b) the tense and modality of the proposition in question. We shall see more of this below.

A term, whether categorematic or syncategorematic, has material supposition, generally speaking, when it is taken to supposit for just one spoken or written expression. Analogously, a term has simple supposition in a given proposition when it is taken to supposit for just one mental expression. Let us take 'term "T" supposits for thing x' as a primitive locution roughly synonymous with 'term "T" denotes a thing x'. Then, since a term with material or simple supposition cannot fail to have a denotatum, we can characterize these two types of supposition as follows:

(P4) A term 'T' has material supposition in a proposition 'P' on reading R if and only if (i) 'T' is an extreme in 'P' and (ii) either (a) 'T' is a spoken or written term and on R 'T' supposits only for itself in 'P' or (b) 'T' is a mental term and on R 'T' supposits in 'P' only for the spoken or written term which is subordinated to 'T'.[8]

(P5) A term 'T' has simple supposition in a proposition 'P' on reading R if and only if (i) 'T' is an extreme in 'P' and (ii) either (a) 'T' is a mental term and on R 'T' supposits only for itself in 'P' or (b) 'T' is a spoken or written term and on R 'T' supposits in 'P' only for the mental term to which 'T' is subordinated.

Hence, on one reading of the written proposition 'Man is a three-

letter word', the term 'man' supposits materially, since it supposits for itself. Again, on one reading of the spoken proposition
'Man is a species', the term 'man' supposits simply, since it supposits for the mental term 'man'. These examples illustrate Ockham's rule that a term may have material or simple supposition
in a given proposition only if the other extreme of that proposition pertains to terms. That is, the other extreme must primarily
signify mental or conventional terms.[9] In the above examples
'three-letter word' primarily signifies written words, and 'species',
given Ockham's anti-Platonism, signifies mental terms primarily.

With these brief remarks about signification and supposition
behind us, we can now turn to Ockham's account of predication.
He begins by discussing the simplest sort of proposition, namely,
a present-tense non-modal singular proposition which is not equivalent to a hypothetical, i.e. compound, proposition and both of
whose extremes are in the nominative case. For ease of reference
let us call such propositions 'S-propositions'.

Ockham deals explicitly with two S-propositions, namely,

(1)   This is an angel
and
(2)   Socrates is a man.

A proposition like (1) or (2) is true, he tells us, just in case its
subject and predicate supposit for the same thing. Since all of
the extremes in these two propositions may have only personal
supposition, we must first formulate the necessary and sufficient
conditions for a term's suppositing personally for a thing in a
given proposition. It is a general rule that a term may supposit
personally only for a thing which it primarily signifies. However,
if we assume for the present that a term may primarily signify
merely past, merely future, and merely possible beings, then it
is not the case that a term always supposits for every individual
that it primarily signifies. In present-tense non-modal propositions, which concern us here, a term supposits personally only
for those of its primary significata of which it is truly predicable
by means of a present-tense verb. Thus,

(P6)   A term 'T' supposits personally for an individual x on reading R
       of a present-tense non-modal proposition 'P' if and only if (i) R

is a reading on which 'T' has personal supposition in 'P' and (ii) 'This is (a) T' is true, where 'this' indicates x.

(From now on I will eliminate reference to readings of propositions when it is clear that the only reading of a given proposition is one in which both extremes have personal supposition.)

Hence, 'angel' in (1) supposits for all presently existing angels (if there are any), and 'man' in (2) supposits personally for all presently existing men (if there are any). Likewise, 'Socrates' in (2) supposits for Socrates (if he exists), and 'this' in (1) supposits personally for whatever presently existing thing (if any) it is taken to indicate by the person who formulates (1).

It is clear from what Ockham says in other places that an affirmative S-proposition is true only if both its subject and predicate supposit for something. Hence, if Socrates does not exist, then even 'Socrates is Socrates' is false. As a result, the most exact formulation of Ockham's account of the truth conditions of (2) is this:

(3)   'Socrates is a man' is true if and only if there is something for which both 'Socrates' and 'man' supposit in 'Socrates is a man'.

(In what follows I will generally omit from the right-hand side the repetition of the proposition whose truth conditions are being given. However, such a repetition should always be understood, since a term has supposition only in a proposition.) Accordingly, (2) is true just in case Socrates exists and is one of the things for which 'man' supposits in (2). A similar account holds for all affirmative S-propositions. Let 'N' stand for a proper name or demonstrative pronoun and let 'P' stand for a term capable of occupying the predicate position of an S-proposition. Then,

(P7)   An affirmative S-proposition, 'N is P', is true if and only if there is something for which both 'N' and 'P' supposit.

(Although 'N is P' is, strictly speaking, a propositional schema rather than a proposition, there is no danger of confusion, I believe, if for the sake of simplicity I allude to it and other propositional schemata as propositions.)

Negative S-propositions are treated as follows:

(P8) A negative S-proposition, 'N is not P', is true if and only if there is
nothing for which both 'N' and 'P' supposit.

Therefore, a negative S-proposition is true just in case any one of
the following conditions obtains: (a) there is nothing for which its
subject supposits, (b) there is nothing for which its predicate supposits, or (c) there is something for which its subject supposits
and something for which its predicate supposits, but nothing for
which both its subject and predicate supposit.

Further, this account also holds for propositions—or for readings of propositions—in which one of the extremes has material
or simple supposition, since such terms play a role analogous to
that of proper names with personal supposition. Hence,

(4) 'Man is a species' (on the reading on which 'man' has simple supposition) is true if and only if there is something for which both
'man' and 'species' supposit.

Given that we are concerned with the reading on which 'man'
has simple supposition, 'man' here supposits for the mental term
'man'. Moreover, the term 'species' has personal supposition in
this proposition and has the term 'man' as one of its supposita,
since it primarily signifies this term. Hence, on this reading the
proposition 'Man is a species' is true.

Given Ockham's account of signification and supposition, it is
not difficult to see that his theory of simple predication is consistent with his avowed anti-realism on the question of universals.
For a close inspection of (P1)–(P8), plus perhaps the treatment
of abstract terms found in Part I of the *Summa Logicae*, reveals
that a term never supposits in an S-proposition for anything that
is not an individual substance or quality. According to Ockham,
then, we do not have to appeal to universals or common natures
in order to explicate the truth conditions of S-propositions.

From what has been said so far it is also clear that Ockham's
account of predication stands in marked contrast to at least two
alternative accounts. According to the first of these alternatives
a common term like 'man' in 'Socrates is a man' supposits for or
denotes a universal.[10] On this account an affirmative S-proposition is true just in case its subject term supposits for something
which stands in the relation of exemplification (perhaps signified

by the copula) to the universal for which the predicate term supposits. By contrast, according to Ockham it is required for the truth of such a proposition that both its subject and predicate supposit for the same thing.

According to the second alternative account, the subject of such a proposition supposits for something which—if the proposition is true—satisfies a function of the form '. . . is F', where 'F' stands for a predicate in Ockham's sense. Hence, the proponent of this alternative account denies that the subject and predicate of an S-proposition both have the role of suppositing for or denoting something. This alternative is, of course, the standard contemporary account of predication and finds its most important formulation in Frege's writings—although certain philosophers claim that at least the rudiments of the Fregean theory can be found in the writings of one or another medieval philosopher.[11] Of course, contemporary philosophers differ over just what ontological consequences this function-argument metaphor has when it is employed in semantics. But whatever these ontological consequences might be, it is clear that Ockham's theory is incompatible with such an account on semantic grounds alone. For even though Ockham does acknowledge in certain cases an asymmetry between the roles of subject and predicate, he insists that this asymmetry merely reflects a difference in the way in which subjects and predicates may be taken to supposit in certain contexts. Hence, even in such contexts both subject and predicate have the property of supposition. Moreover, such asymmetry is absent in the case of S-propositions and thus lends no support, in Ockham's eyes, to the claim that the semantic roles of subject and predicate are in general wholly disparate.

Now if we regard Ockham's account of simple predication as including his account of signification as well as (P7) and (P8), then a third alternative suggests itself. For one might accept (P7) and (P8) with equanimity and yet insist that predicates which are common terms, e.g. 'man' in (2), supposit for individuals only in virtue of the fact that those individuals exemplify or possess the universal or common nature signified by the common term in question. For example, 'man' in (2) supposits for individual men only because those individuals exemplify or possess the universal humanity or human nature. Such a proposal is obviously based on a theory of signification that differs radically from Ockham's. In fact, it employs a distinction between signification and supposition that is roughly equivalent to the distinction between sense and reference as it is used by certain contemporary Platonists. That is, a common term signifies (has as its sense) a universal (property) and supposits for (has as its reference) the individuals which exemplify that universal. It is clear from what has been said that Ockham rejects this account of signification. On the other hand, the proponent of this third alternative agrees with Ockham that the predicates of propositions like (2) have supposition, just as their subjects do.

Ockham appears to have something like this third alternative in mind in chapter 2 of Part II, although this might not at first be evident. Consider the following passage:

> . . . by means of propositions like 'Socrates is a man' and 'Socrates is an animal' it is not asserted that Socrates has humanity or animality. . . .
> Rather, it is asserted that Socrates is truly a man and is truly an animal.
> Nor indeed is it asserted that Socrates is the predicate 'man' or the predicate 'animal'. Rather, it is asserted that he is a thing for which the predicate 'man' or the predicate 'animal' supposits.[12]

Ockham holds that a proposition like (1) or (2) is not exponible. That is, it is not such that it can be expounded in terms of other propositions which reveal more perspicuously its underlying logical form. One reason for this is such a proposition contains only absolute terms. Propositions containing connotative terms, on the other hand, are exponible and thus equivalent to hypothetical propositions. For example, according to Ockham the term 'white' is a connotative term which secondarily signifies individual whitenesses. Hence, 'Socrates is white' is not an S-proposition. Rather, its underlying logical form is most clearly revealed by the following proposition: 'Socrates exists and a whiteness inheres in Socrates'.

Now except for figment terms and infinite terms, common terms belonging to the category of substance, e.g. 'man', 'animal', 'plant', etc., are, according to Ockham, absolute terms, as are proper names and demonstrative pronouns. Hence, propositions which, like (1) and (2), contain no connotative terms and no syncategorematic elements other than the copula, are not exponible. They wear their logical form on their sleeve, as it were, and cannot be rendered more perspicuous by paraphrase. This is the force of Ockham's claim in the above passage that no more is asserted by (2) than that Socrates is truly a man.

However, the alternative account under discussion in effect treats all common terms, including all those in the category of substance, as connotative. For on this account each common term signifies an entity, namely, a universal or common nature, of which it cannot be truly predicated. But if this is so, then even propositions like (1) and (2) are exponible. For example, 'Socrates is a man' is more perspicuously rendered by 'Socrates exists and Socrates has humanity', or by 'Socrates exists and humanity is in Socrates', or by some similar realist variant. And it is precisely the claim that propositions like (2) are exponible which Ockham rejects when he denies that (2) involves the assertion that Socrates has humanity.

Strictly speaking, the proponent of this alternative account would in effect limit the designation 'S-proposition' to at most those propositions in which both the subject and the predicate are either proper names or demonstrative pronouns. Thus, he should not consider (P7) applicable to 'Socrates is a man'. Nevertheless, one who defends this account could agree with Ockham in holding that (2) is true just in case Socrates is a thing for which the predicate 'man' supposits. That is, he could accept with Ockham the following:

(5)   'Socrates is a man' is true if and only if there is some individual for which both 'Socrates' and 'man' supposit.

However, he would also accept

(6)   Socrates is a man if and only if Socrates exists and has humanity.

Ockham spends the better part of chapter 2 trying to show that (6) and other realist variations on it are false. For even on the assumption that Socrates is a man, he argues, propositions like 'Socrates has humanity' and 'Humanity is in Socrates' are, taken literally, false. The reader can judge for himself the cogency of the arguments that Ockham presents in support of this claim. But it is clear all along that Ockham assumes that his opponent accepts (5).

Perhaps, then, a theory of predication is best understood as involving, at least potentially, two sorts of analysis. The first sort, illustrated by (6), takes place at the level of the object language—or at least contains no allusion to the semantic roles of the subject and predicate of the proposition which occurs on its left-hand side. The purpose of such an analysis is to clarify the logical form, and thus the ontological presuppositions, of the simple predication in question. Ockham claims, against his realist opponent, that an S-proposition does not admit of such an analysis or, alternatively, that it is its own such analysis. The second sort of analysis is irreducibly metalinguistic. Its purpose is to explicate the truth conditions of a simple predication in terms of the semantic properties of its components. That is, it explains how those components must be linked to the ontology revealed by the first sort of analysis if the simple predication in question is to be true. (5) serves as an illustration of this second type of analysis. So Ockham's full account of predication differs from the first and second alternatives mentioned above (at least) with respect to the results of this second type of analysis, while it differs from the third alternative with respect to the results of the first sort of analysis.

Before moving on to Ockham's treatment of other types of propositions, I wish to comment briefly on two ways of construing (P7) and (P8) which seem to me to be mistaken and to engender needless difficulties. The first is suggested by Father Boehner, who claims that in chapter 2 of Part II Ockham is explicating the connotation of the term 'true' (as applied to propositions) in terms of the coincidence of the supposition of the subject and predicate terms.[13] This means that Ockham's project is at least in part to formulate the correct nominal definition of 'true' and that the definition he offers is something like 'proposition whose subject and predicate supposit for the same thing'.

The most obvious objection to Boehner's claim is that the definition of 'true' which he takes Ockham to be proposing is inadequate even as applied to S-propositions, since it does not define the truth of negative S-propositions.[14] And even though Ockham—clearly through an oversight—does not deal explicitly with negative S-propositions in chapter 2, (P8) above is a necessary addendum to his account of simple predication and one which is consistent with remarks he makes about negative propositions both in Part I and in later sections of Part II.[15]

However, a more serious objection to Boehner's claim is this: there is simply no good reason to believe that in Part II Ockham is trying to define the term 'true' at all. It seems more likely that he accepts something like the Aristotelian definition, e.g. 'proposition signifying of what is that it is or of what is not that it is not'. In Part II he is trying to formulate the conditions under which various types of propositions fulfill that definition. But the definition of truth remains the same throughout.

This way of viewing Ockham's project obviates one serious problem that Boehner poses for him and other medieval logicians. For if we assume that Ockham is defining truth in terms of the supposition of subject and predicate, then it is not clear how this definition can apply to hypothetical propositions (or even, as we shall see, to certain types of categorical propositions). However, no such problem arises if Ockham accepts throughout something like the Aristotelian definition of 'true' and is simply trying to formulate the conditions under which propositions of various kinds are true. For it is no more surprising that the truth conditions of, say, a disjunctive proposition differ from those of an S-proposition than it is that the truth conditions of an affirmative S-proposition differ from those of a negative S-proposition.

The second issue that I wish to comment on is raised by Marilyn McCord Adams.[16] In the present context the problem can be stated as follows. (P7) and (P8) are circular, at least in cases where both the subject and the predicate have personal supposition. For in (P7) and (P8) truth is defined in terms of supposition and in (P6) a term's suppositing personally for a thing is defined in terms of the truth of propositions of the form 'This is (a) T', which are themselves S-propositions when 'T' stands for an absolute term.

The proper response to this problem is simply to point out that (P6), (P7), and (P8) are not properly construed as definitions. I have already argued this in the case of (P7) and (P8). Likewise, (P6) merely explicates the conditions which must obtain in order for a term to supposit personally for a thing in a present-tense non-modal proposition. However, it does not define the term 'supposit' or even the expression 'supposit personally for something'. Supposition must, I believe, be regarded either

ALLEGHENY COLLEGE LIBRARY

as a primitive notion or as defined in terms of the primitive notion of a term's taking the place of (or being asserted to take the
place of) something within a propositional context.[17]

However, perhaps the problem of circularity can be stated more
forcefully as follows. (P7) and (P8) are meant to provide us with
criteria for determining whether a given S-proposition is true. But
according to (P7) and (P8) we must first know what, if anything,
the subject and predicate terms of the S-proposition in question
supposit for. However, according to (P6) we can know what these
terms supposit for only if we first know the truth value of certain
S-propositions of the form 'This is T'. Thus, (P7) and (P8) can
serve as criteria for determining the truth value of S-propositions
only if we already can determine whether certain S-propositions
are true or false. Thus, Ockham's account of simple predication
suffers from a circularity which renders it useless as a general cri-
terion for determining the truth or falsity of S-propositions.

It is clear, however, that Ockham is not attempting to provide
us here with epistemic criteria for determining the truth value of
S-propositions. In fact, he would surely agree that we can ascertain the truth value of many S-propositions without recourse at
all to the notion of supposition. Rather, he is trying to determine
the semantic relations which obtain between the terms of a given
S-proposition and the individuals which compose the world if and
only if the S-proposition in question is true. Such an account is
independent of our knowing or being able to determine whether
those conditions actually obtain. This latter is a concern for the
theory of knowledge, which Ockham deals with in other places.
Of course, in certain instances the theory of truth conditions
might help us to determine the truth value of a given proposition. But that is not its primary purpose. For in Part II Ockham
is not asking how one determines whether propositions are true.
Rather, he is asking what semantic conditions are necessary and
sufficient for the truth of given types of propositions—whether
or not anyone is actually in a position to determine their truth
values.

3. In chapters 3 through 6 of Part II Ockham discusses present-
tense non-modal particular and universal propositions. A particular
proposition is typically one whose subject is a common term de-

termined by a particular sign, such as 'some' or 'certain', and not preceded by a negation. Examples are 'Some man is Socrates', 'Some man is an animal', and 'Some man is every animal'. Ockham also endorses the view that such a proposition is always interchangeable with the corresponding indefinite proposition, which can be formed in English by replacing the particular sign that determines the subject with the indefinite article. Thus, 'Some man is an animal' is interchangeable with 'A man is an animal'. It is crucial to keep this in mind in order not to be misled by examples in which Ockham uses indefinite propositions. For he is aware that such propositions are sometimes used in Latin, as they are in English, for conditional propositions. For example, 'A man is an animal' is sometimes used for 'If something is a man, it is an animal'. Ockham insists, however, that this is not the proper and literal use of an indefinite proposition. Whether one agrees or not, Ockham himself throughout the *Summa Logicae* is fairly consistent in treating indefinite propositions as interchangeable with the corresponding particular propositions and in distinguishing both from the corresponding conditional propositions. There is no danger of confusion as long as one remembers this.

A universal proposition is typically one whose subject is a common term which is determined by a universal sign such as 'every', 'no', or 'both', and which is not preceded by a negation that determines the whole proposition. Some examples are 'Every man is Socrates', 'Every man is an animal', and 'Every man is every animal'. In this section I will discuss for the most part just those universal propositions in which the universal signs range over any number of individuals distributively. 'Every' and 'no' are such signs.

There are eight different types of present-tense non-modal particular and universal propositions which are such that their truth conditions either are explicitly formulated by Ockham or can be reconstructed from what he does say explicitly. The first four are the traditional A-proposition (universal affirmative), I-proposition (particular affirmative), E-proposition (universal negative) and O-proposition (particular negative). In each of these cases the predicate is either a singular term or a common term that is not determined by a universal sign. Their truth conditions can be formulated as follows:

(P9) A present-tense non-modal A-proposition, 'Every A is B', is true if and only if (i) there is something for which 'A' supposits and (ii) there is nothing for which 'A' supposits and for which 'B' does not supposit.

(P10) A present-tense non-modal I-proposition, 'Some A is B', is true if and only if there is something for which both 'A' and 'B' supposit.

(P11) A present-tense non-modal E-proposition, 'No A is B', is true if and only if there is nothing for which both 'A' and 'B' supposit.

(P12) A present-tense non-modal O-proposition, 'Some A is not B', is true if and only if either (i) there is nothing for which 'A' supposits or (ii) there is something for which 'A' supposits and for which 'B' does not supposit.

As with affirmative S-propositions, an affirmative universal or particular proposition is true only if there is something for which its subject term supposits and something for which its predicate term supposits. Hence, if there are no men, then 'Every man is an animal' is false, while its contradictory, 'Some man is not an animal', and its contrary, 'No man is an animal', are both true. ('Some man is not an animal', however, must be carefully distinguished from 'Some man is a non-animal'. The latter is an I-proposition and thus false if there are no men. The use of infinite terms like 'non-animal' will be discussed below.) Thus, for Ockham the inference from an A-proposition to the corresponding I-proposition is valid whether or not anything exists. The same holds for the inference from an E-proposition to the corresponding O-proposition.

Corresponding to the four traditional forms of universal and particular propositions are four other forms, which I will call A'-propositions, I'-propositions, E'-propositions, and O'-propositions. In all such propositions the predicate is a common term determined by a universal sign. Ockham discusses only the first two of these forms. However, the other two are their contradictories and so it is not difficult to formulate their truth conditions on the basis of what he says explicitly:[18]

(P13) A present-tense non-modal A'-proposition, 'Every A is every B', is true if and only if (i) 'A' supposits for exactly one thing and (ii) 'B' supposits for exactly one thing and (iii) there is something for which both 'A' and 'B' supposit.

(P14) A present-tense non-modal I'-proposition, 'Some A is every B', is true if and only if (i) there is something for which 'A' and 'B' both supposit and (ii) 'B' supposits for exactly one thing.

(P15) A present-tense non-modal E'-proposition, 'No A is every B', is true if and only if either (i) there is nothing for which both 'A' and 'B' supposit or (ii) it is not the case that 'B' supposits for exactly one thing.

(P16) A present-tense non-modal O'-proposition, 'Some A is not every B', is true if and only if either (i) it is not the case that 'A' supposits for exactly one thing, or (ii) it is not the case that 'B' supposits for exactly one thing, or (iii) there is nothing for which both 'A' and 'B' supposit.

The inferential relations which hold among these propositions mirror exactly those which hold among their traditional counterparts. Furthermore, the inferential relations which hold between these propositions and their traditional counterparts can easily be formulated by examining (P9)–(P16).

Ockham thus extends to present-tense non-modal particular and universal propositions the same sort of account which he gives of the truth conditions of S-propositions. And, once again, his theory of predication—construed here to include his theory of significa- tion—guarantees that the truth of particular and universal proposi- tions does not presuppose the existence of non-individual things.

One reason why I have given a prominent place to (P13)–(P16) is that they help to shed some light on a problem which is cur- rently being debated by students of Ockham's logic. The problem is this: how can one relate the above theory of truth conditions for propositions containing quantifiers to the putative rudimen- tary theory of quantification found in Ockham's discussion of the modes of common personal supposition (MCPS) in chapters 69 through 75 of Part I of the *Summa Logicae*?

Some writers suggest that in Part I Ockham is trying to formu- late necessary and sufficient conditions for the truth of proposi- tions containing quantifiers by analyzing such propositions, via the MCPS, into conjunctions and disjunctions of propositions in which only singular terms occur—namely, singular terms composed of a demonstrative adjective and the common terms which served as the subject and predicate of the original proposition.[19] An example might help here. In the I-proposition 'Some man is an animal' both the subject and the predicate, Ockham tells us, have determinate personal supposition. For 'Some man is an animal' implies the disjunctive proposition 'This man is an animal or that man is an animal . . .' and so on for each man. That is, one can validly 'descend' under the term 'man' to a disjunctive proposition, in which singular terms composed of a demonstrative adjective and the term 'man' are the subjects of the various disjuncts. Likewise, 'Some man is an animal' implies the disjunctive proposition 'Some man is this animal or some man is that animal . . .' and so on for each animal. That is, a similar descent can be performed under the term 'animal'. And in both cases any one of the disjuncts implies the original I-proposition. Hence, if we perform both of these descents we can, at least in principle, formulate a proposition which is strictly equivalent to the original I-proposition and in which all the terms are singular terms having discrete supposition. This can be shown somewhat more formally as follows. Let $\{AD/`A\text{'}\}$, following Michael Loux's convention, designate the set of all those things, if any, for which the term 'A' supposits in a present-tense non-modal proposition.[20] Further, replace Ockham's demonstratives with numerical subscripts, so that 'A_1', 'A_2', etc., are singular terms corresponding to 'this A', 'that A', etc. Then we can formulate the truth conditions for an I-proposition, schematized by 'Some A is B', in the following way:

(7) 'Some A is B' is true if and only if
    (i) $\{AD/`A\text{'}\}$ is not empty;
and (ii) $\{[(A_1$ is $B_1)$ or $(A_1$ is $B_2)$ or . . . or $(A_1$ is $B_n)]$
     or $[(A_2$ is $B_1)$ or $(A_2$ is $B_2)$ or . . . or $(A_2$ is $B_n)]$

            .
            .
            .

     or $[(A_n$ is $B_1)$ or $(A_n$ is $B_2)$ or . . . or $(A_n$ is $B_n)]$,
     where A_1-A_n exhaust $\{AD/`A\text{'}\}$ and $B_1$-$B_n$ exhaust $\{AD/`B\text{'}\}\}$.

(7) seems to work fairly well—as well, it seems, as (P10). Moreover, Ockham gives rules for assigning modes of common personal supposition to the subjects and predicates of other types of propositions containing quantifiers. To complete the picture, a term with confused and distributive supposition is such that one (a)

can validly descend from it to a conjunctive proposition of the type in question and (b) cannot validly ascend to it from any of the singular propositions which serve as the conjuncts. A term with merely confused supposition is such that one (a) can validly descend from it only to a proposition with a disjunctive extreme (and not to a disjunctive proposition) and (b) can validly ascend to it from any of the singulars. It appears, then, that in Part I Ockham is giving an account of the truth conditions for propositions containing quantifiers, even though he never explicitly claims that this is the project he has in mind.

Unfortunately, one can attribute such a project to Ockham in Part I only if he is also willing to attribute to Ockham a mistake which a logician of his stature would hardly be expected to make. For, as Gareth Matthews has pointed out, Ockham tells us that the predicate of an O-proposition has confused and distributive supposition.[21] Thus, one can descend under the predicate of 'Some man is not an animal' to the conjunctive proposition 'Some man is not this animal and some man is not that animal . . .' and so on for each animal. However, although such an inference is valid, its converse is clearly not valid. Hence, if Ockham is here attempting to provide us with a theory of quantification, i.e. with an account of the sufficient as well as necessary conditions of the truth of propositions containing quantifiers, then he has blundered by assigning confused and distributive supposition to the predicate of an O-proposition. But surely Ockham would not have made such an elementary mistake. Moreover, a close reading of the text reveals that he never asserts that in every instance a descent of the appropriate type will yield a proposition that is equivalent to the original proposition.

Nevertheless, some who hold that the account of the MCPS constitutes Ockham's theory of quantification have pointed out, correctly, that the defect just alluded to can easily be rectified by assigning merely confused supposition to the predicate of an O-proposition.[22] For the following biconditional is true: 'Some man is not an animal if and only if some man is not this animal or that animal . . .' and so on for each animal. Since this is the only case in which Ockham's own assignment of a mode of common personal supposition does not yield equivalence, it is perhaps

not unreasonable to conjecture that he simply made a careless
mistake in this one isolated instance. Even Matthews does not
seem to regard the objection in question as conclusive. Rather,
he is more concerned with problems that arise when the common
term under which a descent is to be made either is empty or has
exactly one suppositum.

However, we are now in a position to see that the case in question is not an isolated one. For a theory of quantification based
on the account of the MCPS is also clearly inadequate when applied to E'-, A'-, and I'- propositions. Moreover, given Ockham's
interest in propositions of these three forms, it is surely the case
that he would have noticed this deficiency and taken steps to
correct it—if, that is, he had been proposing a theory of quantification in Part I.

Take the E'-proposition 'No man is every animal'. If one attempts to descend first under the predicate 'animal', he finds that
it is impossible to assign any of the three modes of common personal supposition to that predicate. For each of the following inferences is invalid:

(8)   No man is every animal, therefore no man is this animal and no
      man is that animal, etc.

(9)   No man is every animal, therefore no man is this animal or no
      man is that animal, etc.

(10) No man is every animal, therefore no man is this animal or that
      animal, etc.

Suppose that there are many men, that every man is an animal
and that the only animals are men. Then in each of (8), (9), and
(10) the antecedent is true and the consequent false. Moreover,
in Part I Ockham—wisely, as we can now see—does not assign
any of the MCPS to the predicate of an E'-proposition, even
though in Part II he is clearly anxious to give an account of the
truth conditions of propositions of this type.

If Ockham were proposing a theory of quantification in Part I,
he would surely adopt one of two fairly obvious solutions to the
problem posed by E'-propositions. The first solution is to recog-
nize a fourth mode of common personal supposition, in which a
descent is made to a proposition with a conjunctive extreme.[23]
For the following biconditional is true: 'No man is every animal

if and only if no man is this animal and that animal . . .' and so
on for each animal. Ockham discusses propositions with conjunctive predicates in chapter 37 of *Summa Logicae* II and thus could
easily resort to the notion of a conjunctive extreme in this situation. An alternative solution is to adopt a 'priority of analysis'
rule, according to which the descent under the predicate term of
an E'-proposition must be preceded by the descent under the subject term.[24] In the above example the first descent would yield a
conjunctive proposition, each of whose conjuncts is of the form
'This man is not every animal'. And Ockham explicitly, and correctly, assigns determinate supposition to the predicate of such a
proposition.[25] This solution, like the first one, yields both necessary and sufficient conditions for the truth of an E'-proposition.
But Ockham would surely realize this if he were proposing a
theory of quantification in Part I. Yet he nowhere even mentions
either a fourth type of supposition or a priority of analysis rule.

Moreover, neither of these solutions will help in the case of A'-
and I'-propositions. Ockham assigns confused and distributive supposition to the predicates of propositions of this type.[26] However,
since a proposition of this sort is true only if its predicate supposits for exactly one thing, the only descent possible under the
predicate will take the following form: 'Every (some) A is every
B, therefore every (some) A is this B'.[27] But it is clear that the
converse of such an inference is not valid, no matter which type
of common personal supposition—including the fourth type alluded
to above—is attributed to the predicate of the original proposition.
Further, a priority of analysis rule does no good here, since precisely the same problem arises with singular propositions of the
form 'This A is every B'. Here, then, is another indication that
Ockham did not intend his account of the MCPS to be part of
his theory of truth conditions.

However, none of this should be surprising. For Ockham never
claims that his account of the MCPS is part of his theory of truth
conditions, whereas he does explicitly claim that the account of
quantified propositions found in Part II and partially summarized
by (P9)–(P16) above is part of his theory of truth conditions.
What is surprising is that so many recent commentators have not
taken Ockham at his word. The reasons for this phenomenon
need not concern us here. What is important is that Ockham's

avowed theory of quantification, found in Part II, is much
stronger than any theory of quantification that can be constructed from his account of the MCPS—even when that account
is amended along the lines suggested above. First, the theory
found in Part II handles without emendation all the problem
cases cited above. Second, the theory offered in Part II is simpler
than any theory based on the MCPS, since both types of theory
require the notion of supposition, while only the latter requires
in addition the MCPS. Third, as Paul Spade has noted, the theory
offered in Part II enables us to formulate in a finite sentence the
truth conditions for any universal or particular proposition—even
one in which the subject or predicate supposits for infinitely
many things.[28] However, a theory of quantification based on
the account of the MCPS requires that a complete explication
of the truth conditions of a universal or particular proposition
contain an infinitely long proposition if either the subject or the
predicate of the original proposition supposits for infinitely many
things.

The ability to deal successfully with infinite domains is, of
course, a necessary condition for the adequacy of any purported
theory of quantification. In the present context this is sufficient
to corroborate my contention that the theory of quantification
found in Part II is preferable to any theory based on the account
of the MCPS. Moreover, it is interesting to note in passing that
Ockham himself could appreciate the importance of this advantage of the theory proposed in Part II. For although he denies
that there can be an actual infinity of substances or qualities, he
clearly holds that a material substance has an actual infinity of
parts. For instance, in his commentary on Aristotle's *Categories*
he says:

> Although there are infinitely many parts in a continuous thing, it is not
> possible, according to the Philosopher's principles, that there be infinitely
> many things, none of which is a part of another.[29]

In fact, in chapter 50 of *Summa Logicae* I, Ockham employs
the assumption that a piece of wood has an actual infinity of
proper parts in order to show that if there are any relations at
all, then there are infinitely many of them.[30] But since the con-

sequent of this conditional is false, so is the antecedent. Further, he explicitly denies that the parts of such a substance exist only potentially and, hence, that they constitute only a potential infinity. For in that case, he argues, it would be true that an actual substance is composed of non-beings—an obvious absurdity. Hence, Ockham must have realized that his theory of truth conditions had to accommodate the truth, accepted on metaphysical grounds, of certain propositions in which the quantified term supposits for infinitely many things. Indeed, he devotes a whole chapter of Part II to a discussion of the term 'totus', which in its syncategorematic use means 'each part of . . . '.[31]

In light of all this, it is puzzling to find Loux remarking that

> the mathematics of Ockham's day [does not] employ a notion of infinity that is recognizably like that found in contemporary mathematics. It is only plausible to assume, then, that it never occurred to Ockham that there was any need for a stronger theory of generality than that provided by supposition theory.[32]

(By 'supposition theory' here Loux means the account of the MCPS.)

Even if it is the case, as Loux goes on to suggest, that Ockham would have had grave doubts about Cantor's ascending order of infinities, it seems fairly clear that he had no reservations about the existence of actual denumerable (in Cantor's sense) infinities of parts of material things.

Others have argued that Ockham admits into his ontology an actual infinity of possibilia, i.e. unactualized possible things, and hence that his theory of truth conditions must be able to handle infinite domains in order to provide a satisfactory treatment of modal propositions containing quantifiers.[33] I will argue later that there is good reason to believe that Ockham neither accepts nor is commited to the existence (or subsistence) of possibilia.[34] However, if I am mistaken in this claim, then we have another indication that Ockham did not intend the account of the MCPS to be a theory of quantification. For such a theory would not be sufficiently powerful to deal with his antecedent ontological commitments—and he himself would surely have noticed this.

It seems plausible, then, both that the account of quantifica-

tion found in Part II is philosophically preferable to any such
account based on the MCPS and that Ockham himself would have
recognized this fact.

Now perhaps someone will agree that the theory found in Part
II is indeed better, but insist that Ockham himself regarded the
account of the MCPS as a theory of quantification and that he,
albeit mistakenly, took the two theories to be equivalent. For
in Part II, after giving the truth conditions for particular propositions, he adds that it is sufficient for the truth of a particular
proposition that one of its singulars be true.[35] Likewise, after
giving the truth conditions for universal propositions, he adds
that it is commonly said that for the truth of such a proposition it is sufficient that each of its singulars be true.[36] But such
talk of singulars is reminiscent of the account of the MCPS.
Thus, perhaps Ockham proposed two distinct theories of quantification and thought of them as equivalent.

This suggestion, however, is misguided. Ockham's talk of singulars in this section of Part II has to do with singular propositions which are formed by replacing the particular or universal
sign determining the subject with a demonstrative term. Thus,
'This man is an animal' is a singular of both 'Every man is an
animal' and 'Some man is an animal'. Likewise, 'This man is
every animal' is a singular of both 'Every man is every animal'
and 'Some man is every animal'. But the predicate of such a
singular proposition remains the same as the predicate of the
corresponding universal or particular proposition. In terms of
the account of the MCPS, then, Ockham's talk of singulars in
Part II involves only the supposition of the subject term of a
universal or particular proposition—and not the supposition of
the predicate term. But if that is so, then his reference to inferences from singular propositions to their particular and universal counterparts does not constitute an allusion to a full-
blown theory of quantification based on the account of the
MCPS. For, as noted above, such a theory involves descents
to and ascents from propositions which are not only singular
propositions but also propositions in which both the subject
and predicate are singular terms.

Furthermore, Ockham explicitly claims only that the truth
of one (or all) of its singulars is a sufficient condition for the

truth of the particular (or universal) proposition in question. And later in the *Summa Logicae* he emphatically asserts that the truth of one (or all) of its singulars is not a necessary condition for the truth of a particular (or universal) proposition, since some true particular and some true universal propositions have no singulars. Consider the following passage from *Summa Logicae* III–3, chapter 32:

> It should be noted that sometimes a universal proposition has singulars and sometimes it does not have singulars. For when the subject is truly predicated of something, then it has singulars, but when it is not truly predicated of anything, then it does not have singulars.[37]

Two points should be made here. First, it is clear from the context of this passage and from the examples that Ockham uses in this chapter that the singulars to which he is alluding need not have singular terms as their predicates. This is consonant with what I said above.

Second, it is true, as Loux has shown in some detail,[38] that the point made by Ockham in the above passage can be accommodated by a theory of quantification based on the account of the MCPS. This is accomplished by adding the appropriate affirmative or negative existential proposition, as either a conjunct or a disjunct, to the account of the truth conditions for a universal or particular proposition of a given type. Nevertheless, it seems more reasonable to take the account of the MCPS and Ockham's remarks about singulars as belonging to his theory of inference—which presupposes the theory of truth conditions for categorical propositions—rather than as belonging to his theory of truth conditions.[39] There are several considerations in favor of this claim, but I will present only one of them here. Take a universal affirmative proposition like

(11) Each part of this table is a created thing,

in which the subject term supposits for infinitely many beings. As noted above, according to a theory of quantification based on the account of the MCPS the explication of the truth conditions of (11) contains an infinitely long proposition. Since human beings cannot entertain infinitely long propositions, the proposed explication does not render the truth conditions of (11) intelligible

to us. Hence, the theory of truth conditions that yields this explication is not one which we can justifiably accept.

Nevertheless, if we grant that there are or can be infinitely
long propositions (in Ockham's sense of 'proposition'), then
what Ockham says about singulars does commit him to the claim
that (11) may be validly inferred from a certain infinitely long
conjunctive proposition—call it C. But this claim is not philosophically troublesome if it belongs to Ockham's theory of inference. First, both (11) and C can be handled satisfactorily by
the theory of truth conditions found in Part II. The truth conditions of (11) are explicated in accord with (P9) above, and—according to chapter 32 of Part II—C is true just in case each of
its conjuncts is true. Second, even if we cannot entertain infinitely long propositions, we can comprehend the following rule
of inference:

(12) A universal proposition of the form 'Every A is B' in which the
      subject 'A' supposits for infinitely many beings may be validly
      inferred from an infinitely long conjunctive proposition, each of
      whose conjuncts is of the form 'This A is B'.

Hence, if we take the account of the MCPS along with the remarks about singulars to be part of Ockham's theory of truth
conditions, then the resulting theory of truth conditions is seri-
ously defective. On the other hand, if we take them as part of
his theory of inference and take the theory of quantification partially summarized by (P9)–(P16) as part of his theory of truth
conditions, then infinitely long conjunctive (or disjunctive) propositions present no serious problems.

4.   The account of past-tense and future-tense propositions
that Ockham gives in chapter 7 of Part II, even when it is supplemented by his treatment of the conversion of such propositions in chapter 22, is rather sketchy. Nevertheless, these chapters do provide at least a basis for determining the truth conditions which Ockham would assign to various types of past-tense
and future-tense propositions, even though certain ambiguities
remain unresolved. For the sake of simplicity I will limit my
discussion here to past-tense propositions, since on Ockham's
view the semantic account of past-tense propositions corresponds,

mutatis mutandis, to that of their future-tense counterparts. This reflects his insistence that every future-tense proposition is either true now or false now.[40] Thus, the principles given below can be made to apply to future-tense propositions simply by changing each occurrence of the term 'past' to the term 'future' and each occurrence of the verb 'was' to the verb 'will be'.

Ockham's general strategy is to formulate the truth conditions for a past-tense proposition in terms of the past truth of some present-tense proposition. We can represent this strategy schematically as follows, where the verbs embedded in the propositional contexts '. . .' and '_ _ _' are the principal verbs of the propositions in question, and where the blank '_____' is filled by an appropriate temporal determination:

(13) '. . . was . . .' is true if and only if ' _ _ _ is _ _ _' was true at ____ .

In order to provide an account of the truth conditions of a past-tense proposition P, then, one must determine both (a) which present-tense proposition P is correctly mapped onto and (b) which temporal determination is appropriate in the instance of the above schema that pertains to P.

From (13) it is clear that Ockham formulates the truth conditions of past-tense propositions only indirectly in terms of the notion of supposition. That is, his treatment of past-tense propositions is parasitic on his previous treatment of present-tense propositions and is not formulated—appearances sometimes to the contrary—in terms of the supposition of the subject and predicate in a past-tense proposition. I will discuss this general point in more detail below.

The simplest case here is that of a singular past-tense non-modal proposition whose subject is either a proper name or a demonstrative pronoun standing alone, e.g. 'Socrates was white', 'This was running', 'That was hot', etc. Let us call such propositions P-propositions. Then

(P17) An affirmative P-proposition, 'N was P', is true if and only if 'N is P' was true at some past time.

In this case the relevant present-tense proposition is simply the exact present-tense counterpart of the past-tense proposition in question. Further, the temporal determination is suitably indefinite with respect to the past.

Negative P-propositions are somewhat more troublesome. At first glance it seems that a proposition of the form 'N was not P' should be true just in case 'N is not P' was true at some past time. In that case an affirmative P-proposition would not be the contradictory of its negative counterpart, since the relevant present-tense propositions might have been true at different times in the past. For instance, 'Socrates was white' and 'Socrates was not white' would not be contradictories, since 'Socrates is white' might have been true at one time in the past and 'Socrates is not white' might have been true at some other time in the past. However, Ockham claims in chapter 22 that 'Socrates was not white' implies and is implied by 'Nothing which was white was Socrates'. And this latter proposition appears to entail that nothing was ever both white and Socrates. But if this is so, then Ockham would treat a negative P-proposition as follows:

(P18) A negative P-proposition, 'N was not P', is true if and only if 'N is not P' was true at every past time.

Given (P18), an affirmative P-proposition and its negative counterpart are indeed contradictories. Note, however, that on this account an affirmative proposition of the form 'N was non-P' is compatible with the corresponding proposition of the form 'N was P' and thus does not imply the corresponding proposition of the form 'N was not P'. For instance, 'Socrates was non-white' does not imply 'Socrates was not white', even though 'Socrates is non-white' does imply 'Socrates is not white'. So either account of negative P-propositions has the consequence that the inferential relations among P-propositions do not exactly mirror those that obtain among their present-tense counterparts.

If the predicate of a P-proposition contains a more specific temporal determination, as in 'Socrates was white yesterday', then that determination is included in the truth conditions as a modifier of the phrase 'was true'. Hence, 'Socrates was white yesterday' is true just in case 'Socrates is white' was true at some time yesterday. In the same way, 'Socrates was not white yesterday' is true just in case 'Socrates is not white' was true at every time yesterday. The limiting case is one in which a precise moment is specified, as in 'Socrates was white yesterday at 2 P.M.'. This proposition is true just in case 'Socrates is white' was true yesterday at 2 P.M.

In a P-proposition, Ockham tells us, there is no ambiguity with respect to how the terms supposit. For instance, in 'Socrates was white yesterday' the term 'Socrates' is said to supposit for what was Socrates yesterday and the term 'white' is said to supposit for what was white yesterday. (Later I will argue that this manner of speaking is dispensable and thus does not commit Ockham either to the present existence of merely past individuals or to the possibility that a merely past individual stands in relations to a presently existing term.)

However, when a past-tense proposition has a subject which is or includes a common term, further complications arise. Ockham claims that such a proposition is equivocal and "must be distinguished." For its subject term may be taken to supposit either for just those things of which it is truly predicable by means of a present-tense verb or for just those things of which it is truly predicable by means of a past-tense verb. For example, 'Some white thing was black' may be taken as equivalent either to 'Something which is white was black' or to 'Something which was white was black'. Hence, for each past-tense proposition whose subject is or includes a common term we need two accounts of truth conditions, corresponding to the two distinct ways in which its subject may be understood.

The predicates of such propositions, however, do not share in this ambiguity. For the predicate, Ockham emphasizes, "names its form," while the subject does not. This means that the predicate is fixed by the past-tense verb and the further temporal determinations, if any, of that verb. That is, the predicate of a past-tense proposition P must occur unchanged as the predicate of the present-tense proposition in terms of which the truth conditions of P are explicated. Further, the past-tense verb and other temporal determinations, if any, specify the temporal parameters of the truth of that present-tense proposition. Ockham himself says:

> In order for a [past-tense] proposition to be true . . . it is required that the very same predicate be truly predicated of that for which the subject supposits in the manner asserted by means of such a proposition.[41]

Hence, 'Socrates was white' is true only if some instance of the schema '_____ is white' was true, and 'Some white thing was black yesterday' is true only if some instance of the schema '____ is black' was true yesterday.

However, as noted above, when the subject of a past-tense proposition is or includes a common term, it is not fixed in this way. If such a subject is taken to supposit only for those things of which it is truly predicable by means of a present-tense verb, then the same subject will not appear in the relevant present-tense proposition. Rather, a coreferential demonstrative pronoun or proper name will appear in its place. Hence, if its subject supposits only for what is now white, then 'Some white thing was black' is true just in case 'This is black' was once true, where 'this' indicated something for which 'white' now supposits in a present-tense proposition. Accordingly, 'Some white thing was black', so understood, may be true, even though 'Some white thing is black' was never true.

In general, when the subject of a past-tense proposition is taken to supposit for what is now such-and-such, we must guarantee that the subject of the relevant present-tense proposition picked out what the subject of the past-tense proposition is intended to pick out—no matter what changes have taken place. What we need, in short, is a term which picks out one and the same thing at every moment at which it exists. Such a term serves, in contemporary parlance, as a rigid designator across all the times at which its referent exists.

With this in mind, we can now proceed to formulate the truth conditions of past-tense propositions in which the subject is or includes a common term. First we will deal with cases in which the subject is taken to supposit for what is now such-and-such. Let a Q-proposition be a past-tense non-modal proposition in which the subject is a singular term composed of a demonstrative adjective and a common term. Then

(P19) An affirmative Q-proposition, 'That A was B', where 'that A' is taken to supposit only for something which is now A, is true if and only if (i) there is something for which 'that A' supposits and (ii) 'This is B' was true at some past time, where 'this' indicated the thing for which 'that A' supposits.

(P20) A negative Q-proposition, 'That A was not B', where 'that A' is taken to supposit only for something which is now A, is true if and only if either (i) there is nothing for which 'that A' supposits or (ii) 'This is not B' was true at every past time, where 'this' indicated (or was asserted to indicate) the thing for which 'that A' supposits.

Note that 'This is not B' is true whenever the thing for which 'this' is taken to supposit does not exist. Ockham seems to treat demonstrative pronouns on a par with proper names. Since on his view a proper name can fail to supposit for anything in a meaningful and genuinely singular proposition, the same holds for a demonstrative pronoun.

Universal and particular propositions of the sort in question may be treated in the following way:

(P21) A past-tense non-modal A-proposition, 'Every A was B', where 'A' is taken to supposit only for what is now A, is true if and only if (i) there is something for which 'A' supposits and (ii) 'This is B' was true at some past time, no matter which of the supposita of 'A' was indicated by 'this'.

(P22) A past-tense non-modal I-proposition, 'Some A was B', where 'A' is taken to supposit only for what is now A, is true if and only if (i) there is something for which 'A' supposits and (ii) in at least one instance in which 'this' indicated something for which 'A' supposits, 'This is B' was true at some past time.

(P23) A past-tense non-modal E-proposition, 'No A was B', where 'A' is taken to supposit only for what is now A, is true if and only if either (i) there is nothing for which 'A' supposits or (ii) 'This is not B' was true at every past time, no matter which of the supposita of 'A' was indicated (or asserted to be indicated) by 'this'.

(P24) A past-tense non-modal O-proposition, 'Some A was not B', where 'A' is taken to supposit for what is now A, is true if and only if either (i) there is nothing for which 'A' supposits or (ii) in at least one instance in which 'this' indicated (or was asserted to indicate) something for which 'A' supposits, 'This is not B' was true at every past time.

This account can easily be extended to propositions which contain more specific temporal determinations and also to propositions in which the predicate is modified by a universal sign.

When the subject term of such a past-tense proposition is taken to supposit for what was such-and-such, a problem of interpretation arises. Take, for instance, the past-tense I-proposition 'Some white thing was black'. Ockham tells us that when the subject of this proposition is taken to supposit for what was white, then this proposition is equivalent to 'Something which was white was black'. However, this latter proposition is ambiguous. One way to read it is as follows: 'Something which was white at some past time was black at some past time'. On this reading the proposition in question is possibly true, since it does not imply that something was both white and black at the same time. A second way to read it is this: 'Something was both black and white at the same time in the past'. On this construal the proposition in question is necessarily false.

It is difficult to know which reading Ockham took to be the correct one, since his examples are inconclusive on this point. Loux appears to adopt the first of these readings in his brief discussion of past-tense propositions.[42] However, it seems to me that the second reading is more natural, and so I will interpret such propositions accordingly. Although this move will simplify my discussion, nothing essential depends on it. For the principles pertaining to past-tense propositions in Ockham's semantic theory provide us with the resources to handle the propositions in question, no matter how they are interpreted.

One further problem is this. Ockham's talk of a term being taken to supposit for what was such-and-such seems at first glance to commit him to the possibility that things which no longer exist stand in relations to presently existing terms. For, it appears, even if Socrates no longer exists, the subjects of the following propositions supposit for him: 'Socrates was a man' and 'Some man was white', where 'man' is taken to supposit only for what was a man. Nevertheless, Ockham seems to have accepted—and correctly, I believe—the metaphysical principle that only actually existing things can have properties or stand in relations. For, as we shall see below, he insists that a proposition can have a truth value—or, presumably, properties in general—only if it exists. And he often talks in a way which indicates that he would extend this principle to all substances and qualities. But if this is so, then if Socrates no longer exists, no presently existing term can now supposit for him. What, then, does 'Socrates' now supposit for in 'Socrates was a man'?

One solution to this dilemma is to claim that merely past (and merely future) entities do in fact exist in the present, even though they are not 'present in the present'. It is not immediately obvious how to understand this suggestion. Perhaps it entails that all moments of time exist eternally and become present successively. Likewise, each being exists eternally, although some, like Socrates, are at first merely future beings, become present beings for a short while, and then become merely past beings. Hence, strictly speaking, we should not say that Socrates no longer exists but rather that he is no longer present. Further, it is not the fact that God exists eternally which distinguishes him from mortals like ourselves. Rather, God, unlike a creature, is such that he is always present and never merely past or merely future.

Whether this proposal can be made entirely coherent is a moot point. It is clear, however, that Ockham would not accept it. For in his commentary on Aristotle's *Categories* he explicitly denies that the past and future exist:

> Furthermore, no part of time exists, since neither the past nor the future exists. Therefore, time itself is not some existent thing totally distinct from other things.[43]

Moreover, the picture painted above has theological consequences that Ockham clearly could not accept. For it entails that no being can either come into existence or pass out of existence. To say, in ordinary parlance, that a thing comes into existence is merely, on the proposed view, to say that it becomes present after having been merely future. Likewise, to say that a thing passes out of existence is merely, on the proposed view, to say that it becomes merely past after having been present. Hence, God cannot now either create a new being from nothing or completely annihilate any existing being. But Ockham would surely reject such a limitation on God's power. Hence, he could not accept the proposal in question.

At this point someone familiar with the entire *Summa Logicae* might object that the problem that I have constructed is not really a problem for Ockham at all. For he himself alludes

to cases in which a term may supposit for a non-being. Specifically, in Part III–4, chapter 13, he says:

> [In the inference] 'The Antichrist is not, therefore the Antichrist is not
> thought of by you' . . . there is a fallacy of relative and absolute. For
> one argues from the verb 'to be' taken by itself to the same verb followed
> by a predicate. And the predicate in question is able to agree with a term
> which supposits for a non-being as well as with a term which supposits
> for a being.[44]

Hence, Ockham does not accept the general principle attributed
to him above, namely, that a thing cannot stand in relations to
existing terms unless it itself exists. But if this is so, then there
is no reason why a term cannot supposit for a non-being in a
past-tense proposition like 'Socrates was white'.

Before responding to this point I will list a few other examples
of invalid inferences that Ockham cites in the context of the passage quoted above. They are: 'The Antichrist does not exist,
therefore the Antichrist is not possible'; 'A is producible by God,
therefore A exists'; 'A does not exist, therefore A is not producible by God'; 'The Antichrist does not exist, therefore the Antichrist is not foreknown by God'; 'The Antichrist is foreknown
by God, therefore the Antichrist exists'. It should be clear that
each of these cases involves modality, either alethic or epistemic.

What Ockham says in the passage quoted above is, if taken
literally, clearly inconsistent with the account in *Summa Logicae*
II of the truth conditions of propositions containing infinite
terms. For, as we will see below, he makes it clear that he takes
every singular proposition of the form '_____ is a non-being' to
be necessarily false. Yet the passage just cited commits him to
the thesis that there are non-beings, i.e. things which do not actually exist. So the account of truth conditions found in Part II
is incompatible with his claim here that a term may supposit for
a non-being.

Moreover, as noted above, the inferences which Ockham is
concerned with here all involve modal notions. In the next section I will argue that his treatment of modality in Part II does
not commit him to the thesis that there are things which do not
actually exist. My own inclination, then, is to take the theory
of truth conditions found in Part II as canonical and then to

argue that that theory can, without making the assumption that there are non-beings, yield the result that each of the inferences listed above is indeed invalid. *Summa Logicae* III–4 constitutes Ockham's tract on fallacies. His main purpose in the above passage, then, is simply to point out that the inferences he cites are invalid. On my view, however, the reason for their invalidity is stated rather carelessly. And although I will not return to this problem in the present essay, I believe that the invalidity of such inferences can be adequately explicated within the framework of the modal semantics outlined below, supplemented by Ockham's account of intentionality in those cases which involve epistemic modality.[45]

It should also be noted in the present context that none of the examples cited by Ockham involves a past-tense or future-tense proposition. Hence, it is not clear that he intends the point he is making to apply to such propositions in general.

In view of all this, I will concentrate in this essay on the following question: does Ockham's theory of truth conditions as presented in Part II of the *Summa Logicae* involve an irrevocable commitment to the thesis that there are merely past, merely future, or merely possible entities?[46] And I will assume for now that the theory presented in Part II can adequately explain the reason for the invalidity of the inferences alluded to above.

With this in mind, we can return to our original problem: if Socrates no longer exists, then what does the term 'Socrates' supposit for in 'Socrates was a man'? The solution to this problem is, I believe, suggested by the fact that Ockham explicates the truth conditions of past-tense propositions in terms of the past truth of present-tense propositions rather than directly in terms of the supposition of subjects and predicates in past-tense propositions. A close examination of (P17) and (P18) reveals that at no point is there mention of a term suppositing at present for a past individual. Rather, the occurrence of terms which are taken to supposit for what was such-and-such points back, as it were, to previous occurrences of those same terms in present-tense propositions.[47] For example, Ockham does not say that 'Socrates was white' is true now just in case 'Socrates' supposits for a past individual which 'white' also supposits for. Rather, this proposition is true, he tells us, just in case 'Socrates is white' was once true, i.e. just in case the terms 'Socrates' and 'white' once supposited for the same individual in the present-tense proposition 'Socrates is white'. The same treatment is accorded the predicate terms in propositions of the forms explicated in (P19)–(P24).

Hence, talk about merely past individuals—in fact, talk about a past individual in general, whether or not it has ceased to exist—can be dispensed with in favor of talk about the semantic relations which terms once entered into in the context of present-tense propositions. Thus, in order to give truth conditions for past-tense propositions, Ockham has to talk only of what terms once supposited for in present-tense propositions—and not of what terms now supposit for in past-tense propositions. And this interpretation is suggested straightforwardly by the essential role that Ockham assigns to present-tense propositions in his account of the truth conditions of past-tense (and future-tense) propositions.

With this in mind we can proceed to an explication of those past-tense propositions in which the subject is or includes a common term and is taken to supposit for what was such-and-such:

(P25) An affirmative Q-proposition, 'That A was B', where 'that A' is taken to supposit for something which was A, is true if and only if 'That A is B' was true at some past time.

(P26) A negative Q-proposition, 'That A was not B', where 'that A' is taken to supposit for something which was A, is true if and only if 'That A is not B' was true at every past time.

(P27) A past-tense non-modal A-proposition, 'Every A was B', where 'A' is taken to supposit only for what was A, is true if and only if (i) 'Every A is B' was true at some past time and (ii) 'Every A is B' was true at every past time at which there was something for which 'A' supposited.

(P28) A past-tense non-modal I-proposition, 'Some A was B', where 'A' is taken to supposit only for what was A, is true if and only if 'Some A is B' was true at some past time.

(P29) A past-tense non-modal E-proposition, 'No A was B', where 'A' is taken to supposit only for what was A, is true if and only if 'No A is B' was true at every past time.

(P30) A past-tense non-modal O-proposition, 'Some A was not B', where 'A' is taken to supposit only for what was A, is true if and only if either (i) 'Some A is not B' was true at every past time or (ii) 'Some A is not B' was true at some past time at which there was something for which 'A' supposited.

Someone might object that the left-hand side of each of (P25)–(P30) still contains the problematic phrase "where 'A' is taken to supposit only for what was A." However, locutions of this sort are meant merely to disambiguate past-tense propositions in which the subject is or includes a common term. But the ambiguity of such propositions can be adequately characterized in syntactic terms alone, without any reference to the notion of supposition, for this ambiguity is in essence a scope ambiguity. In an ambiguous past-tense proposition the past-tense verb (including its more specific temporal determinations, if any) may have as its scope either the whole proposition or just the predicate alone.[48] And the scope of the verb, as we have seen, determines just which present-tense proposition it is that the past-tense proposition in question is to be mapped onto. When the scope of the verb is the whole proposition, then both the subject and the predicate will appear unchanged in the relevant present-tense proposition. On the other hand, when the scope of the verb is the predicate alone, only the predicate will appear unchanged in the relevant present-tense proposition. The ambiguity in question is, in fact, like that between the sense of composition and the sense of division in the case of modal propositions with a dictum. This latter ambiguity will be discussed below.

Hence, we could rewrite (P22) and (P28), for example, as follows:

(P22*) 'Some A was B', taken in the sense of division, is true if and only if (i) 'Some A is a being' is true and (ii) in at least one instance in which 'this' indicated something for which 'A' supposits in 'Some A is a being', 'This is B' was true at some past time.

(P28*) 'Some A was B', taken in the sense of composition, is true if and only if 'Some A is B' was true at some past time.

An Ockhamistic semantics, then, is not irrevocably committed to the existence of either merely past or merely future individuals. And there is at least some evidence to suggest that Ockham himself understood this.

There is much more that could be said about Ockham's account of past-tense and future-tense propositions. However, I will limit the present discussion to one problem that might occur to

the reader of Part II. Ockham, as we have seen, attempts to explicate the present truth of past-tense propositions in terms of
the past truth of present-tense propositions. However, as noted
above, in several places he explicitly denies that propositions are
eternal entities. In order to have a truth value a proposition must
exist, and in order to exist it must be formulated by some person.[49] Now according to the principles laid out above, the present
truth of a given past-tense proposition entails that some specific
present-tense proposition was true in the past, and hence that it
existed in the past, i.e. was formulated by someone. But it is
surely implausible to believe that every true past-tense proposition is such that the present-tense proposition that appears in
the account of its truth conditions was once uttered or thought
or otherwise expressed by someone. Even the simplest case serves
to illustrate this fact. Suppose that Socrates was white yesterday.
It surely does not follow that anyone, including Socrates, formulated the proposition 'Socrates is white' at some time yesterday. And suppose that no one did formulate it. Then it was not
true at any time yesterday—and thus, on Ockham's account
'Socrates was white yesterday' is false, even though we assumed
that Socrates was white yesterday. The problem obviously becomes more acute when we are dealing with past-tense propositions—of the sort to be found in geological and cosmological
writings—which make ostensibly true claims about times at which
no intelligent creature existed. It seems, then, that Ockham's
strategy in dealing with past-tense and future-tense propositions
is, though clever, doomed to failure.

One interesting response to this problem would be an attempt
to recast (P17)–(P30) above directly in terms of the supposition
of the subjects and predicates of past-tense propositions. For instance, the truth conditions of an affirmative P-proposition might
be reformulated as follows:

> (14) An affirmative P-proposition, 'N was P', is true if and only if 'N'
>   supposits for what was N and 'P' supposits for what was P and
>   there was something for which both 'N' and 'P' supposit.

In this way we could avoid any reference to a proposition other
than the past-tense proposition which is being explicated.

First of all, however, it is not clear to me whether this wholesale revision of Ockham's theory could be carried out successfully. Second, even if it could be, the proposal itself raises anew the question of whether it is generally true that the terms of past-tense propositions may supposit for merely past beings. In light of our previous discussion of this issue, it seems best to regard the suggestion in question as one which should be adopted only if there is no workable alternative.

A more attractive response to the problem in question is to resort to subjunctive conditionals of the form

(15) If proposition 'P' were to exist in the future at such-and-such a time, then it would be true

and

(16) If proposition 'P' had existed at such-and-such a time in the past, then it would have been true.

Ockham himself, in fact, makes use of such conditionals at one point in chapter 7. Adopting this suggestion, we could change the general form of the explication of the truth conditions of a past-tense proposition to

(17) Past-tense proposition 'P' is true if and only if either (i) present-tense proposition 'Q' was true at such-and-such a past time or (ii) if 'Q' had existed at every past time, it would have been true at such-and-such a past time.

We could then reformulate (P17)–(P30) accordingly.

However, there is a further problem here. Suppose that 'Socrates is white' was formulated yesterday and was true. Then, given (17), it follows that a certain past-tense proposition, namely, 'Socrates was white', is true today. Hence, it follows that that past-tense proposition is formulated today. But even if 'Socrates is white' was true yesterday, it is clearly possible that no one will formulate the proposition 'Socrates was white' today. In that case, one who endorses (17) is forced to admit that it is possible for a proposition to be true even when it does not exist.

The only escape from this difficulty is to employ subjunctive conditionals on both sides of a principle like (17), as in

(18)   Past-tense proposition 'P' is true, or would be true if it now
        existed, if and only if either (i) present-tense proposition 'Q'
        was true at such-and-such a past time or (ii) if 'Q' had existed
        at every past time, it would have been true at such-and-such a
        time.

(18) at least tries to accommodate the commonsense intuition
that there are unexpressed truths about the past. But a moment's
reflection reveals that we must make an analogous move in the
treatment of present-tense propositions in order to accommodate
the intuition that there are unexpressed truths about the present.
This may not be an insuperable objection to the suggestion in
question, but it is obvious that the resulting theory of truth conditions would be enormously complicated. Unfortunately, this
might be the price that Ockham has to pay in order to remain
consistent.

In any case, it is certainly true that Ockham's theory would
be greatly simplified by the assumption that every proposition
exists at every moment of time. In fact, he often proceeds as if
this were the case. Apparently, his main reason for denying that
every proposition always exists is his reluctance to posit entities
that are both eternal and independent of God. But it is not immediately clear why he cannot hold that certain propositions—
namely, those formed by God—are eternal but dependent entities. Further, such propositions would be individuals, just as
are the propositions formed by angels and men.[50]

However, Ockham's understanding of the notion of divine simplicity seems to rule out this alternative. For such propositions
would have to be individual qualities of God's intellect, and
there would be an infinite number of them. But God can
have no such qualities—and, moreover, he knows everything
by means of one act of knowing which is identical with
his essence.

Nevertheless, Ockham often speaks of God's knowing propositions.[51] That is, in order to explicate the notion of God's omni-
science, Ockham speaks as if God has a divine language, analogous
to human language, in which he formulates propositions. God is
omniscient in that he knows with respect to every proposition
whether it is true or false. If we take such talk literally, then

God's being necessarily omniscient appears to entail that he forms propositions. In that case, the assumption that he formulates every proposition at every moment, and hence that every proposition exists at every moment, is unexceptionable.

The relevant question, of course, is this: should we take literally the notion of a divine language? Is the above picture of God's mental life compatible with Ockham's construal of the notion of divine simplicity? If so, then the above solution is available to him. If not, then some version of the proposal to introduce subjunctive conditionals into the explication of truth conditions appears to be his most promising escape from the problem we have been discussing. In that case, however, Ockham's failure to treat explicitly the truth conditions of subjunctive conditionals takes on added significance.

5. Ockham's complete account of modal propositions—scattered as it is through the various parts of the *Summa Logicae*—is much too extensive to be treated fully here. Nevertheless, I will try to sketch its basic features and discuss certain questions to which it gives rise.

It should first be noted that on Ockham's view any term which can be truly predicated of a whole proposition is a mode and is capable of rendering a proposition modal. Hence, all of the following are modes: 'necessary', 'possible', 'impossible', 'contingent', 'true', 'false', 'written', 'spoken', 'thought', 'known', 'believed', 'opined', etc. In the present context I will concentrate on the first four of the modes just mentioned. Moreover, since Ockham takes 'contingent' to mean 'neither necessary nor impossible' (or: 'possible but not necessary') and 'impossible' to mean 'not possible', we can simplify matters by limiting our discussion to the modes 'necessary' and 'possible'.

Ockham's strategy in dealing with modal propositions is analogous to his strategy in dealing with past-tense and future-tense propositions. In each case he explicates the truth conditions of the modal proposition in question in terms of the modal status of some non-modal proposition.[52] This strategy is captured by the following schema, where '. . .' and '_ _ _' are propositional contexts:

(19) 'It is necessary (possible) that . . .' is true if and only if this is necessary (possible): '_ _ _ '.

Roughly speaking, just as the past and future tenses were relegated to the metalanguage in the explication of the truth conditions of past-tense and future-tense propositions, so too modal
terms are now relegated to the metalanguage in the semantic account of the truth conditions of modal propositions. They become, in fact, metalinguistic predicates.[53] So in order to determine the truth conditions for a given modal proposition we must
map that proposition onto the appropriate non-modal proposition
and predicate the appropriate modal term of the latter.

Let us assume for now that the standard form of a *de necessario* proposition is

(20) It is necessary that P,

and that the standard form of a *de possibili* proposition is

(21) It is possible that P,

where 'P' takes indicative sentences as substitutes. A proposition
of the form of (20) or (21) is said to be a modal proposition
'with a dictum', where 'that P' in English corresponds to the
Latin accusative-with-infinitive construction, which medieval
logicians called the dictum of such a proposition. According to
Ockham and others, a proposition of the form of (20) or (21)
is ambiguous, since it may be understood in either the sense of
composition or the sense of division. When such a proposition
is taken in the sense of composition (or composed sense), it is
asserted that the modal term is truly predicable of the proposition which corresponds to the dictum. Hence, we can formulate
the following principles, which hold no matter which proposition
is substituted for 'P':

(P31) 'It is necessary that P', taken in the sense of composition, is true
if and only if this is necessary: 'P'.

(P32) 'It is possible that P', taken in the sense of composition, is true
if and only if this is possible: 'P'.

Ockham later asserts that a proposition is necessary just in
case, if it exists, it is true and cannot be false. On the other

hand, a proposition is impossible just in case its existence entails its being false.[54] From this we can infer that a proposition is possible just in case its existence is compatible with its being true.

Unfortunately, Ockham's insistence that propositions are neither eternal nor necessary existents leads to difficulties here, just as it did in the case of past-tense and future-tense propositions. In fact, the problem is somewhat more intractable with respect to modal propositions.[55] Take the proposition 'No proposition is negative'. Its contradictory, namely, 'Some proposition is negative', is not necessary, since it could exist and be false if God were to destroy all negative propositions. But if its contradictory is not necessarily true, then we should expect that 'No proposition is negative' is possible. However, the latter is impossible according to the above characterization of a proposition's being impossible, since it cannot exist without being false. For it constitutes its own counterexample. Moreover, many other such puzzles are generated by the above characterization of necessity and impossibility.

The obvious—and ultimately, perhaps, the best—solution to this problem is simply to admit that propositions exist necessarily and eternally.[56] However, we have already seen that Ockham is reluctant—on theological grounds—to make such a move. Excluding this radical solution, the most ingenious alternative is suggested by Buridan, who distinguishes a proposition's being possible from its being possibly true and a proposition's being necessary from its being necessarily true.[57] A full discussion of this proposal would take us too far afield. However, there are some interesting treatments of Buridan's distinctions in recent philosophical literature, and the interested reader may wish to consult them.[58]

I will simply sidestep this issue for the present by assuming that propositions are necessary beings. This will at least provide us with the chance to look at other aspects of Ockham's treatment of necessity and possibility. One final point on this matter is, however, in order. Ockham here and in other places emphasizes that it is not sufficient for a proposition's being necessary that it always be true (or even that it be true whenever it exists). Rather, it must also be such that it cannot be false. Moreover, even though Ockham acknowledges a type of necessity which is had by every true (genuinely) past-tense proposition, once again the key is not that such a proposition will always be true in the future, but rather that it cannot be made false in the future— even by the power of God.[59] (I will not be discussing this latter type of necessity, sometimes called "necessity *per accidens*," in this introduction, since Ockham does not talk about it specifically in Part II—even though a few of his examples presuppose it. Rather, he is mainly concerned with logical necessity and logical possibility. Hence, in what follows 'necessary' and 'possible' should be read as 'logically necessary' and 'logically possible'.)

With all this in mind, take a simple S-proposition, e.g. 'Socrates is a man'. This proposition is necessary just in case it cannot be false. Since it entails that Socrates exists, it is necessary only if 'Socrates exists' is necessary. But, according to Ockham, 'Socrates exists' can indeed be false, since Socrates can cease to exist. Hence, 'Socrates is a man' is not necessary. (The same holds, interestingly enough, for 'Socrates is Socrates'.) On the other hand, 'God exists' is necessary, since God is not a contingent being. However, 'God is a creator' is not necessary, since God could have chosen not to create anything, in which case 'God is a creator' would have been false.

When propositions of the form of (20) or (21) are taken in the sense of division (or divided sense), the explication of their truth conditions becomes more complicated. In such cases the modal term does not have as its scope the whole embedded proposition. Rather, it determines only the predicate. Hence, a modal proposition with a dictum, taken in the sense of division, is equivalent to a modal proposition without a dictum. A proposition of this latter type takes the following form:

(22) S is _____ P,

where 'S' and 'P' stand for the subject and predicate of the proposition embedded in the corresponding proposition with a dictum, and the blank is to be filled by the adverbial form of the mode in question. Some examples are 'Some man is necessarily an animal' and 'This white thing is possibly black'. Hence, a modal proposition of the form of (20) or (21) is ambiguous in a way analogous to that in which a past-tense or future-tense proposition is ambiguous when its subject is or includes a common term. Ockham notes this analogy at several places in the *Summa Logicae.* And he deals with the ambiguity of modal propositions with a dictum in the same way. That is, he maps propositions taken in the sense of composition onto their exact non-modal counterparts; and he maps propositions taken in the sense of division onto non-modal propositions in which the subject term is a demonstrative pronoun or a proper name.

In *Summa Logicae* III–3, chapter 14, Ockham divides *de necessario* and *de possibili* propositions without a dictum into those which are primary and those which are derived.[60] In each instance a primary proposition has a derived counterpart to which it is equivalent in virtue of the interrelations between the modes of necessity and possibility. Although this division will strike the contemporary reader as somewhat arbitrary, it proves to be a convenient ordering principle. According to Ockham, a modal proposition is primary just in case its modal term is not preceded by a negation. Ockham himself divides only particular and universal propositions in this way, but we can easily extend the distinction in question to singular propositions—both those whose subject is a proper name or demonstrative pronoun and those whose subject includes a common term.

Let an R-proposition be a singular present-tense *de possibili* or *de necessario* proposition without a dictum, whose subject is a proper name or demonstrative pronoun. R-propositions can be of one of four primary forms listed below (with their respective derived forms in parentheses):

(23) N is necessarily P   (N is not possibly not P)

(24) N is necessarily not P   (N is not possibly P)

(25) N is possibly P   (N is not necessarily not P)

(26) N is possibly not P   (N is not necessarily P)

From what Ockham says about such propositions we can conclude that (23) and (26) are contradictory forms, as are (24) and (25).

The following captures Ockham's account of the truth conditions of R-propositions:

(P33) An affirmative *de necessario* R-proposition, 'N is necessarily P',
   is true if and only if this is necessary: 'N is P'.

(P34) A negative *de necessario* R-proposition, 'N is necessarily not P',
   is true if and only if this is necessary: 'N is not P'.

(P35) An affirmative *de possibili* R-proposition, 'N is possibly P', is
   true if and only if this is possible: 'N is P'.

(P36) A negative *de possibili* R-proposition, 'N is possibly not P', is true
   if and only if this is possible: 'N is not P'.

Hence, in giving the truth conditions for an R-proposition,
Ockham maps the R-proposition in question onto its exact non-
modal counterpart. One interesting consequence of this treatment
is that 'Socrates is necessarily a man' turns out to be equivalent
to 'It is necessary that Socrates is a man', taken in the sense of
composition. As we have already seen, the latter is false. Thus,
the former is also false.

This result appears to place in doubt Ockham's commitment to
an essentialist account of substance, i.e. to the thesis that a substance is characterized necessarily (or essentially) in certain ways
and only contingently (or accidentally) in other ways. For the
truth of propositions like 'Socrates is necessarily a man' is often
thought to be crucial to such an account. According to Ockham,
however, an affirmative *de necessario* R-proposition is true only
if its subject term supposits for a necessary being. And the only
necessary being is God.[61]

Nevertheless, there is really no problem here. For Ockham can
and does accept propositions such as

(27) Socrates is a man and Socrates is necessarily not a non-man

and

(28) Socrates is a man and it is necessary that if Socrates is a being,
      Socrates is a man.

But it is precisely propositions like (27) and (28) which the essentialist typically takes to be equivalent to 'Socrates is necessarily a man' and which are themselves the cornerstone of an
essentialist account of substance. The only disagreement between
Ockham and these other essentialists, then, centers on the claim
that (27) or (28) is equivalent to 'Socrates is necessarily a man'.

Ockham can deny such an equivalence and yet remain an essentialist by accepting propositions like (27) and (28) themselves.

It is also interesting to note that Ockham apparently does not believe that an R-proposition of the form 'N is possibly P' entails the corresponding proposition of the form 'N exists' or 'N is a being'. The reason for this is that, given (P35), the proposition 'Socrates is possibly a carpenter', for instance, is equivalent to 'It is possible that Socrates is a carpenter', taken in the sense of composition. But the latter itself does not, on Ockham's view, entail that Socrates exists. For it is reasonably clear that Ockham believes that a proper name, once imposed on a given individual, continues (or, at least, may continue) to function as a proper name even after that individual has ceased to exist. Hence, even though Socrates no longer exists, the term 'Socrates' is a proper name in our language, and the proposition 'Socrates is a carpenter' is a meaningful, albeit false, singular proposition in our language. But 'Socrates is a carpenter' is not impossible. Therefore, 'Socrates is possibly a carpenter' is true, even though Socrates does not exist.

This result is somewhat counterintuitive, since one might be tempted to think that the proposition in question is equivalent to the claim that Socrates has the characteristic of being possibly such that he is a carpenter. But given that Socrates has no characteristics at all unless he exists, this claim entails that he does indeed exist. Ockham, on the other hand, is apparently not tempted to think of 'Socrates is possibly a carpenter' in this way.

We are now ready to treat singular propositions of the type in question in which the subject includes a common term. Let a T-proposition be a singular present-tense *de necessario* or *de possibili* proposition without a dictum, in which the subject term is composed of a demonstrative adjective and a common term. T-propositions may be divided into primary and derived forms as follows:

(29) That A is necessarily B   (That A is not possibly not B)

(30) That A is necessarily not B   (That A is not possibly B)

(31) That A is possibly B   (That A is not necessarily not B)

(32) That A is possibly not B   (That A is not necessarily B)

(29) and (32) are contradictory forms, as are (30) and (31). The account of the truth conditions of (29) and (30) are relatively straightforward. In *de possibili* propositions of this type, however, the subject term may be taken to supposit only for what is actually such-and-such or for that which is possibly such-and such as well. This distinction raises some rather interesting semantic and philosophical problems. However, I will postpone a discussion of them until later. For the present I will concentrate on the less problematic cases, i.e. those in which the subject term is taken to supposit for what is actually such-and-such. As far as I can tell, Ockham takes this reading of (31) and (32) to be the one on which they are the contradictories of (30) and (29), respectively. With this in mind, we can formulate the truth conditions for T-propositions as follows:

(P37) An affirmative *de necessario* T-proposition, 'That A is necessarily B', is true if and only if (i) there is something for which 'that A' supposits and (ii) 'This is B' is necessary, where 'this' indicates the thing for which 'that A' supposits.

(P38) A negative *de necessario* T-proposition, 'That A is necessarily not B', is true if and only if either (i) there is nothing for which 'that A' supposits or (ii) 'This is not B' is necessary, where 'this' indicates the thing for which 'that A' supposits.

(P39) An affirmative *de possibili* T-proposition, 'That A is possibly B', where 'that A' is taken to supposit for something which is actually A, is true if and only if (i) there is something for which 'that A' supposits and (ii) 'This is B' is possible, where 'this' indicates the thing for which 'that A' supposits.

(P40) A negative *de possibili* T-proposition, 'That A is possibly not B', where 'that A' is taken to supposit for something which is actually A, is true if and only if either (i) there is nothing for which 'that A' supposits or (ii) 'This is not B' is possible, where 'this' indicates the thing for which 'that A' supposits.

Since the subject term of a T-proposition includes a common term, the non-modal proposition onto which it is mapped has as its subject a demonstrative pronoun (or proper name) that supposits for the same thing that the subject of the T-proposition supposits for. Hence, 'This white table is possibly black' is true just in case 'This is black' is possible, where 'this' and 'this white table' supposit for the same thing. On the reasonable assumption that this latter proposition is indeed possible, 'This white table is possibly black' is true, even though 'This white table is black' is impossible.

The situation is similar with respect to universal and particular modal propositions without a dictum. Such propositions are divided into primary and derived forms as follows:

(33)	Every A is necessarily B	(No A is possibly not B)
(34)	Every A is necessarily not B	(No A is possibly B)
(35)	Some A is necessarily B	(Some A is not possibly not B)
(36)	Some A is necessarily not B	(Some A is not possibly B)
(37)	Every A is possibly B	(No A is necessarily not B)
(38)	Every A is possibly not B	(No A is necessarily B)
(39)	Some A is possibly B	(Some A is not necessarily not B)
(40)	Some A is possibly not B	(Some A is not necessarily B)

I will again take the *de possibili* propositions to be such that their subject terms are understood to supposit for what is actually such-and-such. Hence, the following pairs are contradictory: (33) and (40), (34) and (39), (35) and (38), and (36) and (37). And, Ockham tells us, the following pairs are related as logical contraries: (33) and (34), (33) and (36), and (34) and (35). These relationships are captured by the following:[62]

(P41) A present-tense *de necessario* A-proposition, 'Every A is necessarily B', is true if and only if (i) there is something for which 'A' supposits and (ii) 'This is B' is necessary, no matter which of the supposita of 'A' is indicated by 'this'.

(P42) A present-tense *de necessario* E-proposition, 'Every A is necessarily not B', is true if and only if (i) there is nothing for which 'A' supposits or (ii) 'This is not B' is necessary, no matter which of the supposita of 'A' is indicated by 'this'.

(P43) A present-tense *de necessario* I-proposition, 'Some A is necessarily B', is true if and only if (i) there is something for which 'A' supposits and (ii) in at least one instance in which 'this' indicates something for which 'A' supposits, 'This is B' is necessary.

(P44) A present-tense *de necessario* O-proposition, 'Some A is necessarily not B', is true if and only if either (i) there is nothing for which

'A' supposits or (ii) in at least one instance in which 'this' indicates
something for which 'A' supposits, 'This is not B' is necessary.

(P45) A present-tense *de possibili* A-proposition, 'Every A is possibly B',
where 'A' is taken to supposit only for what is actually A, is true
if and only if (i) there is something for which 'A' supposits and
(ii) 'This is B' is possible, no matter which of the supposita of 'A'
is indicated by 'this'.

(P46) A present-tense *de possibili* E-proposition, 'Every A is possibly not
B', where 'A' is taken to supposit only for what is actually A, is
true if and only if either (i) there is nothing for which 'A' supposits
or (ii) 'This is not B' is possible, no matter which of the supposita
of 'A' is indicated by 'this'.

(P47) A present-tense *de possibili* I-proposition, 'Some A is possibly B',
where 'A' is taken to supposit only for what is actually A, is true
if and only if (i) there is something for which 'A' supposits and
(ii) in at least one instance in which 'this' indicates something for
which 'A' supposits, 'This is B' is possible.

(P48) A present-tense *de possibili* O-proposition, 'Some A is possibly not
B', where 'A' is taken to supposit only for what is actually A, is
true if and only if either (i) there is nothing for which 'A' supposits or (ii) in at least one instance in which 'this' indicates something for which 'A' supposits, 'This is not B' is possible.

(P41)–(P48) constitute, I believe, a faithful rendering of what
Ockham has in mind.

But how are we to deal with a proposition like 'Some A is
possibly B' when 'A' is taken to supposit for what can be or is
possibly A? Does Ockham believe that the subject of such a proposition may have among its supposita merely possible beings? And,
given that he believes some such propositions to be true, is he
thereby committed to the thesis that there are merely possible
beings, i.e. unactualized possible beings?

These questions are rather difficult to settle on textual grounds
alone. However, I believe that a strong case can be made for each
of the following claims: (a) that Ockham explicitly rejects in the
Summa Logicae the thesis that there are merely possible things;
and (b) that his treatment of modal propositions in the *Summa
Logicae* does not commit him, as it were unwillingly, to that
thesis.

One way to understand the claim that there are merely possible things is as follows: among the things which populate our world some are actual beings and others are merely possible beings. The latter might have actually existed if things had turned out differently, e.g. if God had decided to create things other than those which he has created and will create. The term 'being' signifies both actual and merely possible beings, then, in the affirmative present-tense proposition

(41) Some beings are merely possible.

This proposition is taken to be a non-modal proposition whose subject is 'being' and whose predicate is 'merely possible (being)'. This predicate signifies beings which are, so to speak, real but not actual.

Now it is clear beyond doubt that Ockham rejects the claim that there are merely possible beings when it is interpreted in this way. The clearest indication of this comes in chapter 38 of *Summa Logicae* I, where he says the following:

> Similarly, being is divided into being in potency and being in act. This should not be understood to mean that something which does not actually exist but possibly exists is truly a being, and that something else which does actually exist is also a being. Rather, in dividing being into potency and act in *Metaphysics* V, Aristotle meant that the term 'being' is predicated of some (terms) by means of the word 'is' in a proposition that is simply non-modal and not equivalent to a *de possibili* proposition, e.g. 'Socrates is a being' and 'A whiteness is a being'; but of other (terms) it is not predicated except in a *de possibili* proposition, e.g. 'The Antichrist is possibly a being' or 'The Antichrist is a being in potency'. Hence, in the passage in question he wants to say that 'being', like 'knowing' and 'sleeping', is predicable both potentially and actually—and yet nothing knows or sleeps unless it actually knows or sleeps.[63]

Again, in chapter 31 of *Summa Logicae* III-1 Ockham explicitly asserts that 'Every being is actual' is a necessary proposition.[64] Hence, (41) and the equivalent

(42) Some merely possible beings are beings

are false if taken to be non-modal propositions, since the term 'being' in such a proposition supposits only for things which actually exist. Ockham, then, pretty clearly rejects the claim that there are merely possible beings.

Perhaps, however, there is another way to understand the claim in question. As we saw in section 3, Ockham rejects the suggestion that the parts of material objects are only potential beings, since in such a case a being would be composed of non-beings. It may be that he uses the term 'being' in such a way that it is equivalent to 'actual thing'. Hence, it is not surprising that he rejects (41) and (42). Nevertheless, he might consistently admit there are merely possible things and that these things are non-beings, where 'thing' is a term which signifies both beings and non-beings.

This proposal is tantamount to the suggestion that Ockham might consistently take the following proposition to be true:

(43) Some things are non-beings and some non-beings are (merely) possible things.

However, if there are non-beings, then it might be thought that their number includes impossible as well as merely possible things. Yet Ockham explicitly denies that

(44) A chimera is a non-being

is true.[65] But even if we prescind from impossibilia, it is clear from what Ockham says about infinite terms that he takes every instance of the schema '_____ is a non-being' to be necessarily false. Hence, it is also clear that he does not accept (43). Moreover, it seems doubtful to me that there is any other coherent interpretation of the claim that there are merely possible things which does not entail either (40) or (43).

But even though Ockham does not accept the thesis that there are merely possible things, it may still be the case that his treatment of modal propositions presupposes that there are such entities. Just how, then, does he explicate the truth conditions of 'Some A is possibly B' when 'A' is taken to supposit for what is possibly A?

There is no easy answer to this question, since the few hints which he does give us are open to divergent interpretations. In chapter 25 of Part II Ockham claims that the proposition 'Someone living on earth is possibly damned', where 'living on earth' is taken to supposit for what possibly lives on earth, is equivalent to 'Someone who is possibly damned is possibly living on earth'.[66]

This suggests that, in general, a proposition of the form 'Some A is possibly B', where 'A' is taken to supposit for what is possibly A, entails that something actually exists and that some actually existent being is both possibly A and possibly B. Likewise, 'Every A is possibly B', where 'A' is taken to supposit for what is possibly A, is true just in case some actual existent is possibly A and every actual existent which is possibly A is also possibly B. O- and E-propositions of this sort could be treated along the same lines, with the stipulation that they are true if no actual existent is possibly such that the subject of the O- or E-proposition in question is truly predicated of it.

On this interpretation, then, the correct account of the truth conditions of such propositions does not presuppose that there are merely possible things. Rather, such propositions, like their counterparts explicated above in (P45)–(P48), make assertions only about possibilities which pertain to actually existing things.

Unfortunately, this interpretation conflicts with what Ockham says in later sections of the *Summa Logicae*. For example, in expounding his theory of demonstration he asserts that

(45) Every man is possibly something which laughs

is necessarily true, as long as 'man' is taken to supposit for what is possibly a man. That is, (45) would be true if there were no men—in fact, it would be true even if there were no creatures at all. But if that is so, then 'man' in (45) must, it seems, have merely possible men among its supposita.

One might object at this point that God exists necessarily and, given the doctrine of the Incarnation, is both possibly a man and possibly something which laughs. Hence, (45) would still be necessarily true even on the interpretation suggested above. For even if there are no creatures, there is an actual being, namely, God, who is the sole thing which is possibly a man, and who is also possibly something which laughs. Furthermore, perhaps Ockham believes that God may assume any nature at all, e.g. that of a stone or of a donkey. In that case, each proposition like (45) that Ockham takes to be necessarily true can be handled in a similar fashion.

However, it is clear that Ockham cannot accept this rather quaint suggestion. First of all, he would surely accept as necessarily true

(46) Every whiteness is possibly a color

where 'whiteness' is taken to supposit for what is possibly a whiteness. But he explicitly claims that

(47) God is a whiteness

is necessarily false.[67] Hence, the above proposal would not afford him with a perfectly general account of propositions like (45). Moreover, he claims that the proposition

(48) Some donkey is possibly a man,

where 'donkey' is taken to supposit for what is possibly a donkey, is necessarily false.[68] But the proposal under discussion has as a consequence the claim that (48) is true, indeed necessarily true. For if God can assume any nature at all, then there is a necessary existent, namely, God, who is both possibly a donkey and possibly a man. Hence, Ockham cannot accept the account given above of the truth conditions for *de possibili* propositions in which the subject term supposits for what is possibly such-and-such. But in that case, if he takes (45) to be necessarily true, he must, it seems, be presupposing that there are merely possible men.

Nevertheless, although Ockham never gives a complete account of the truth conditions for propositions like (45), such propositions can be adequately treated within the framework of his semantic theory in a manner consistent with his avowed denial that there are merely possible beings. The first step is to show that such propositions are equivalent to propositions which are not of the type under discussion. The second step is to show that the latter propositions themselves do not entail the thesis that there are merely possible beings.

Ockham does give us one clue which proves helpful in the explication of the truth conditions for the *de possibili* propositions in question. In chapter 23 of *Summa Logicae* III–1 he admits that with respect to affirmative *de possibili* propositions that are ambiguous, it is more correct to say that the subject term is *asserted* to be able to supposit for what is possibly such-and-such than to say that the subject term *is* able to supposit for what is possibly such-and-such.[69] Analogously, he notes in other places that with respect to an affirmative S-proposition like

'Socrates is a man', it is more correct to say that its subject is asserted to supposit for Socrates rather than to say that its subject does supposit for Socrates. For if Socrates does not exist, then 'Socrates is a man' is both meaningful and false. Similarly, in the present case Ockham seems to be claiming that a proposition of the form 'Some A is possibly B' or of the form 'Every A is possibly B', where 'A' is taken to supposit for what is possibly A, implies that it is possible that there be A's. It is not clear whether he wishes to extend this condition to O- and E-propositions of this type as well. I will simply assume that he does not, i.e. that such propositions are true if it is impossible that their subject terms supposit for anything in a present-tense non-modal affirmative proposition. However, this assumption is incidental to my present argument, which can accommodate the contrary assumption just as easily.

Universal *de possibili* propositions of this type embody assertions about "every possible such-and-such." (45), for example, makes an assertion about every possible man. It tells us, to put it somewhat vaguely, something necessary about men. This intuition is, I think, adequately captured if we take 'Every A is possibly B', where 'A' is taken to supposit for what is possibly A, as equivalent to

(49) This is possible: 'Some being is A', and this is necessary: 'If a being is A, then it is possibly B'.

Note that in 'If a being is A, then it is possibly B', the subject of the consequent is taken to supposit for what is actually A. The second conjunct of (49) in effect asserts that a proposition of the form 'This is A' entails a proposition of the form 'This A is possibly B', when 'this' and 'this A' supposit for the same thing. The second of these propositions is then explicated in accordance with (P39) above.

Similarly, 'Every A is possibly not B', where 'A' is taken to supposit for what is possibly A, is equivalent to

(50) Either   (i) this is necessary: 'No being is A'
      or   (ii) this is possible: 'Some being is A', and this is necessary: 'If a being is A, then it is possibly not B'.

Comments analogous to those in the previous paragraph apply to the second conjunct of (ii) in (50). Here (P40) above is relevant.

Particular *de possibili* propositions of this type can be handled as follows. 'Some A is possibly B', where 'A' is taken to supposit for what is possibly A, is equivalent to

(51) This is possible: 'Some A is possibly B',

where 'A' in the embedded proposition is taken to supposit for what is actually A. The truth conditions for this embedded proposition are explicated as in (P47) above.

Lastly, 'Some A is possibly not B', where 'A' is taken to supposit for what is possibly A, is equivalent to

(52) Either   (i) this is necessary: 'No being is A'
        or   (ii) this is possible: 'Some being is A', and this is possible:
                   'Some A is possibly not B'.

The truth conditions for the second of conjunct of (ii) in (52) are explicated as in (P48) above.

As should be expected, (52) follows from (50), and (51) follows from (49). Again, as one should expect, each of (49)–(52) is compatible with each of the others.

As I noted, the truth conditions for each of the *de possibili* propositions without a dictum that is embedded in (49)–(52) can be explicated without presupposing that there are merely possible beings. For in each of these propositions the subject term is taken to supposit for what is actually such-and-such. The only remaining question is this: does Ockham's treatment of *de necessario* and *de possibili* propositions taken in the sense of composition presuppose that there are merely possible beings?

Take the following proposition, which Ockham admits as true when it is taken in the sense of composition:

(53) It is necessary that no man is a donkey.

What does the term 'man' supposit for in (53)? It cannot be the case that it supposits just for all actual men, since one cannot validly infer (53) from the proposition 'No man is a donkey'. Likewise, (53) cannot be inferred from the conjunctive proposition 'No man is a donkey and no man was a donkey and no man will be a donkey', where the last two conjuncts are taken in the sense of composition. For the sense of (53) is this: it has never been true, is not now true, and never will be true that some man is a donkey, and even if there were men other than those that now exist, have existed, and will exist, it would still not be true that some man is a donkey. That is, even if God had chosen, as he could have, to create human beings other than those whom he has created or will create, it would still be true that no man is a donkey. Hence, it seems that 'man' in (53) supposits for all possible men, including some that are merely possible.

Nevertheless, it is clear upon reflection that Ockham's account of the truth conditions of (53) does not commit him irrevocably to the thesis that there are merely possible things. For he explicates those truth conditions in terms of a present-tense non-modal proposition, in which the term 'man' supposits only for actually existing human beings. Thus,

> (54) 'It is necessary that no man is a donkey', taken in the sense of composition, is true if and only if this is necessary: 'No man is a donkey'.

An Ockhamistic semantics need not assign supposition directly to the terms of a modal proposition taken in the sense of composition. Rather, the terms of the dicta of such propositions point, as it were, to their own occurrence in present-tense non-modal propositions and to the semantic relations which they have entered into, now enter into, will enter into, or might have entered into in virtue of their use in such propositions. Thus, Ockham might accept the following as a full explication of the truth conditions of (53):

> (55) 'It is necessary that no man is a donkey', taken in the sense of composition, is true if and only if it is impossible that there be something for which 'man' and 'donkey' both supposit in the present-tense non-modal proposition 'No man is a donkey'.

In general, discourse about merely possible beings can be dispensed with in favor of discourse about the semantic relations that terms might have entered into. Consider the following:

> (56) 'There might have been beings other than those which have existed, now exist, or will exist' is true if and only if the term 'being' might have supposited in a present-tense non-modal proposition for beings

other than those which it has supposited for, now supposits for,
or will supposit for in such a proposition.

Ockham would presumably find the metaphysical basis for the
truth that there might have been other beings in the operation of
God's will and intellect. However, this is one metaphysical problem which a semantic account of the modalities of necessity and
possibility should not be expected to address.[70]

The above interpretation of Ockham's semantics for modal propositions taken in the composed sense might seem strained to some.
Nonetheless, it is clearly suggested by the fact that Ockham himself explicates the truth conditions of such propositions in terms
of the modal status of non-modal propositions—and not directly
in terms of the supposition of subjects and predicates in the
modal propositions themselves.

Moreover, as we have seen, he ultimately explicates the truth
conditions of propositions of all types in terms of the truth
(past, present, or future) and/or modal status of present-tense
non-modal propositions.[71] And this indicates that he could easily
dispense with all discourse about non-actual beings in favor of
discourse about the semantic relations which terms did enter into,
will enter into, or might have entered into when used in present-
tense non-modal propositions.

In fact, Ockham's general strategy in dealing with past-tense,
future-tense, and modal propositions suggests the thesis that,
strictly speaking, terms other than modal terms (construed
broadly to include 'true' and 'false') and the names of propositions have supposition only in present-tense non-modal propositions.[72] For the latter are the only propositions whose truth
conditions are explicated directly in terms of the notion of supposition. Further, the truth conditions for more complex propositions can be explicated entirely in terms of the semantic
properties of present-tense non-modal propositions. This picture
of Ockham's semantics is the basis of my somewhat vague assertion that terms in more complex propositions "point to"
their past or future or possible uses in present-tense non-modal
propositions.

The only serious objection to this view of Ockham's semantics
is that he himself explicitly speaks of the supposition of subject

terms in certain past-tense, future-tense, and modal propositions. But I pointed out before that in the case of past-tense and future-tense propositions such talk can be eliminated in favor of talk about scope distinctions. My suspicion is that the same holds true in the case of modal propositions as well.

6.   After treating modal propositions Ockham goes on to deal with exponible propositions, i.e. propositions which, though categorical in appearance, are really equivalent to disjunctive and conjunctive propositions. At this point in Part II he has already provided us with the basics of a semantic account of the truth conditions for all types of non-exponible categorical propositions. Now he wants to show that exponible categorical propositions are equivalent to conjunctions or disjunctions of the sorts of propositions already treated.[73] Hence, the sort of analysis in which he now engages differs in kind from the sort of analysis found in previous sections of Part II. We have already seen the distinction between these types of analysis in the discussion of predication above. I will now elaborate on it a bit further.

Until now Ockham has been formulating the truth conditions of categorical propositions by using the following schema:

(57)   'P' is true if and only if _____ ,

where the quotes surround an indicative sentence and the blank is filled by a proposition which is strictly equivalent to " 'P' is true" and which provides the necessary and sufficient semantic conditions for the truth of 'P'. Further, as we have just seen, a full characterization of these truth conditions can ultimately be formulated in terms of how the subject and predicate of the proposition to be explicated do supposit or did supposit or will supposit or might supposit in one or more relevant present-tense propositions.

The sort of analysis which Ockham now engages in, by contrast, has the following form:

(58)   'P' is true if and only if 'Q and (or) R' is true,

where 'P' is replaced by an exponible categorical proposition and where the hypothetical proposition on the right-hand side has as its parts the "exponents" of 'P'. This hypothetical proposition

typically contains no allusion—either explicit or implicit—to semantic properties. In fact, if a biconditional of the form of (58)
is true, then a corresponding biconditional, namely, one of the
form

(59) P if and only if (Q and [or] R),

which lacks the semantic trappings of (58), will also be true. On
the other hand, a biconditional of the form of (57) has no such
counterpart in the object language. Further, a hypothetical proposition which occurs in an analysis of the form of (58) still stands
in need of the sort of semantic analysis illustrated by (57).

One might even make the stronger claim that the two sides of
an analysis of the form of (58) are, if the analysis is correct,
strictly synonymous with one another, whereas it is fairly clear
that this is not the case in an analysis of the form of (57). Within the framework of Ockham's theory of language, such a claim
is tantamount to the assertion that the mental language contains
no exponible propositions. I will not discuss this suggestion here,
but only note that it is rather controversial.[74]

It is not difficult to see that Ockham's analysis of exponible
propositions is similar to Russell's analysis of sentences containing definite descriptions. The analyzanda, it is claimed, do not
perspicuously exhibit their true logical form. Thus, they must
be expounded in terms of simpler sentences in order for their
truth conditions to be explicated fully.

I will not attempt to survey all the types of exponible propositions which Ockham discusses. Instead I will merely try to illustrate his method by examining briefly his treatment of two
types of exponible propositions, namely, those containing infinite terms and those containing figment terms.

An infinite term is formed by prefixing the particle 'non-' to
a categorematic term, as in 'non-man', 'non-white', etc. Such
terms do not affect the quality of a proposition, i.e. its being
affirmative or negative. In this way they are similar to positive
terms. Thus, we must distinguish 'Socrates is a non-donkey'
from 'Socrates is not a donkey', and 'Some animal is a non-
man' from 'Some animal is not a man'. The first member of
each of these pairs is an affirmative proposition and hence is
true only if there is something for which its subject term sup-

posits. The second member of each pair, on the other hand, is a negative proposition which is true if there is nothing for which its subject term supposits.

Ockham uses as an example the indefinite proposition 'A donkey is a non-man'. The nominal definition of 'non-man' is 'something that is not a man'. The proposition in question, he tells us, is thus equivalent to the conjunctive proposition 'A donkey is something and a donkey is not a man'. The force of 'A donkey is something' is clearly existential. In fact, given Ockham's insistence, noted above, that 'being' supposits for all and only those things which actually exist when it is used in a present-tense non-modal proposition, we may read 'A donkey is something' as 'A donkey is a being'. Thus

(60) 'A donkey is a non-man' is true if and only if 'A donkey is a being and a donkey is not a man' is true.

Hence, 'Every donkey is a man' and 'A donkey is a non-man', though contraries, are not contradictories, for they are both false if there are no donkeys. Likewise, 'Socrates is a man' and 'Socrates is a non-man', though contraries, are not contradictories, since they are both false if Socrates does not exist. Again, 'Some man is a non-man' is true only if there is a man who is not a man—and for this reason it is impossible. However, 'Some man is not a man' is possible, since it is true if there are no men.

As noted in previous discussions, this account has the consequence that every proposition of the form '_____ is a non-being' is necessarily false. For the nominal definition of 'non-being' is 'something that is not a being'. Using (60) above as a guide, we can expound the proposition 'The Antichrist is a non-being' as follows:

(61) 'The Antichrist is a non-being' is true if and only if 'The Antichrist is a being and the Antichrist is not a being' is true.

But the proposition embedded in the right-hand side of (61) is a straightforward contradiction. Hence, 'The Antichrist is a non-being' is impossible.

Thus, Ockham's logical theory recognizes the distinction between propositional negation and terminal negation, which is not captured by standard first-order predicate logic as normally presented. Further, this distinction is philosophically important. For instance, in *The Nature of Necessity* Alvin Plantinga claims that in order to understand singular negative existential propositions we must distinguish between what he calls the predicative and impredicative senses of sentences like 'Socrates does not exist'.[75] And this distinction corresponds exactly to the distinction which Ockham draws between 'Socrates is a non-being', which is impossible, and 'Socrates is not a being', which is possible.

Figment terms are categorematic terms which are such that it is impossible that there be anything for which they supposit personally in a present-tense non-modal proposition. 'Chimera' is Ockham's favorite example of such a term. As noted above, its nominal definition is 'animal composed of a goat and a cow'. Although this example is rather controversial, my purpose here is not to specify just which terms are figment terms but merely to outline Ockham's analysis of propositions in which figment terms occur. One who objects to Ockham's example may substitute a more obvious instance of a figment term, e.g. 'round square'.

Since figment terms are necessarily empty, there is no true affirmative proposition in which such a term has personal supposition. For each such proposition implies that there is or was or will be or might be something of which the figment term in question is truly predicable. Take, for example, the affirmative proposition 'A chimera is a non-being'. Although this proposition radiates an aura of truth, it is necessarily false, since it entails the necessarily false proposition 'An animal composed of a goat and a cow is a being'. On the other hand, each negative proposition in which a figment term has personal supposition is necessarily true, since there can be nothing for which such a term supposits. For example, 'A chimera is not a man' is necessarily true, even though 'A chimera is a non-man' is necessarily false.

Thus, as Ockham emphasizes, there is no need to posit a universe of impossible entities in order to explicate the truth conditions of propositions containing figment terms. For all such affirmative propositions are false and all such negative propositions are true simply in virtue of the fact that there can be no such entities. Still, figment terms do have signification, namely, secondary signification, and thus differ in signification from one another insofar as their nominal definitions differ from one another. On Ockham's view, then, the fact that no figment term can personally supposit for anything does not entail that all such terms are equivalent in signification. This way of dealing with figment terms is surely elegant if nothing else.

One further feature of this section of Part II merits comment here. In the chapters on exclusive propositions, exceptive propositions, and propositions containing the verbs 'begin' and 'cease', Ockham assigns modes of common personal supposition to the subjects and predicates of the propositions in question. He does so, however, only after analyzing them into their exponents. Thus, it is clear that the account of the modes of common personal supposition plays no essential role in the explication of the truth conditions of these propositions—or of any others. For the three chapters just alluded to contain the only substantive discussion of the modes of common personal supposition in Part II. However, I wish to suggest, without pursuing the matter here, that a close study of these chapters might provide a clue to the mystery of just what role the account of the modes of common personal supposition is meant to play in the *Summa Logicae* as a whole.

7. In the last section of Part II Ockham deals with hypothetical propositions, i.e. propositions composed of two or more categorical propositions joined by one or more proposition-forming conjunctions or adverbs. Since exponible categorical propositions, as we have seen, are equivalent to hypothetical propositions, this section of Part II also constitutes a necessary step in the formulation of a complete semantic account of the truth conditions of exponible propositions.

Ockham divides hypothetical propositions into six species: conditional, conjunctive, disjunctive, causal, temporal, and local. I will concentrate here on the first three types. (Ockham's treatment of the last three types is, in any case, open to serious objections which go beyond the scope of this introduction.)

In each instance Ockham's strategy is to explicate the truth conditions of the hypothetical proposition in question in terms of the truth or modal status of its components or in terms of the logical relations of those components to one another. When one or more of these components are themselves hypothetical propositions, the same procedure applies to them. Hence, ultimately the truth conditions for any hypothetical proposition can be spelled out in terms of the truth or modal status of categorical propositions or in terms of the logical relations of given categorical propositions to one another. Ockham's account of hypothetical propositions, then, is continuous with and builds upon his treatment of categorical propositions.

There has been some debate about whether Ockham had the notion of material implication.[76] This issue will not be discussed here, since such a discussion would take us far beyond Part II to Ockham's fullest treatment of conditional propositions (or consequences) in Part III–3 of the *Summa Logicae*. In Part II he consistently treats conditional propositions as strict implications, i.e. as propositions which are true if and only if it is impossible both that the antecedent be true and the consequent false. I believe, in fact, that it can be shown that Ockham treats all conditional propositions along these lines, although such a claim requires support. However, even if he does treat some conditional propositions as material implications, the truth conditions for such propositions can still be formulated in terms of the truth of negative conjunctive propositions. So I will proceed directly to a consideration of conjunctive propositions.

Let 'P' and 'Q' stand for propositions and let 'not-P' and 'not-Q' stand for their respective negations. Ockham gives the following rules for conjunctive propositions:

(P49) An affirmative non-modal conjunctive proposition, 'P and Q', is true if and only if (i) 'P' is true and (ii) 'Q' is true.

(P50) A negative non-modal conjunctive proposition, 'It is not the case that P and Q', is true if and only if either (i) 'not-P' is true or (ii) 'not-Q' is true.

(P51) An affirmative *de necessario* conjunctive proposition, 'It is necessary that P and Q', is true if and only if (i) 'P' is necessary and (ii) 'Q' is necessary.

(P52) An affirmative *de possibili* conjunctive proposition, 'It is possible that P and Q', is true if and only if (i) 'P' is possible and (ii) 'Q' is possible and (iii) 'P' and 'Q' are neither contraries nor contradictories.

(P53) An affirmative *de impossibili* conjunctive proposition, 'It is impossible that P and Q', is true if and only if either (i) 'P' is not possible or (ii) 'Q' is not possible or (iii) 'P' and 'Q' are either contraries or contradictories.

Ockham gives the following rules for disjunctive propositions:

(P54) An affirmative non-modal disjunctive proposition, 'P or Q', is true if and only if either (i) 'P' is true or (ii) 'Q' is true.

(P55) A negative non-modal disjunctive proposition, 'It is not the case that P or Q', is true if and only if (i) 'not-P' is true and (ii) 'not-Q' is true.

(P56) An affirmative *de necessario* disjunctive proposition, 'It is necessary that P or Q', is true if and only if either (i) 'P' is necessary or (ii) 'Q' is necessary or (iii) 'P' and 'Q' are either subcontraries or contradictories.

(P57) An affirmative *de possibili* disjunctive proposition, 'It is possible that P or Q', is true if and only if either (i) 'P' is possible or (ii) 'Q' is possible.

(P58) An affirmative *de impossibili* disjunctive proposition, 'It is impossible that P or Q', is true if and only if (i) 'P' is not possible and (ii) 'Q' is not possible.

(P50) and (P55) are actually somewhat misleading, since Ockham never mentions propositions of the form 'It is not the case that P and Q' or 'It is not the case that P or Q'. Rather, he simply says that the contradictory of a conjunctive proposition is a disjunctive proposition whose parts are the contradictories of the parts of that conjunctive proposition, and that the contradictory of a disjunctive proposition is a conjunctive proposition whose parts are the contradictories of the parts of that disjunctive proposition. This point is perhaps significant, since it may explain why Ockham makes no mention of past-tense and future-tense conjunctive or disjunctive propositions, e.g. 'It was the case that Socrates is white and Plato is black' or 'It will be the case that Socrates is white or Plato is black'. Perhaps conjunctive propositions of this sort could be treated as temporal propositions, while disjunctive propositions of this type could be treated as disjunctive propositions in which each disjunct is past-tense or future-tense.

In any case, it should be clear from this brief discussion how Ockham's treatment of hypothetical propositions is related to his earlier treatment of categorical propositions.

Finally, I do not wish to leave the impression that Ockham has successfully completed in every respect the project on which he embarked in Part II of the *Summa Logicae*. His theory of predication, for instance, has been characterized by some as one of the most catastrophic mistakes in the history of logic.[77] Again, he spends depressingly little time discussing the truth conditions of relational propositions, i.e. propositions in which one extreme includes a term in an oblique case. His account of reduplicative propositions has been called inadequate[78] and his treatment of exceptive propositions question begging.[79] The list of complaints goes on.

Nevertheless, the project itself is of enduring philosophical importance. And in view of the renewed interest among contemporary philosophers in the theory of truth conditions, Ockham's attempt to carry out this project warrants close study.

NOTES

1. Ockham's most extensive treatment of the problem of universals occurs in the *Ordinatio* I, dist. 2, ques. IV-VIII. This section of the *Ordinatio* is found in Stephen Brown and Gedeon Gál, eds., *Ockham: Opera Theologica*, vol. II (St. Bonaventure, N.Y., 1970), pp. 99-292.

2. These three distinctions are discussed in chapters 3, 4, and 10, respectively, of Part I of the *Summa Logicae* (hereafter: *SL*). For excellent expositions of the first and third of these distinctions, cf. Trentman (30) and Spade (25).

3. This revision of (P1) would consist of three principles. The first captures the first sense of "primarily signify" found in *SL* I, chap. 33:

    (a)   A term 'T' *primarily signifies* a thing x if and only if 'This is (a) T' is true, where 'this' indicates x.

In order to accommodate the objection that on (a) the signification of a common term might constantly change in virtue of changes in things, Ockham gives a second sense to "primarily signify" which (P1) is meant to capture. On the proposed revision the point of this second sense would be captured by the following:

    (b)   A term 'T' *has primary signification* if and only if it is possible that there be an x such that 'T' primarily signifies x.

We then add:

    (c)   Term 'T' *differs in primary signification from* term 'T*' if and only if (i) both 'T' and 'T*' have primary signification and (ii) it is possible that there be an x such that 'T' but not 'T*' primarily signifies x, or 'T*' but not 'T' primarily signifies x.

The objection in question is thus avoided, since, for instance, the term 'man' as used on one occasion will never differ in primary signification from the same term as used on another occasion, even though two uses of the same term may primarily signify, in the sense defined by (a), different individuals. Note also that although terms like 'triangular' and 'trilateral' would not differ in primary signification, they would still differ in secondary signification in the sense characterized by (P2) below. If my contention, argued below, that Ockham's semantics is not commited irrevocably to the existence or subsistence of merely past, merely future or merely possible things is correct, then the above account may be taken as a possible—and perhaps even plausible—interpretation of the first part of *SL* I, chap. 33.

4. On this point and others in the discussion of secondary signification I have borrowed heavily from Spade (25).

5. Cf. Spade (25), p. 73.

6. This claim is itself somewhat problematic, as Spade notes in (24), esp. pp. 66-68.

7. (P3) can be simplified by replacing condition (ii) with the stipulation that 'T' is a categorematic term. I have chosen this more clumsy condition in order to emphasize that a demonstrative pronoun may have personal

supposition, even though it is not clear whether such a term can properly
be said to signify anything primarily.

8. Some may object to the claim that a mental term can have material
supposition, but it is clear that Ockham holds this view. See *SL* I, chap.
64, lines 59–62. (Line references are to the critical edition of the *Summa
Logicae* found in Philotheus Boehner, G. Gál, and S. Brown, eds., *Ockham:
Opera Philosophica*, vol. I [St. Bonaventure, N.Y., 1974].) Also, Loux in
(14), p. 44, fn. 2 mentions a somewhat technical difficulty with what Ockham says about material supposition in *SL* I, chap. 63. I will not discuss
this problem here, although (P4) might have to be amended slightly to accommodate precisely what Ockham says about propositional dicta which
have material supposition.

9. This seems to be what Ockham has in mind in *SL* I, chap. 65, lines
8–10, when he claims that a term can have material or simple supposition
"tantum quando terminus talis comparatur alteri extremo quod respicit
intentionem animam vel vocem vel scriptum." It is tempting—though not
unproblematic—to take "respicit" here as equivalent to "significat." For in
a subsequent passage Ockham claims that 'man' in 'Man is a species' may
have simple supposition, since 'species' signifies ("significat") intentions of
the soul. If this suggestion is correct, then it seems that in (2), p. 382 Adams
is mistaken in claiming that the term 'man' may have material supposition
in both 'This is man' (where 'this' indicates a term) and 'Man is man'. For
'this', as noted above, does not appear to signify anything primarily, and
'man' signifies only human beings primarily. Ockham does occasionally use
propositions like 'The term "man" is the term "man" '. But in such a proposition the whole extreme, namely, 'the term "man"', has personal supposition. One might be tempted to say that at least part of this extreme has
material supposition, but in *SL* I, chap. 72, lines 155–161 Ockham denies
that a part of an extreme can properly be said to have supposition. (On
this point, however, cf. Spade (26), pp. 265–268.)

10. An account of predication of this sort is proposed by Bergmann in
(6), p. 208.

11. See Trentman (29), pp. 362–363; Geach (11), p. 300; and Tweedale
(32), pp. 307–327.

12. *SL* II, chap. 2, lines 22–31.

13. See Boehner (8), p. 260. In (31) Turnbull agrees that Ockham is
attempting to define truth.

14. This shortcoming of Boehner's proposal is noted by Adams in (2),
p. 388, fn. 12.

15. See, for example, *SL* I, chap. 72, lines 121–126 and *SL* II, chap.
3, lines 13–16.

16. See Adams (2), esp. pp. 375–381. Although Adams believes that
Ockham's characterization of supposition does not fall victim to the circularity charge, she does not distinguish the two versions of that objection
which are developed below.

17. Adams indicates that neither the notion of supposition nor the notion of a term's being posited for a thing in a proposition is a suitable can-
didate for a primitive notion. See (2), p. 384. However, it is clear that an
appeal to speakers' intentions, discussed briefly at the conclusion of (2),
will not help here. For although Ockham sometimes appeals to speakers'

intentions in order to disambiguate equivocal propositions in which the same term can be taken to supposit in two or more ways, such intentions only help determine which thing or things a speaker intends the term in question to stand for. The basic notion of a term's standing for or being posited for a thing remains itself undefined.

18. A complete account of quantification would also include a treatment of singular propositions in which the predicate is determined by a universal sign, e.g. 'Socrates is every man' and 'This substance is not every animal'. The truth conditions for such propositions parallel exactly those given here for I'- and O'- propositions. Also, it is not clear whether Ockham's theory of truth conditions can successfully deal with relational statements containing multiple quantifiers, e.g. 'Some boy loves every girl'. On this point see Priest and Read (20), p. 113 and Geach (10), chap. 4. My own suspicion is that this problem is parasitic on the problem of how Ockham's theory can adequately deal with relational propositions in general. A solution to this latter difficulty would, I believe, yield a solution to the former.

19. This view is either suggested or presupposed in Boehner (7), p. 38; Turnbull (31), pp. 321–322; Scott (22), p. 586; Swiniarski (28), pp. 205 ff.; Loux (14), p. 30; Priest and Read (10), p. 310; and Spade (26). It is tentatively accepted by Adams in (2), p. 387, fn. 2. Matthews held this view in (15), but later rejected it in (16). In (9) I presupposed this picture of Ockham's account of the MCPS but have since come to reject it in light of my study of Part II and comments made on (9) by Calvin Normore at the APA West meetings in April 1978.

20. See Loux (14), p. 25.

21. See *SL* I, chap. 74, lines 12–15. This feature of Ockham's account was noted in the early 1970s by both Matthews in (16) and Swiniarski in (28), although only the former urged that the thesis that Ockham's account of the MCPS is his theory of quantification ought to be abandoned.

22. See Priest and Read (20) and Spade (26).

23. In (28) Swiniarski discusses the possibility of using this fourth mode of common personal supposition to solve the problem posed by O-propositions but correctly rejects it in that context. Such a mode of reference is discussed in some detail by Geach in (10), pp. 71 ff.

24. In (28) Swiniarski proposes such a rule to solve the problem posed by O-propositions, even though he admits that Ockham never mentions a rule of this type. For a response to this strategy, see Spade (26).

25. See *SL* I, chap. 74, lines 29–30.

26. See *SL* I, chap. 74, lines 23–29.

27. This problem is similar to the one raised by Matthews in his discussion of 'monoreferential' terms in (16), p. 21.

28. See Spade (27), p. 86.

29. *Expositio in Librum Praedicamentorum Aristotelis*, chap. 10, lines 116–118. (Line references here are taken from the critical edition of this work edited by Gedeon Gál and found in *Ockham: Opera Philosophica*, vol. II [St. Bonaventure, N.Y., 1978], pp. 135–339.)

30. See *SL* I, chap. 50, lines 14–35.

31. See *SL* II, chap. 6.

32. Loux (14), p. 46, fn. 13.

33. See Priest and Read (20), pp. 109–110. In (3) Adams claims that

Ockham is committed to the existence of infinitely many possibilia and that
he has no obviously consistent way of reducing possibilia to anything actual,
e.g. mental acts. See Adams (3), pp. 163–175.

34. See section 5 below.

35. *SL* II, chap. 3, lines 16–17.

36. *SL* II, chap. 4, lines 57–60.

37. *SL* III–3, chap. 32, lines 5–8.

38. See Loux (14), esp. pp. 33–37.

39. The thesis that the account of the MCPS is best relegated to the
theory of inference was first suggested to me by Calvin Normore.

40. Ockham discusses this point in the *Summa Logicae* at II, chap. 33,
lines 6–11 and III–3, chap. 32, lines 46–163. Both of these passages are
found in translation in Adams and Kretzmann (4).

41. *SL* II, chap. 7, lines 36–40.

42. In (14), pp. 38–40 Loux claims in effect that even if the subject of
a proposition of the form 'This A was this B' is taken to supposit for what
was A, 'this A' does not appear as the subject of the relevant present-tense
proposition.

43. *Expositio in Librum Praedicamentorum Aristotelis*, chap. 10, lines
164–166.

44. *SL* III–4, chap. 13, lines 16–17, 20–23.

45. In (3) Adams discusses at length the two theories of intentionality
which Ockham held during his philosophical career, namely, the "objective-
existence" theory and the "mental act" theory.

46. This question is important in its own right, since Adams looks to
SL II for evidence that Ockham retained a commitment to possibilia even
in his later philosophical writings. See Adams (3), p. 173.

47. At the end of section 5 I will try to make clearer the force of the
expression "points back to" as I am using it here.

48. As noted above, propositions of the sort in question are still ambiguous even after it is made clear that the subject term is taken to supposit for what was such-and-such. This indicates that the scope of a past-
tense verb may be understood in three distinct ways when its subject is
or includes a common term.

49. It should be mentioned at this point that there is a type-token ambiguity in Ockham's use of the term 'proposition'. In what follows I am
assuming that a proposition-type may be said to exist just in case at least
one proposition-token of that type exists. For more on the use of the term
'proposition' by medieval logicians, see Kretzmann (12).

50. The claim here is that the propositions said to be formulated by God
would be proposition-tokens and that the corresponding proposition-type
would exist eternally in virtue of the fact that God either formulates a
token of that type at every moment or conserves a token of that type in
existence at every moment.

51. See especially the *Tractatus De Praedestinatione et De Praescientia
Dei et De Futuris Contingentibus*, ques. 2. This work can now be found in
a critical edition in *Ockham: Opera Philosophica*, vol. II (St. Bonaventure,
N.Y., 1978). This edition is based on the edition previously published by
Philotheus Boehner, with some corrections made by Stephen Brown. Also,
this entire work is found in English translation in Adams and Kretzmann (4).

52. Ockham does not explicitly deal with propositions containing iterated modalities. However, it is clear that what he says can be extended to accommodate such propositions.

53. Loux in (14), p. 43 notes that Ockham tends to take propositions of the form '"P" is necessary' as singular propositions, whether or not the proposition substituted for 'P' is itself a singular proposition. This seems to me essentially correct despite what Ockham says at *SL* II, chap. 9, lines 50–66. However, on p. 46, fn. 17, Loux goes on to suggest that such a move "effectively denies that the proposition 'Every A is B' has any internal structure in '"Every A is B" is necessary' [and thus] makes it difficult to explain just how the proposition figures in inferential contexts." Nevertheless, it is not obvious that Ockham has a problem here. For on his view '"Q" is necessary' follows from 'If P, then Q' and '"P" is necessary' via the following rule of inference: 'If the antecedent is necessary, then the consequent is necessary'.

54. These characterizations of necessity and impossibility are found at *SL* II, chap. 9, lines 72–74 and 80–81.

55. I wish to thank Paul Spade for pointing out to me that this problem is more serious than its analogue in the case of past-tense and future-tense propositions.

56. Again I am assuming that a proposition-type is a necessary being just in case it is necessary that one of its tokens exist.

57. See Scott (23), chap. 8.

58. See esp. Prior (21), pp. 202–214.

59. See Adams and Kretzmann (4), p. 36.

60. See *SL* III-3, chap. 13, esp. lines 39–43 for Ockham's own characterization of this distinction. He then applies the distinction to *de necessario* and *de possibili* propositions in chap. 14.

61. See, e.g., *SL* III-2, chap. 5, lines 26–34.

62. Ockham's examples at various points in the *Summa Logicae* indicate that the existential implications of (33)–(36) are correctly rendered by (P41)–(P44). But if that is so, then the subjects of the *de possibili* derived forms of (33)–(36) are such that they are taken to supposit for what is actually A. For this reason I have assumed that the logical relations just noted hold when the subject terms of (37)–(40) are taken to supposit for what is actually such-and-such.

63. *SL* I, chap. 38, lines 54–66. Someone may object to my parenthetical insertion of the word 'terms' into the translation, since Ockham says only that the term 'being' is predicated of something ("de aliquo") actually and of something potentially. However, the insertion of the word 'term' here is necessary to preserve his point and is in any case consistent with his often repeated insistence that only terms are predicable and that they are predicable only of other terms. See, e.g., *SL* I, chap. 30, lines 20 ff. Unfortunately, Ockham himself sometimes talks in a way which indicates that extramental things are the subjects of propositions and of predication. But it is clear that he does not believe this.

64. *SL* III-1, chap. 31, lines 85–86.

65. *SL* II, chap. 14, lines 33–35.

66. *SL* II, chap. 25, lines 31–32. Although Ockham explicitly says only that the second of these propositions follows from the first, it is clear from the rules governing conversion that in this case the conversion is mutual as

long as the subject of the first proposition is taken to supposit for what is possibly someone who is living on earth.

67. *SL* III–1, chap. 31, lines 70–72.

68. *SL* III–1, chap. 34, lines 39–42.

69. *SL* III–1, chap. 23, lines 27–28. A similar point is made less clearly at *SL* II, chap. 27, lines 170–178.

70. Such a question is tantamount to asking, for instance, why it is that a necessary truth is true in all possible worlds. However, philosophers of Ockham's time were discussing the following question: Is something possible because God can bring it about or is it rather that God can bring it about because it is possible? For an account of the debate over this question and Ockham's opinion on this matter, see Wolter (33).

71. A complete Ockhamistic semantics would, of course, need rules to deal with propositions which are both modal and past-tense or future-tense. Such rules would establish orderings of the operations already discussed.

72. It is not clear from what Ockham says in Part II just how he would formulate the truth conditions for the metalinguistic propositions in terms of which the truth conditions for object-language propositions are formulated. This is why I have excluded modal terms and names of propositions from the thesis suggested here. However, it seems reasonable to believe that Ockham would extend the strategies outlined above to metalinguistic propositions. For instance, the proposition 'This was true: "Socrates is white"' would be true if and only if this was true: 'This is true: "Socrates is white"'. In that case it would also be true that modal terms and names of propositions have supposition, strictly speaking, only in present-tense propositions— although such propositions would still be modal in Ockham's sense. Also, a full defense of this thesis, especially if it is taken as an interpretation of what Ockham says, should include a discussion of passages such as *SL* I, chap. 72, lines 37–57, where he explicitly speaks of the supposition of terms in past-tense, future-tense, and modal propositions.

73. This is not entirely accurate, since in certain cases conditional propositions occur as parts of such conjunctive or disjunctive propositions.

74. See Ashworth (5), esp. pp. 137–142.

75. See Plantinga (19), pp. 144–152.

76. Cf. Boehner (8), pp. 319–351; Moody (17), pp. 64–80; Adams (1); and Mullick (18).

77. Geach makes this claim in several places, e.g. (10), pp. 34–36 and (11), pp. 44–61 and 289 ff.

78. See Geach (11), p. 295.

79. See Leff (13), p. 263, fn. 126.

REFERENCES

(1) Adams, Marilyn McCord. "Did Ockham Know of Material and Strict Implication? A Reconsideration." *Franciscan Studies* 33 (1973), 5–37.

(2) ———. "What Does Ockham Mean by 'Supposition'?" *Notre Dame Journal of Formal Logic* 17 (1976), 375–391.

(3) ———. "Ockham's Nominalism and Unreal Entities." *Philosophical Review* 76 (1977), 144–176.

(4) ——— and Kretzmann, Norman, trans. *Predestination, God's Foreknowledge, and Future Contingents.* New York, 1967.

(5) Ashworth, E. J. "The Doctrine of Exponibilia in the Fifteenth and Sixteenth Centuries." *Vivarium* 11 (1973), 137–167.

(6) Bergmann, Gustav. *Meaning and Existence.* Madison, Wisc. 1967.

(7) Boehner, Philotheus. *Medieval Logic.* Manchester, England, 1952.

(8) ———. *Collected Articles on Ockham*, E. Buytaert, ed. St. Bonaventure, N.Y., 1958.

(9) Freddoso, Alfred J. "O-Propositions and Ockham's Theory of Supposition." *Notre Dame Journal of Formal Logic* 20 (1979), 741–750.

(10) Geach, Peter T. *Reference and Generality.* Ithaca, N.Y., 1962.

(11) ———. *Logic Matters.* Berkeley, Calif., 1972.

(12) Kretzmann, Norman. "Medieval Logicians on the Meaning of 'Propositio'." *Journal of Philosophy* 67 (1970), 767–787.

(13) Leff, Gordon. *William of Ockham.* Manchester, England, 1975.

(14) Loux, Michael J., trans. *Ockham's Theory of Terms: Part I of the Summa Logicae.* Notre Dame, Ind., 1974.

(15) Matthews, Gareth. "Ockham's Supposition Theory and Modern Logic." *Philosophical Review* 73 (1964), 91–99.

(16) ———. "Supposition and Quantification in Ockham." *Nous* 7 (1973), 13–24.

(17) Moody, Ernest A. *Truth and Consequence in Medieval Logic.* Amsterdam, 1953.

(18) Mullick, Mohini. "Does Ockham Accept Material Implication?" *Notre Dame Journal of Formal Logic* 12 (1971), 117–124.

(19) Plantinga, Alvin. *The Nature of Necessity.* Oxford, 1974.

(20) Priest, Graham, and Read, Stephen. "The Formalization of Ockham's Theory of Supposition." *Mind* 87 (1977), 109–113.

(21) Prior, A. N. *Papers in Logic and Ethics*, P. T. Geach and A. J. P. Kenny, eds. Amherst, Mass., 1976.

(22) Scott, T. K. "Geach on Supposition Theory." *Mind* 75 (1966), 586–588.

(23) ———. trans. *John Buridan: Sophisms on Meaning and Truth.* New York, 1966.

(24) Spade, Paul Vincent. "Ockham's Rule of Supposition: Two Conflicts in his Theory." *Vivarium* 12 (1974), 63–73.

(25) ———. "Ockham's Distinctions between Absolute and Connotative Terms." *Vivarium* 13 (1975), 55–76.

(26) ———. "Priority of Analysis and the Predicates of O-form Sentences." *Franciscan Studies* 36 (1976), 263–270.

(27) ——. "Review of Michael J. Loux, trans., *Ockham's Theory of Terms: Part I of the Summa Logicae.*" *Nous* 12 (1978), 82–87.

(28) Swiniarski, John. "A New Presentation of Ockham's Theory of Supposition and an Evaluation of Some Contemporary Criticisms." *Franciscan Studies* 30 (1970), 181–217.

(29) Trentman, John. "Lesniewski's Ontology and Some Medieval Logicians." *Notre Dame Journal of Formal Logic* 7 (1966), 361–364.

(30) ——. "Ockham on Mental." *Mind* 79 (1970), 586–590.

(31) Turnbull, Robert G. "Ockham's Nominalistic Logic: Some Twentieth Century Reflections." *New Scholasticism* 36 (1962), 313–329.

(32) Tweedale, Martin. *Abailard on Universals.* Amsterdam, 1976.

(33) Wolter, Allan B. "Ockham and the Textbooks: On the Origin of Possibility." *Franziskanische Studien* 32 (1950), 70–96.

Summa Logicae
PART II:
ON PROPOSITIONS

1: On the Classification of Propositions in General

Now that something has been said about terms, we must discuss propositions. First, some classifications should be given; second, we should see what is necessary and sufficient for the truth of propositions; and, third, we must examine carefully some things concerning the conversion of propositions.

Concerning the first point it should be noted that one way to divide propositions is into categorical propositions and hypothetical propositions. A categorical proposition has a subject, predicate, and copula, and it does not include more than one such proposition. A hypothetical proposition is one which is composed of more than one categorical proposition. According to the usual view hypotheticals are divided into five species: conjunctive, disjunctive, conditional, causal, and temporal.

A conjunctive proposition is one which is composed of two or more propositions—either categoricals or hypotheticals, or one categorical and the other hypothetical—joined by the conjunction 'and'. An example of the first is 'Socrates is running and Plato is debating'. An example of the second is 'If Socrates exists, an animal exists, and Socrates is running and Plato is debating'. An example of the third is 'If a man is running, an animal is running, and Socrates is debating'. But since these last two types are rarely used, I intend to talk only about conjunctive propositions of the first type, namely, those which are composed of two categoricals.

A disjunctive proposition is composed of two or more propositions joined by the conjunction 'or'.

A conditional proposition is one composed of two or more propositions joined by the conjunction 'if', as in 'If Socrates is running, an animal is running' or 'A man exists if Socrates exists'. For it does not matter whether the conjunction in question is placed before the first proposition or between the propositions.

A causal proposition is one composed of two or more propositions joined by the conjunction 'since', as in 'Since a man is running, a man is moving'.

79

A temporal proposition is one composed of two propositions joined by some temporal adverb, as in 'When Socrates is running, Plato is debating' and, similarly, 'While Socrates is running, John is a man', and so on for the others.

Another way of dividing propositions is into non-modal (*de inesse*)[1] propositions and propositions *de modo* or modal propositions. A modal proposition is one in which a modal term occurs. A non-modal proposition is one without a modal term.

All the best thinkers seem to agree that there are only four modes, namely, 'necessary', 'impossible', 'contingent', and 'possible'. The reason is that the Philosopher did not mention more modes, nor did he specify more modes in the *Prior Analytics* when he treated the conversion of such propositions and the syllogisms composed of them.[2] Nevertheless, since he did not deny that there are other modes, it can be said, speaking more generally, that there are more modes which make propositions modal than these four.

On this point it should be noted that a proposition is called modal because of the addition of a mode to the proposition. But not any mode is sufficient to make a proposition modal. Rather, it is necessary that the mode be predicable of a whole proposition. Therefore, properly speaking, the mode of a proposition is, as it were, truly predicable of the proposition itself. And it is in virtue of such a mode or the adverbial form of such a predicable—if it has an adverbial form—or its verbal form that a proposition is said to be modal. But there are more such modes than the four mentioned above. For just as one proposition is necessary, another impossible, another possible, another contingent, so too one proposition is true, another false, another known, another not known, another spoken, another written, another thought, another believed, another opined, another doubted, etc. Therefore, just as a proposition is called modal in which the mode 'possible' or 'necessary' or 'contingent' or 'impossible' or the adverbial form of any of them occurs, so too a proposition in which one of the above mentioned modes occurs can just as reasonably be called modal. Thus, just as 'That every man is an animal is necessary' and 'Every man is necessarily an animal' are modal propositions, so too are 'That every man is an animal is known' and 'Every man is known to be an animal' and propositions such as 'That every man is an animal is true'—and so on for the others.

If someone should ask why the Philosopher did not deal with these propositions, it should be replied that the Philosopher, striving for brevity, did not want to treat these propositions extensively, for what he said about the others can be applied to these. Now in what follows it will become clear in what way many things which were said about the other modal propositions can be applied to these.[3]

A third way to divide categorical propositions is into those which are equivalent to hypothetical propositions—even though they are categoricals—and those which are not equivalent to hypothetical propositions. Exceptives, exclusives, reduplicatives, and certain others are propositions of the first kind. In fact, whenever a concrete term in the first mode[4] is the subject or predicate, the proposition in question is equivalent to a hypothetical proposition, as will become clear. Some examples of propositions of the second kind are 'An angel is a substance', 'God exists', 'God is the Father', etc.

Another division is this: some propositions are universal, some particular, some indefinite, and some singular. A universal proposition is one whose subject is a common term determined by a universal sign—whether the proposition is affirmative or negative—as in 'Every man is running', 'No man is running', 'Both of them are running', and so on. A particular proposition is one whose subject is a common term determined by a particular sign, e.g. 'Some man is running', 'A certain man is running', and so on. An indefinite proposition is one whose subject is a common term without either a universal or a particular sign, e.g. 'A man is an animal', 'An animal is running', and so on. A singular proposition is one whose subject is the proper name of something, or a demonstrative pronoun, or a demonstrative pronoun with a common term. An example of the first is 'Socrates is running'; an example of the second is 'He is running', pointing to someone; an example of the third is 'This man is an animal'.

Nevertheless, with respect to many propositions one may be uncertain as to what their quantity is. The following are examples:

(1) 'They are running'.[5]

(2) 'One of the two is running'.

(3) Likewise, a part of a conjunctive proposition in which the subject is some relative pronoun, as in 'Socrates is running and he is debating'.

(4) Similarly, propositions such as 'It is not the case that every man is running', 'It is not the case that no man is an animal', and so on.

(5) Likewise, propositions such as 'Man is a species', 'Animal is a genus', 'Man is in the nominative case', and so on.

(6) Similarly, propositions such as 'God creates', 'God generates', 'God is the Father and the Son and the Holy Spirit'.

(1) To the first of these it should be said that 'They are running' is a singular proposition, since such a demonstrative pronoun supposits for specific things.

Now someone might claim that it is never proper to add a universal sign to a singular proposition. Hence, just as 'Every Socrates is running' is not well-formed, neither is 'Every that is an animal' or 'Every he is running'. But it is proper to say 'All these are running'. Therefore, the proposition 'They are running' is not singular.

It should be replied that according to the common way of speaking it is proper to add such a sign to a plural term, even if the latter is a demonstrative pronoun—although perhaps, strictly speaking, such a sign should not be added, since 'They are running' and 'All these are running' are totally equipollent. If the latter is proper, then nothing more is conveyed by the one that by the other. Still, just as sometimes the same expression is repeated within the same subject or predicate for some particular reason, so too a universal sign is added to a plural pronoun for the sake of greater expression or emphasis or for some other such reason—although, literally and properly speaking, it should not be so added.

(2) To the second it should be said that 'One of the two is running' is an indefinite proposition, just as 'Both of them are running' is universal. For a universal sign like this, which distributes over only two things, can be added to a plural pronoun and render a proposition universal. And thus what was said earlier, namely, that a proposition whose subject is a demonstrative pronoun is singular, should be understood to apply when that pronoun is in the nominative case. However, when it is in an

oblique case the proposition need not be singular, but can be universal or indefinite. And, in the same way, when it is said that a proposition whose subject is a common term with a universal sign is a universal proposition, it should be understood that a proposition is also universal when such a sign is added to a pronoun in the genitive case. Therefore, propositions such as these are universal: 'Both of them are running', 'Each of them is a man', and so on. Likewise, propositions such as the following are particular: 'Some of them are running' and 'Some of them are animals'. For the particular sign is added to a pronoun in the genitive plural and the sign itself is in the nominative case.

(3) To the next one it should be said that when a relative pronoun has as its antecedent a discrete name it renders the proposition singular. When it has as its antecedent a common name it renders the proposition indefinite. Thus, in 'Socrates is running and he is debating'—if it is properly formed—the second part of the conjunctive is singular. But the second part of the conjunctive proposition 'A man is running and he is debating' is indefinite, since the relative supposits for the same thing or things that its antecedent supposits for. Therefore, whether the proposition is singular or indefinite depends on whether the antecedent of the relative term is a discrete or proper name or a common name.

(4) To the fourth it should be said that propositions like 'It is not the case that every man is running' and 'It is not the case that no man is an animal' are particular, since the negation precedes the universal sign. Therefore, when it is said that a particular proposition is one whose subject is a common term, etc., the following should be added: ". . . unless a negation precedes the particular sign; and a proposition is particular when its subject is a common term with a universal sign preceded by a negation." Hence, propositions such as these are particular: 'It is not the case that every man is running' and 'It is not the case that no man is an animal'. And propositions such as these are universal: 'It is not the case that some man is running' and 'It is not the case that a certain man is not running' and so on.

(5) To the fifth uncertain case: with respect to propositions like 'Man is a species', 'Animal is a genus', and 'Man is in the nominative case'—and, in general, with respect to any proposition in which a term supposits simply or materially—it can be said

arbitrarily, as it were, either that they are singular or that they are indefinite. For this depends more on how one decides to use the terms 'singular proposition' and 'indefinite proposition' than on any substantive issue.

Hence, if one wishes to say that a proposition whose subject is a common term without a sign and without a preceding negation is always indefinite, then he should say that all propositions like those in question are indefinite. On the other hand, if one wants to use these terms in another way, then he should say something else. For he should say that it is not sufficient that the subject be a common term of this sort, but that it is necessary to add that such a common term is suppositing personally. And in that case all propositions in which terms supposit simply or materially are singular.

(6) Almost the same thing holds for the last uncertain case. For if one wants to call every proposition in which the subject is a term predicable of two or more really distinct supposita an indefinite proposition, then he should say that propositions like 'God creates', 'God generates', etc., are indefinite. The reason for this is that 'God' is a term predicable of more than one suppositum. On the other hand, if one wants to say that a proposition is not indefinite unless the common term may be predicated of several supposita which are not simply one thing, then he should say that 'God creates' and other propositions of this sort are singular and not indefinite.

Therefore, it should be said that a universal proposition is (a) one in which the subject is a common term determined by a universal sign and not preceded by a negation—this is needed because of propositions like 'It is not the case that every man is running' and 'It is not the case that no man is an animal'; or (b) one in which the subject is a common term without a universal sign but with a preceding negation—this is needed because of propositions like 'It is not the case that some man is running' and 'It is not the case that a man is an animal', which are universal; or (c) one in which the subject is a demonstrative pronoun in the genitive plural with a universal sign but with no preceding negation—this is needed because of propositions like 'Both of them are running' and 'Each of them is a man'; or (d) one in which the subject is a relative pronoun whose antecedent has confused and distributive supposition—this is needed because of propositions like 'Every man is running and he is debating', since the second part of the conjunctive is universal in the same way that the first part is. And according to one view it should be added that such a common term is suppositing personally. Hence, on that opinion the following are not universal: 'Every man is a common term with a universal sign' and 'Every man is composed of a common term and a universal sign'. But one who holds this opinion must concede that, strictly speaking, numerically the same proposition is universal and singular, because in numerically the same proposition the same term can supposit simply (or materially) and personally. If the term supposits simply or materially, the proposition will be singular. If it supposits personally, the proposition will be universal. For example, assume that I have two respondents and that to one of them I specify that when I utter the proposition 'Every man is a common term determined by a universal sign', I want the expression 'every man' to supposit materially. In that case he would concede that the proposition is singular. To the other, let us assume, I specify that I want the subject to supposit personally. In that case he would concede that the proposition is universal. So in the posited circumstances a single proposition is uttered, and yet one person, responding correctly, will say that it is singular, and the other will say that it is universal. Consequently, a single proposition will be singular and universal. But this is no more inappropriate than saying that numerically the same proposition is known and not known because it is known by one person and not known by another. In the same way, one who holds the opinion under discussion should concede, strictly speaking, that numerically the same proposition is true and false, necessary and impossible, and that the same syllogism is demonstrative and yet sophistical and incorrect in form.

But what should be said about these cases will become clear in what follows.

From what has been said one can easily tell which propositions are universal, which are indefinite, and which are singular.

A sixth division of propositions can be made. For some propositions are present-tense, e.g. 'A man is an animal', 'A man is running', etc.; some are past-tense, e.g. 'Socrates was a man', 'Soc-

rates was white', etc.; and some are future-tense, e.g. 'A man will
be white', etc. Some propositions are present-tense in form but
equivalent to past-tense or future-tense propositions, e.g. 'This is
future' and 'This is past' and others like them.

Another division is this. Some propositions are such that both
of their extremes are in the nominative case, and some are such
that one of their extremes is in an oblique case. Sometimes the
oblique case occurs in the subject, as in 'Hominem videt asinus',[6]
and sometimes it occurs in the predicate, as in 'A donkey belongs
to a man'.[7]

2: What is Required for the Truth
of a Singular Non-Modal Proposition

Now that the foregoing classifications, which are not subordinated to one another, have been given for propositions, we
must see what is required for the truth of propositions. We will
first discuss singular non-modal present-tense propositions whose
subjects and predicates are both in the nominative case and
which are not equivalent to hypothetical propositions.

On this point it should be noted that for the truth of such a
singular proposition which is not equivalent to several propositions it is not required that the subject and predicate be really
identical, or that the predicate be in reality in the subject or
that it really inhere in the subject, or that the predicate be
united to the subject itself outside the mind. Thus, for the truth
of 'This is an angel' it is not required that the common term
'angel' be really identical with what is posited as the subject, or
that it be really in that subject, or anything of this sort. Rather,
it is sufficient and necessary that the subject and predicate supposit for the same thing. And, therefore, if in 'This is an angel'
the subject and predicate supposit for the same thing, the proposition will be true. Thus, it is not asserted that this thing has

angelhood or that angelhood is in it—or anything of this sort.
Rather, it is asserted that this thing is truly an angel—not, indeed,
that it is the predicate, but that it is that for which the predicate supposits.

Similarly, by means of propositions like 'Socrates is a man'
and 'Socrates is an animal' it is not asserted that Socrates has
humanity or animality. Nor is it asserted that humanity or animality is in Socrates, or that man or animal is in Socrates, or
that animal is part of the quidditative concept of Socrates. Rather,
it is asserted that Socrates is truly a man and is truly an animal.
Nor, indeed, is it asserted that Socrates is the predicate 'man' or
the predicate 'animal'. Rather, it is asserted that he is a thing
for which the predicate 'man' or the predicate 'animal' stands
or supposits. For both of these predicates stand for Socrates.

From this it is clear that, literally speaking, all propositions
such as these are false: 'Man is of the quiddity of Socrates',
'Man is of the essence of Socrates', 'Humanity is in Socrates',
'Socrates has humanity', 'Socrates is a man in virtue of humanity'—and many other such propositions which are considered
true, it seems, by everyone. Their falsity is obvious. For I take
one of them, namely, 'Humanity is in Socrates', and I ask: what
does 'humanity' stand for? Either for a thing or for an intention,
i.e. by means of this proposition it is asserted either that a real
extramental thing is in Socrates or that an intention of the soul
is in Socrates. If it supposits for a thing, then I ask: for which
thing? Either for Socrates, or for a part of Socrates, or for a
thing which is neither Socrates nor a part of Socrates. If for
Socrates, then the proposition is false, since nothing which is
Socrates is in Socrates—for Socrates is not in Socrates, even
though Socrates is Socrates. And in the same way humanity is
not in Socrates but is Socrates, if 'humanity' supposits for a
thing which is Socrates. On the other hand, if 'humanity' stands
for a thing which is a part of Socrates, then the proposition is
false, because anything which is a part of Socrates is either matter or form or a composite of matter and form—and just one
human form and not another—or it is an integral part of Socrates. But humanity is no such part, as is clear inductively. For
humanity is not an intellective soul. For if it were, then real
humanity would have remained in Christ in the tomb, and

humanity would have been really united to the Word in the tomb, and, consequently, he would really have been a man—which is false. Similarly, humanity is not matter. Nor is humanity the body of Socrates or his foot or his head, and so on for the other parts of Socrates. For no part of Socrates is humanity—rather, it is only a part of humanity. As a result, 'humanity' cannot supposit for a part of Socrates. If it supposits for a thing which is neither Socrates nor a part of Socrates, then, since such a thing could only be an accident or some other thing which is not in Socrates, 'humanity' would supposit for an accident of Socrates or for some other thing which is neither Socrates nor a part of Socrates—and it is clear that that is false. If, moreover, 'humanity' supposits for an intention of the soul, then the proposition is clearly false. For an intention of the soul is not in Socrates. And so it is clear that 'Humanity is in Socrates' is false no matter how it is understood.

One can argue in the same way with respect to all the other propositions noted above. For if man or humanity is of the essence of Socrates, I then ask: what does 'man' or 'humanity' supposit for? Either for Socrates, in which case it would be asserted that Socrates is of the essence of Socrates—which is not true. Or if it supposits for a thing other than Socrates, then it supposits either for a part of Socrates—but this cannot be, since no part of Socrates is a man or humanity—or for something else which is neither Socrates nor a part of Socrates—but it is clear that no such thing is a man or humanity unless it is Plato or John or some other man. And it is manifest that no man other than Socrates is of the essence of Socrates. On the other hand, if it supposits for an intention of the soul or for a spoken word, it is clear that in that case it is not of the essence of Socrates. And so it is obvious that all such propositions are literally false.

Now someone might claim that humanity is in Socrates and is of the essence of Socrates, and that, nevertheless, it is neither Socrates, nor matter, nor form, nor an integral part—rather, it is a common nature which enters into a composition with the individual difference of Socrates. Hence, it is a part of Socrates but neither matter nor form.

I argue against this view at length in several places, namely, in my commentaries on the first book of the *Sentences*, on the book of Porphyry, and on the *Categories*.[1] At present I will offer some arguments against it.

The first is this. If humanity were something different from singular things and of the essence of singulars, then the same thing, while remaining unchanged, would be in many singular things. And so the same thing, while remaining naturally unchanged, would be in many distinct places without a miracle. But it is obvious that this is false.

Similarly, in that case the same thing, while remaining unchanged, would be damned in Judas and saved in Christ. And so there would be something miserable and damned in Christ—which is absurd.

Likewise, in that case God would not be able to annihilate an individual unless he annihilated or destroyed every individual of the same genus. For when something is annihilated, nothing of it remains and, as a result, such a common nature does not remain. Consequently, no individual in which it is remains, and so each individual would be annihilated or destroyed.

Further, I take that humanity which you posit in Socrates and in every other man, and the donkeyhood which you posit in every donkey. And let that humanity be called A, so that A stands just for that humanity; and let that donkeyhood be called B, so that B stands just for that donkeyhood. Then I ask: are A and B just two things, or more than two things, or not more than one thing? It cannot be said that they are not more than one thing. For in that case necessarily either they are one thing, or neither A nor B is a thing, or A is not a thing, or B is not a thing. It is clear, even according to those who hold this position, that the first answer cannot be given. Nor can the second answer be given, since these same people deny it when they claim that humanity is a real thing and, likewise, donkeyhood. Nor can the third answer be given, since there is no more reason for claiming that B is not a thing than for claiming that A is not a thing, and conversely. Therefore, it is absolutely necessary to say that A and B are more than one thing. Further, it cannot be claimed that they are more than two things. For if they are more than two things and if they are not more than two universal things, then they are more singular things. And, as a result, they are not distinguished absolutely from singular things. Therefore, the only remaining alternative is that they are two things and no more. Consequently, each of them is one in number, since each will be one thing in such a way that it is not many things. And this is what it is to be one in number, namely, to be one thing and not many. For that ought to be the description of being one in number. For if this were to be denied, I might just as easily claim that Socrates is not numerically one thing even if he is one thing and not many things.

Hence, it is the opinion of the Philosopher as well as the truth that the predicate 'is one in species' or 'is one or the same in genus' is never predicated except of an individual or individuals, each of which is one in number. Thus, 'Socrates and Plato are one in species' and 'Socrates and this donkey are one in genus' are true. And nothing other than individuals is one in species or in genus. And so it is the case that that humanity which is posited in every man is one thing and not more than one thing and, consequently, that it is one in number. From this it follows that numerically one thing would be in every man.

Moreover, I think that in other places I have sufficiently responded to arguments which seem to contravene the view I have set forth.

Nor does it help to claim that the humanity of Socrates is only formally distinct—and not really distinct—from Socrates. For such a distinction should not be posited in creatures, although it can in some sense be posited in the divinity. This is so because among creatures it is impossible to find any numerically one thing which is really more than one thing and is each of those things, as is the case with God. For in God the divine essence is three persons and it is each of those persons, and yet one person is not another. For to say that the essence and a person are formally distinguished, in the true sense, is nothing other than to say that the essence is three persons and a person is not three persons. Similarly, I understand the proposition, 'The essence and the Paternity are formally distinguished' to mean nothing other than the proposition 'The essence is the Filiation and the Paternity is not the Filiation and yet the es-

sence is the Paternity'. Likewise, to say that the Paternity and
the Active Procession are formally distinguished is nothing other
than to say that the Paternity is not the Filiation and that the
Active Procession is the Filiation and yet that the Paternity is
the Active Procession.

And so, generally, when two things are truly said to be formally distinguished, this is nothing other than to say that something is truly affirmed of the one and truly denied of the other,
and yet that one of those two things is truly affirmed of the
other—without any variation or equivocation or verification for
different things, as happens in particular and indefinite propositions. But this can never occur except when one simple thing is
more than one thing, as a single divine essence is three persons
and as a single Active Procession is the Paternity and the Filiation. And since it cannot happen among creatures that one thing
is more than one thing and is each of them, a formal distinction
ought not be posited in creatures. And so it is clear that it should
not be claimed that the humanity of Socrates is formally—but
not really—distinguished from Socrates. The same holds for propositions like 'Animality is distinguished from a man', and so on
for the others. In the commentary on the first book of the *Sentences,* distinction two I proved, moreover, that such a formal
distinction must not be posited in creatures.[2]

3: What is Required for the Truth of an
Indefinite Proposition and of a Particular Proposition

Now that we have seen what suffices for the truth of a singular
proposition, we must see what is required for the truth of an indefinite proposition and of a particular proposition.

It should first be noted that if a proposition is not called indefinite or particular except when its subject term supposits per-

sonally, then an indefinite and a particular are always interchangeable. For example, the following are interchangeable: 'A man is running' and 'Some man is running'; 'An animal is a man' and 'Some animal is a man'; 'An animal is not a man' and 'Some animal is not a man'. And it is sufficient for the truth of such a proposition that the subject and predicate supposit for some same thing if the proposition is affirmative and a universal sign is not added to the predicate—I mention this because of propositions like 'Some animal is every man' and 'Some angel is every angel'. On the other hand, if such a proposition is negative, then it is required that the subject and predicate not supposit for all the same things. In fact, it is required either that the subject supposit for nothing or that it supposit for something for which the predicate does not supposit. This is so because the truth of any of its singulars is sufficient for the truth of such a proposition. For example, the truth of 'This animal is a man' or 'That animal is a man' is sufficient for the truth of 'Some animal is a man'. Similarly, the truth of 'This animal is not a man', referring to any animal, is sufficient for the truth of 'An animal is not a man'. This is so because a consequence—without distribution—from an inferior to a superior is always valid. And this should be understood to apply when the superior is predicated of the inferior—for otherwise one cannot properly argue from an inferior to a superior. Thus, if there are no men and if there are no animals except for a donkey, then this consequence is not valid: 'A man is not a donkey; therefore some animal is not a donkey'. Similarly, unless the proposition 'A white man is a man' is true, this does not follow: 'A white man is not an animal; therefore a man is not an animal'. Still, the affirmative counterparts of such consequences are valid, whether or not the superior is predicated of the inferior. For whether or not a man is an animal, this always follows: 'A man is running; therefore an animal is running'. Similarly, whether or not a man is white, this is valid: 'A white man is an animal; therefore a man is an animal'.

And so it is clear in what way an indefinite or particular proposition is true if the subject supposits for something that the predicate does not supposit for. However, this is not always required. Rather, it is sometimes sufficient that the subject of an indefinite or particular negative supposit for nothing. For example, if no man is white, then 'A white man is not a man' is true, even though the subject supposits for nothing. For it supposits for neither a substance nor an accident.

From these considerations it is clear that if the proposition 'God generates God' is indefinite, then according to the view spoken of above[1] it should be conceded without qualification that the Father, who is God, generates God. In the same way one can properly concede 'God does not generate God', since it has the true singulars 'The Son does not generate God' and, similarly, 'The Holy Spirit does not generate God'. Thus, one argues from an inferior to a superior in 'The Son does not generate God; therefore God does not generate God', just as one does in 'This angel does not understand; therefore an angel does not understand'. Still, it should not be thought that in God something is superior and something is inferior. For the superiority and inferiority under discussion are found only among terms, whether the terms are spoken words or concepts or intentions of the soul.

Still, it might be true that certain saints sometimes deny propositions such as 'God does not generate God' and 'God does not proceed from God' because of certain heretics, i.e. in order that they not appear to be denying 'God generates God'. Nevertheless, according to the view in question it is not necessary, properly speaking, to deny this proposition. However, according to the other view something else should be said.

Second, it should be noted that if anyone claims that every proposition is indefinite in which the subject is a common term without a sign—whether it supposits personally or simply or materially—then it follows that he should say that a particular and an indefinite are not always interchangeable. This happens when the subject of the indefinite supposits simply and the subject of the particular supposits personally. For example, these two propositions are not interchangeable: 'Man is a species' and 'Some man is a species'. For in 'Man is a species', 'man' can supposit simply, but in 'Some man is a species', the term 'man' can supposit only personally, since a particular sign is added to it and it is not matched with something which pertains to a particular sign.[2] And so 'Man is a species' must be distinguished, since 'man' can

supposit either simply or personally. However, 'Some man is a
species' should not be distinguished, since in it the term 'man'
can supposit only personally. The reason is that a particular sign
is added to it. However, in 'Some man is composed of a common
term and a particular sign', the term 'man' can supposit either
personally or materially. Thus, this proposition and ones just like
it must be distinguished—but not the others.

But what is sufficient for the truth of such an indefinite proposition—if, indeed, it is indefinite? It should be said that it is sufficient for the truth of such a proposition that the subject and
predicate supposit for the same thing if the proposition is affirmative, or that they not supposit for the same thing if the proposition is negative. Thus, what suffices for the truth of a singular
proposition suffices here, for our understanding with respect to
such a proposition is the same as that with respect to a singular
proposition. Thus, it is commonly claimed that such a proposition is singular—and this claim is reasonable enough.

Now someone might object that if in such a proposition the
subject and predicate supposited for the same thing, then the
same thing would be predicated of itself. It should be responded
that this does not follow. For although both the subject and
predicate supposit for the same thing, still that which supposits
is not the same. Hence, even in the proposition 'Socrates is this
man' the same thing is not predicated of itself, although the subject and predicate supposit precisely for the same thing. For a
proper name and a demonstrative pronoun with a common term
are not the same thing. And one of them is just the subject and
the other is just the predicate. And so the same thing is not
predicated of itself, although the terms supposit precisely for
the same thing.

Likewise, in 'Every man is risible' the subject and the predicate
supposit precisely for the same thing, and yet the same thing is
not predicated of itself. The reason is that that which is the subject is not the same as that which is the predicate, since that
which supposits and that for which it supposits are different. And
so even though that for which both terms supposit is the same, it
is still not the case that that which supposits is the same.

Finally, it should be noted that although I have been using as
examples propositions which are equivalent to hypothetical propo-

sitions—and what has been said is true of them—still what has been said is also true of indefinite and particular propositions which are not equivalent to hypotheticals, e.g. 'God creates', 'God generates', 'An angel is a spirit', 'Some angel is a substance', and others of this sort.

4: On Universal Propositions

Third, we must discuss universal propositions.

It should first be noted that there are several types of universal propositions, corresponding to the diversity of universal signs. Now some posit a manifold distinction of universal signs. For it is said that some are distributive indifferently over substance and accident, e.g. 'every', 'any', 'each one', 'no', 'both', 'neither', and so on. Others are distributive only over accidents, e.g. 'any kind of', 'however often'—and perhaps there are others.

But this distinction can be understood either correctly or incorrectly. For if it is thought that 'any kind of' is simply distributive over accidents in the same way that 'every' or some such sign is distributive over substance and accident, this is false, as will become obvious. However, if it is thought that it is distributive in a certain way, namely, disjunctively among species or conjunctively among species or in some such way, then the point can be conceded.

Another division of universal signs which is posited is that some are distributive over subjective parts and some over integral parts. The first type are those like 'every', 'no', 'both', 'neither', and so on. The second type are those like 'whole'. But how this distinction should be understood will be discussed in what follows.[1]

Another posited division of universal signs is that some can distribute over any number of things, e.g. 'every', 'no', and others of this type, and some can distribute over only two things, e.g. 'both' and 'neither'.

Thus, we should first discuss those signs which distribute in-differently over substance and accident and over subjective parts and over any number of things—like 'every', 'no', 'anyone', 'any-thing', 'each one', etc.—and we should discuss the propositions in which such signs occur.

It should first be noted that no such sign signifies anything by itself or is imposed to signify anything determinately. Rather, it is used to make the term to which it is added stand for all its significata and not just for some. That is why it is called a syn-categorematic term. The same holds for many other terms and, in general, for all terms which, when taken by themselves, cannot be extremes of any proposition—if they are understood signifi-catively, as was said earlier.[2]

Second, it should be noted that the sign 'every' differs from the signs 'any' and 'each', since the sign 'every' can only be added to a term which agrees with it in case, so that the term to which it is added and the sign are in the same case. For example, these are properly formed: 'Every man is an animal', 'Socrates sees every man', 'A donkey belongs to every man'. However, the signs 'each' and 'any' can be added to a term which is in the same case and to a term which is in a different case, namely, the genitive plural. For example, 'Each man is running' is properly formed, and so are 'Any and each of them is running' and 'Any of the men is an animal'. However, 'Every of them is running' is not properly formed.

And if anyone wants to know the reason for this diversity, it should be said that in this case, as in many others in both grammar and logic, there is no reason other than the decisions of those who instituted the terms and those who use them.

Third, we must posit certain rules which are common to the signs 'every', 'any', 'each', and others like them, if there are any others. These rules are also common to many propositions which are equivalent to hypothetical propositions, e.g. 'Every man is an animal', 'Every white thing is running', etc., as well as to others which are not equivalent to such hypotheticals, e.g. 'Every God exists', 'Every angel exists', and others of this type.

It should first be noted that for the truth of such a universal proposition it is not required that the subject and predicate be in reality the same thing. Rather, it is required that the predicate

supposit for all those things that the subject supposits for, so
that it is truly predicated of them. And if this is the case, then
the universal proposition is true—unless some special cause inter-
venes. And what is commonly said is that for the truth of such a
universal proposition it is sufficient that each of its singulars be
true.

From this it is clear that certain claims which are made by
some thinkers are false.[3] One is that the sign 'every' requires
three appellata. For suppose that only one angel understands
and that no man understands. In that case 'Every creature which
understands is an angel' is true, and yet there are not three things
of which the name 'creature which understands' is truly predicated.
And I can prove that the proposition in question is true: each of
its singulars is true. Similarly, the predicate truly supposits for
each thing that the subject supposits for and it is truly predicated
of each thing that the subject is truly predicated of. Therefore,
the proposition is simply true.

Similarly, if there are only two men and they are white, then
'Every man is white' is true, since it has no false singular—and
yet it does not have three appellata.

From this it is clear that some thinkers incorrectly solve the
sophism 'Every phoenix exists' when they claim (a) that that
proposition is false because 'every' requires three appellata, and
(b) that 'Some phoenix does not exist' is true because 'phoenix'
supposits equally for a being and a non-being.[4] For I ask: in
what sense does 'every' require three appellata? They might
mean that it requires three real things, in which case 'Every
colored thing exists' would be false if there were only one
colored thing. But this cannot be conceded, since its contradictory, 'Some colored thing does not exist', is false—for it
has no true singular. Nor can it be claimed that 'colored thing'
supposits equally for a being and a non-being. For it is obvious
that it does not supposit for a non-being—just as it is not ·
predicated of a non-being. Hence, just as 'A non-being is
colored' is false, so is ' "Colored thing" supposits for a non-
being.' For it was explained before that a term never supposits
for something unless it is truly predicated of that thing.[5] Moreover, if 'every' requires three appellata in the sense that the
term to which it is added supposits for three things, then it is

not the case that 'Every phoenix exists' is false just because only one phoenix exists. For according to that thinker 'phoenix' supposits equally for a being and a non-being—and no more for one non-being than for two. Therefore, it supposits for at least three things, and so 'every' has three appellata in this case.

Furthermore, if 'phoenix' supposited equally for a being and a non-being, then so would 'animal' for the same reason. Consequently, 'Every animal exists' would be false—which that thinker denies in another place.[6]

Therefore, it should be said that it is not the case that the proposition 'Every phoenix exists' or any other is false for the reason given above, just as it is not the case that their contradictories are true for the reason given above. Hence, if no man is laughing except Socrates, then 'Some laughing thing is not a man' is not true—indeed it will be false. Consequently, its contradictory, 'Every laughing thing is a man', will be true. Likewise, if no man is white except Socrates, then 'Some white man is not a man' will be false and, consequently, 'Every white man is a man' will be true—even though there are not three white men.

Nor does it help to object that, given the situation just posited, 'Every white man is a man' and 'Some white man is not a man' are not contradictories. For a change among things does not alter the form of propositions or, consequently, bring it about that certain propositions are contradictories at one time and not at another.

From these considerations it also follows that these thinkers make a false claim when they say that if there is only one white thing and only one black thing and only one gray thing, then each of these is false: 'Every white thing exists', 'Every black thing exists', 'Every gray thing exists'. And they also deny this syllogism: 'Every colored thing exists; every white thing is colored; therefore every white thing exists'.

Similarly, on the assumption that there are no donkeys, they deny this syllogism: 'Every animal is a man; every donkey is an animal; therefore every donkey is a man'. They claim that the verb 'to be' is equivocal in these syllogisms, since in the major premises it is taken for an operation of a being—and this is the 'to be' of what exists—whereas in the minor premises it is taken for the 'to be' of condition or consequence. The verb 'to be' in this sense occurs when one says: 'If it is white, then it is colored'.

This claim is completely irrational, for it amounts to destroying every syllogistic form. For whenever it pleases me, I will say that 'to be' is equivocal in the propositions, and I will ascribe at will a fallacy of equivocation to every syllogism.

Similarly, just as a syllogism holds for all terms, so it holds no matter how things change. But according to Aristotle this is now a good syllogism: 'Every colored thing exists; every white thing is colored; therefore every white thing exists'. Similarly, this syllogism is now in fact good: 'Every animal is a man; every donkey is an animal; therefore every donkey is a man'. For these syllogisms are regulated by the rules governing 'every' (*dici de omni*).

And surely, whoever denies such syllogisms is incapable of perceiving any truth whatsoever. Therefore, even if every white thing and every donkey were destroyed, these would still be good syllogisms. And they would still in that case conform to the rules governing 'every' (*dici de omni*), just as they now do.

Hence, distinctions such as that between the 'to be' which is an operation of a being and the 'to be' of condition are frivolous, and they are posited by those who do not know how to distinguish between a categorical proposition and a conditional proposition. Hence, these propositions are distinct: 'A donkey is an animal' and 'If a donkey exists, an animal exists'. For the one is categorical and the other is conditional and hypothetical—and they are not interchangeable. Rather, one can be true while the other is false. In the same way, 'A non-creating God is God' is now false, and yet these conditionals are true: 'If a non-creating God exists, then God exists' and 'If this is a non-creating God, then it is God'.

Similarly, no reason can be found why 'to be' bespeaks condition or consequence in one categorical proposition rather than in another. And so in an equiform proposition it will either always or never bespeak condition or consequence. And so either every such proposition will be interchangeable with a conditional, or none will be. But not none, according to that thinker; therefore, all of them. And, as a result, in the case posited above 'Every animal is a man' is false, since, according to him, this conditional

is false: 'If an animal exists, a man exists'.[7] And so in the same
tract he said manifestly contradictory things and seemed not to
know the proper thing to say.

From what has been said it is also clear that all propositions
like the following are, properly speaking, false: 'Every animal is
healthy', assuming that one lion is healthy and one ox and one
man, and so on; 'Every animal was in Noah's ark'; and so on for
many others. For they have many false singulars, and it is not
the case that the predicate agrees with all those things for which
the subject supposits. Nevertheless, when such propositions or
ones just like them are posited by authors, they should be glossed—
even though they are, properly speaking, false. In the same way,
authentic words are often false in the sense which they convey,
i.e. in their literal and proper sense, and yet they are true in the
sense in which they were uttered or written. The reason for this
is that authors frequently speak equivocally and improperly and
metaphorically. And thus in exposing philosophical authorities
one ought mainly to penetrate their underlying meaning and
thought processes and intention rather than to take the words as
they sound, i.e. literally. And for the authorities in question the
following distinction, which is posited by some, is helpful: when
the sign 'every' is joined to a common term which contains many
species under it, the distribution can be made either over the
singulars of the genus or over the genera of the singulars, i.e.
either over immediate or remote parts, or either over parts according to species or according to number, or either over species
or individuals. But this must not be understood to be the literal
meaning of such a sign. For a sign never distributes a term over
anything except those things for which the term supposits. But
it has just now been said that such a term supposits only for individuals and not for species. Therefore, it is distributed only
over individuals and not over species. And, therefore, the distinction in question should be understood in the following way. By
means of such a proposition either it is asserted that the predicate agrees with all the individuals—and this is the literal sense;
or it is asserted that the predicate agrees with the species taken
particularly, i.e. it is asserted that the predicate is predicated of
each species taken particularly and not of each species taken
universally—and, consequently, it is not asserted that the predicate

agrees with all the individuals. But this is not what the words themselves convey. Rather, it is what was intended by the author. Thus, properly speaking, by means of the proposition 'Every animal is healthy' it is asserted that every man is healthy and that every ox is healthy, and so on for the others. For otherwise the following syllogism, which is in the first mode of the first figure and which is regulated by the rules governing 'every' (*dici de omni*) would not be valid: 'Every animal is healthy; every man is an animal; therefore every man is healthy'. But it is an optimal syllogism. Nevertheless, according to the intention of some speaker the proposition in question can be used to assert just that the following are true: 'A man is healthy', 'A lion is healthy', 'An ox is healthy'. In this way 'healthy' is predicated of each species, not for itself but for an individual, since no species is healthy—rather, only an individual is healthy. But this sense is not the literal sense of the proposition. Thus, if we take the proposition in this sense, then this argument is not valid: 'Every animal is healthy; every man is an animal; therefore every man is healthy'. And it is not inappropriate that a syllogism, which, when taken literally, is perfect, is not good when taken according to the intention of some speaker—just as this is not inappropriate with respect to the truth of a proposition, as was said earlier.[8]

Second, it should be noted that every universal proposition in which the predicate is taken universally is false if the subject or predicate is predicated of more than one thing. However, if the predicate were predicated of exactly one thing and if the same held for the subject, then the proposition could be true. Hence, if there were only one animal, say one man, then 'Every man is every animal' would be true, as would 'Every animal is every man'. But if there were more than one man or if there were any number of animals greater than one, then these propositions would be false. Therefore, 'Every phoenix is every animal' is false, even though 'Every phoenix is every phoenix' is true. Still, sometimes an indefinite or particular proposition, in which a universally taken predicate is predicated, can be true, even though the subject has many things contained under it. For example, if there were only one man, then even if there were many animals, 'Some animal is every man' would be true.

Third, it should be noted that when the sign 'all' is taken in the plural, it can have either a collective or a distributive sense. If it is taken distributively, then it is asserted that the predicate truly belongs to all those things of which the subject is truly predicated. For example, by means of 'All the apostles of God are twelve' it is asserted that the predicate 'twelve' is truly said of each thing of which the subject 'apostles' is truly predicated. And so, since Peter and Paul are apostles, it follows that Peter and Paul are twelve. But if 'all' is understood collectively, then it is not asserted that the predicate agrees with each thing of which the subject is truly predicated. Rather, it is asserted that the predicate belongs to all the things—taken at once—of which the subject is truly predicated. Hence, it is asserted that these apostles, referring to all the apostles, are twelve.

5: On Universal Propositions in which the Sign Distributes over Two Things Only

Concerning signs which distribute not over any number of things but over two things only, e.g. 'both' and 'neither', it should be noted that for the truth of such a proposition it is required that the predicate truly belong to each of the things referred to— if the proposition is affirmative—or that it be denied of each—if the proposition is negative. For example, for the truth of 'Both of them are running' it is sufficient that this one is running and that one is running. And for the truth of 'Neither of them is running' it is required that this one is not running and that one is not running.

And it should be noted that a universal proposition in which 'both' occurs differs from a universal proposition in which 'every' occurs in the following way: a proposition in which 'both' occurs can never be true when the predicate is taken universally—whether the predicate is taken with the sign 'every' or with the sign 'both'.

Hence, these propositions can in no way be true: 'Both of them are every man' and 'Both of them are both of them'—no matter which things are referred to. Still, the following can be true: 'Every man is every man' and, likewise, 'Every white thing is every white thing', and 'Every animal is every animal'. For if there were only one man or only one animal or only one white thing, then the proposition in question would be true.

The reason for this difference is that the sign 'every' can properly be added to a term which has one suppositum, while 'both' always requires two supposita, namely, the two things referred to. And so if the predicate in 'Both of them are every man' had only one suppositum, the proposition would obviously be false. For in the subject it is required that two things be referred to—but not two men, therefore one man and one non-man, or two non-men. Whichever alternative is chosen, the proposition is clearly false. And so it is clear for all the other cases.

6: On Universal Propositions in which the Sign Distributes over Integral Parts, e.g. the Sign 'Whole'

With respect to a sign which distributes over integral parts—the sign 'whole' is said to be of this type[1] —it should be noted that the sign 'whole' can sometimes be taken categorematically and sometimes syncategorematically. If it is taken categorematically, then it signifies the same thing signified by 'complete' or 'composed of all its parts'. And when it is so taken, then insofar as the truth of what is said is concerned, not adding it has the same effect as adding it. Hence, whatever is said of a term taken with 'whole' understood categorematically can be said of that term taken without 'whole'. For if the whole Socrates is running, then Socrates is running; and if a whole man is an animal, then a man is an animal.

Nevertheless, it could be said that it is properly added only to a term which in some way introduces something composite. Thus, perhaps the following is not properly formed: 'The whole God is seen'. For this seems to imply that God is composed of parts. And in that case a consequence from a term taken without 'whole' to the term taken with 'whole' is not valid. Thus, 'God is seen; therefore the whole God is seen' is not valid, for in this case it is implied in the consequent that God is composed of several distinct things.

On the other hand, if 'whole' is understood syncategorematically, then it is a sign which is distributive over integral parts—in fact, over the parts, properly speaking, of the thing which is introduced by the term to which it is added. For example, 'Totus Sortes est minor Sorte'[2] is equivalent to 'Each part of Socrates is less than Socrates'; and 'Totus Sortes currit' is equivalent to 'Each part of Socrates is running'. And in this case no such proposition can be true unless the predicate agrees with each part of that whole which is introduced by the term to which the sign is added. In that case it is properly a sign and is said to distribute over integral parts, while other signs distribute over subjective parts.[3] This should be understood as follows: these other signs distribute over the things contained under a term, which things are not parts properly speaking, but parts only in a broad and extended sense. But the sign 'whole' distributes over parts properly so called, whether they are parts with the same definition or parts with different definitions. And 'whole' distributes in this way over the parts of that which is introduced by the term to which it is added. For example, in 'Totus Sortes est pars Sortis' a distribution is made over each part of Socrates, namely, over his matter and form, over his hands and feet, and so on for the others.

Nevertheless, it should be noted that sometimes—I don't care whether it is due to the strict sense of the term, or to the way in which it is used, or to the decision of someone who uses it— 'whole' distributes only over integral parts and not over essential parts. (Form and matter are called parts of this latter sort.) Sometimes, however, it distributes over all parts, whether they are integral or essential or of any other kind.

Now with respect to signs which are said to be distributive over accidents it should be noted that such terms as 'any kind of' and others of this type are not properly signs. Rather, they are equivalent to a phrase composed of a sign and other terms. For example, 'any kind of' is the same as 'having from among every species of quality some one quality'. Thus, it is proper for some sign to be added to it. For it is proper to say 'Anyone of any kind is running', in the same way that it is proper to say 'Anyone who has some one quality from among every species of quality is running'. And in such a case it is clear what is necessary and sufficient for the truth of such a proposition.

Such signs are not used very much in theology, so I mention them only in passing.

7: On Past-Tense and Future-Tense Propositions

Fourth, we must examine past- and future-tense propositions.

It should first be noted that any past- or future-tense proposition in which the subject is a common term, or a demonstrative pronoun with a common term, or a discrete term which introduces some composite thing, must be distinguished. For the subject can supposit either for that which is such-and-such or for that which was such-and-such, if the proposition is past-tense; or it can supposit either for that which is such-and-such or for that which will be such-and-such, if the proposition is future-tense. In either case, if the proposition is affirmative, it is required that the predicate under its proper form, i.e. the very same predicate, be truly predicated—by means of a verb of the appropriate tense—of that for which the subject supposits. Thus, it is required that a proposition in which the predicate is predicated of a pronoun referring precisely to that for which the subject supposits was true at some time (if the proposition is past-tense) or will be true at some time (if the proposition is future-

tense). For example, if the proposition 'A white thing was Socrates' is true and if 'white thing' supposits for that which is white,
then it is not required that 'A white thing is Socrates' was true
at some time. Rather, it is required that 'This is Socrates' was
true, referring to that for which the subject supposits in 'A white
thing was Socrates'. Hence, if Socrates is now white for the first
time, then 'A white thing was Socrates' is true, as long as the
subject is taken for that which is white—and yet 'A white thing
is Socrates' was never true. Rather, 'This is Socrates', referring to
Socrates, was true. And since 'white thing' in 'A white thing was
Socrates' supposits for Socrates, this latter proposition is true.
Similarly, 'A being which creates was from eternity God' is now
true, and yet 'A being which creates is God' was not true from
eternity. Rather, this was true from eternity—or would have been
true if it had been formed: 'This is God', referring to that for
which 'being which creates' supposits in 'A being which creates
was from eternity God'.

Similarly, 'A boy will be an old man' is true, and yet 'A boy
is an old man' will never be true. Rather, 'This is an old man'
will be true, referring to that person who is now a boy. And the
same holds for other such propositions.

Hence, there is this difference between present-tense propositions and past- and future-tense propositions: in a present-tense
proposition the predicate stands in the same way that the subject
does, unless something added to it prevents this; but in past- and
future-tense propositions there is a variation, since the predicate
does not simply stand for those things of which it is truly predicated in a past-tense proposition and a future-tense proposition.
For in order for such a proposition to be true it is not sufficient
that that of which the predicate is truly predicated—whether by
means of a past-tense verb or a future-tense verb—be that for which
the subject supposits. Rather, it is required that the very same
predicate be truly predicated of that for which the subject supposits in the manner asserted by means of such a proposition. For
example, assume that Socrates is now white and that he has been
white for this whole day but not before. In that case 'Socrates was
white yesterday' is false, and yet 'white' is truly predicated of
Socrates and, likewise, it was truly predicated of Socrates. But

since it was not predicated of Socrates yesterday, the past-tense proposition 'Socrates was white yesterday' is now false.

Likewise, if Socrates is now white for the first time, then 'Socrates was white' is false—and yet Socrates was that of which 'white' is now truly predicated. But since 'Socrates is white' was not true, it follows that 'Socrates was white' is now false. And the reason for this is that the predicate names its form in the way explained previously.[1] But it is not so with the subject, since for the truth of a past-tense proposition it is not required that some proposition be true in which the predicate—or that for which the predicate supposits—is predicated by means of a present-tense verb of that subject. For example, if Socrates is now white for the first time, then 'A white thing was Socrates' is true, and yet no present-tense proposition in which the predicate 'Socrates'—or that for which it supposits—is predicated of the subject 'white thing', was ever true before. For these propositions were never true: 'A white thing is Socrates', or 'A white thing is this', referring to that for which the predicate supposits in 'A white thing was Socrates'. Nevertheless, some proposition was true in which 'Socrates' is predicated of a pronoun referring precisely to that for which the subject supposits in 'A white thing was Socrates'. For in 'A white thing was Socrates' the term 'white thing' supposits for Socrates, who is now white. And 'This is Socrates', referring to Socrates, was true before.

From these remarks it is clear that 'A being which creates was always God' should be conceded. For a proposition in which 'God' is predicated of a pronoun referring to that for which 'being which creates' supposits in 'A being which creates was always God', was always true—or would have been true if it had been formed. For 'This is God' was always true. Still, 'A being which creates is God' was not always true, since before the creation of the world it was false. And 'God was always a being which creates' is simply false for the reason just stated. And the same holds for many other precisely similar propositions. And future-tense propositions should be dealt with in the same way, *mutatis mutandis,* that past-tense propositions have been dealt with.

8: How to Find Out when a Proposition, One of Whose Extremes is in an Oblique Case, is True or False

Now what has been said above is not sufficient for finding out when a proposition, one of whose extremes is an oblique term, is true or false. Rather, on this matter it is necessary to have special rules. Here are some useful grammatical rules, which I will just quickly mention.

Hence, it should be noted that just as in an affirmative proposition in which both terms are in the nominative case, for the truth of the proposition it is required that the subject and predicate supposit for the same thing, so too sometimes for the truth of a proposition in which one term is oblique, it is required that the subject and predicate not supposit for the same thing or that they not supposit for all the same things. Still, sometimes they can supposit for the same thing, depending on differences among the words and among the rules for an oblique case. Hence, when the oblique case has the force of possession, then for the truth of the proposition it is required that the subject and predicate supposit for distinct things, although this is not always sufficient. Therefore, 'Socrates belongs to Socrates' is false, and yet 'Some donkey belongs to Socrates' can be true. And just as it is with this case, so it is with many others. But sometimes the proposition can be true despite the fact that the subject and predicate supposit for the same thing, or despite the fact that the nominative term and the oblique term supposit for the same thing. For example, 'Socrates sees Socrates' is true. And the same thing can happen in many other cases. And in these cases it is not easy to give a general and firm rule.

9: What is Required for the Truth of Modal Propositions

After non-modal propositions[1] we must deal with modal propositions. And it should first be noted that sometimes a proposition is called modal because the dictum of the proposition is taken with such a mode. This is clear in the following cases: 'That every man is an animal is necessary', 'That every man is running is contingent', 'That every man is an animal is *per se* in the first mode', 'That everything necessary is true is known', 'That Socrates is running is unknown', and so on for the others. However, some propositions are called modal in which the mode occurs without such a dictum of a proposition.

A modal proposition of the first type must always be distinguished with respect to composition and division. In the sense of composition it is always asserted that such a mode is truly predicated of the proposition corresponding to the dictum in question. For example, by means of 'That every man is an animal is necessary' it is asserted that the mode 'necessary' is truly predicated of the proposition 'Every man is an animal', the dictum of which is 'That every man is an animal'. For something is called the dictum of a proposition when the terms of the proposition are taken in the accusative case and the verb in the infinitive mood.[2] However, the sense of division of such a proposition is always equipollent to a proposition taken with a mode and without such a dictum. For example, 'That every man is an animal is necessary' in the sense of division is equipollent to 'Every man is of necessity (or necessarily) an animal'. Similarly, 'That Socrates is an animal is known' in the sense of division is equipollent to 'Socrates is known to be an animal'—and so on for the others.

Hence, we should say a few things first about such propositions taken in the sense of composition and then about the others.

It should first be noted, as was just said, that by means of such a proposition it is always asserted that such a mode is truly predicated of the whole proposition which corresponds to the dictum. Certain things follow from this. One is that a universal *de necessario* proposition of this sort can be necessary even though each of its singulars is contingent or false. For instance, in the sense of composition 'That every true contingent proposition is true is necessary' is true and necessary, and yet each of its singulars is false. For 'That this true contingent proposition is true is necessary', referring to any of them, is false, since this true contingent proposition can be false. But if this is so, then the singular proposition in question is false and, consequently, is not now necessary.

But that it is necessary is asserted by means of such a singular proposition.

Similarly, 'That every false contingent proposition is false is true' is true and necessary, and yet each of its singulars is contingent, as is obvious inductively. Likewise, sometimes such a universal proposition is impossible, and yet each singular is possible and contingent. This is clear in the case of 'That both of these are true is true', referring to two contingent propositions which are contradictories. Similarly, it is clear in the case of 'That all of these are false is true', referring to all future contingent propositions—and yet each of the singulars is contingent.[3]

But in response to all these examples it can be claimed that no such proposition is universal but that each such proposition is singular. For in each such proposition the subject is a single proposition or something which supposits for one proposition.

To this it should be said that we should not worry much at present about whether, strictly and properly speaking, such a proposition is universal or particular, on the one hand, or singular, on the other. For at least Aristotle calls such propositions universal and particular, as will be shown later[4] —and I have been speaking in the same way in the present discussion. But I do not much care whether Aristotle was in that instance speaking broadly and improperly or strictly and properly. And so I claim that a proposition is universal when the dictim of a proposition is the subject with respect to the proposition as a whole and when a common term with a universal sign is the subject with respect to the subordinate construction.[5] For example, in 'That every man is an animal is necessary' the phrase 'that every man is an animal' is the subject with respect to the main verb 'is', but the common term 'man' with the sign is the subject with respect to the subordinate construction. And this is sufficient for what I have claimed. Hence, if anyone wishes to hold that such propositions are properly universal, he can easily claim that it is sufficient that a common term be the subject with respect to the subordinate construction.

From these remarks it is clear that in order to know what is required for the truth of such propositions, it is sufficient to know what is required for it to be the case that some proposition is necessary, or for it to be the case that a proposition is contingent or true or impossible or known or unknown or believed, and so on for the others—it would take too long to examine all of them in detail.

However, with respect to a necessary proposition it should be noted that a proposition is called necessary not because it is always true, but because it is true if it exists and cannot be false. Hence, the mental proposition 'God exists' is necessary, not because it is always true—for if it does not exist, it is not true—but because if it exists, then it is true and cannot be false. Similarly, the spoken proposition 'God exists' is necessary, and yet it is not always true—for when it does not exist, it is then neither true nor false. But if it is uttered, then it is true and it cannot be false, unless the signification of the terms is altered.

Something analogous should be said of an impossible proposition, namely, that it is a proposition which, if it exists, is false—and yet it is not false unless it is a proposition. And the same holds, *mutatis mutandis,* for a contingent proposition. But in order for a proposition to be known or believed, etc., more is required. However, what is required pertains to the *Posterior Analytics* and to other books.[6]

10: On Modal Propositions without a Dictum

With respect to modal propositions without a dictum of a proposition, which are altogether equipollent to propositions with a dictum in the sense of division, it should be noted that such propositions are not interchangeable with the first type discussed. In fact, one can be true even if the other is false, and conversely. For example, in Aristotle's opinion 'That every man is an animal is necessary' is true in the sense of composition, while 'Every man is necessarily an animal' is false.[1] Likewise, in Aristotle's opinion 'That every truth is true is necessary' is true, and yet 'Every truth is necessarily true' is false. And so it is with many others.

For this reason it should be noted that for the truth of such propositions it is required that the predicate under its proper form belong to that for which the subject supposits, or to a pronoun referring to that for which the subject supposits. Thus, it is required that the mode expressed in such a proposition be truly predicated of a non-modal proposition in which the very same predicate is predicated of a pronoun referring to that for which the subject supposits—just as it was explained in the case of past-tense and future-tense propositions.[2] For example, for the truth of 'Every truth is necessarily true' it is required that each proposition be necessary in which the predicate 'true' is predicated of anything for which the subject 'truth' supposits. That is, it is required that each proposition like the following be necessary: 'This is true', 'That is true', referring to something for which the subject supposits. And since it is not the case that each such proposition is necessary, 'Every truth is necessarily true' is simply false.[3]

Similarly, by means of 'A being which creates is possibly not God' it is not asserted that 'A being which creates is not God' is possible, since in that case this *de possibili* proposition would be true. Rather, it is asserted that this is possible: 'This is not God', referring to that for which 'being which creates' supposits in 'A being which creates is possibly not God'. And this is simply impossible, since 'being which creates' supposits for God, in 'A being which creates is possibly not God'. And, surely, 'This is not God', referring to God, is impossible. Similarly, by means of 'A being which creates is necessarily God' it is asserted that 'This is God' is necessary, referring to that for which 'being which creates' supposits in the *de necessario* proposition in question. And this is true. Therefore, that *de necessario* proposition is true. But it is not necessary. Rather, it is contingently true, since on the assumption that God ceased to create, it would then be false—just as its non-modal counterpart, namely, 'A being which creates is God', would be false.

And there is nothing improper in the fact that a true *de neces-sario* proposition is contingent, as is clear in the above example. And just as a true *de necessario* proposition can be contingent, so too a true *per se* proposition can be true accidentally and contingently. For example, 'A being which creates is *per se* God' is true, and yet it is true accidentally and contingently. And so it is with many others. Still, despite the fact that these propositions are true, propositions like 'God is necessarily a being which creates' are false and propositions like the following are true: 'God is contingently a being which creates', 'God is able not to be a being which creates', 'God is possibly a being which does not create', etc. This is so because no proposition in which the predicate 'being which creates' is predicated of a pronoun referring to that for which the term 'God' supposits is necessary. Rather, it is contingent. For every proposition like 'This is a being which creates' and 'That is a being which does not create', referring to God, is contingent.

Similarly, it should be said that the following propositions are all false: 'God possibly assumes a human suppositum', 'God is possibly united to a human suppositum', 'God possibly performs a meritorious act by himself', 'God possibly makes a white thing without whiteness', and others of this kind. For each proposition in which one of the above things is predicated of a pronoun referring to that for which the subject supposits is simply impossible. For 'A suppositum is assumed' is impossible, since this follows: 'A suppositum is assumed; therefore a suppositum depends upon another'—and further, 'therefore a suppositum is not a suppositum'. But it is implied that it is a suppositum. Therefore, 'A suppositum is assumed' is impossible. Similarly, 'This is united to a suppositum', referring to God, is impossible. And, likewise, 'God performs a meritorious act by himself' is impossible, since this follows: 'God performs a meritorious act by himself; therefore a meritorious act is performed only by God; consequently, it is not performed by the will of the person whose act it is, and, consequently, it is not a meritorious act'.

Despite this fact, however, the following propositions are true, unless some logical or grammatical reason prevents it: 'A suppositum is possibly assumed by the Word', 'A suppositum is possibly

united to the Word', 'A meritorious act is possibly performed by
God alone'. For by means of these propositions it is asserted only
that a proposition in which the predicate is predicated of a pronoun referring to that for which the subject supposits is possible—
and this is true. For in the proposition 'A suppositum is possibly
assumed' the subject 'suppositum' supposits for this human nature,
since this human nature, in virtue of the fact that it does not de-
pend on or require the support of another, is now truly a suppositum. And so 'suppositum' truly supposits for this nature, just
as 'white thing' in 'A white thing is running' truly supposits for Socrates if Socrates is white. But if that human nature is being referred
to, then 'This is assumed by a divine suppositum' is a possible proposition. Therefore, 'A suppositum is possibly assumed' is true, just as
'A white thing is possibly black' is true. For 'This is black', referring
to something for which 'white thing' supposits, is possible—and yet
'A white thing is black' is impossible.

Likewise, in the same sense all propositions such as these are
true: 'A man is possibly assumed', 'A thing caused by a created
agent is possibly caused by God alone', 'A thing seen by Socrates
and Plato is possibly seen by Socrates alone', and so on. And yet
these propositions are impossible: 'A man is assumed', 'A thing
caused by a created agent is caused by God alone', 'A thing seen
by Socrates and Plato is seen by Socrates alone', and so on.

Second, it should be noted that such propositions *de modo*
are related to their singulars in exactly the same way that non-
modal propositions are. Therefore, it is impossible for such a universal proposition to be true or necessary or contingent unless
each of its singulars is true or necessary or contingent.

Similarly, just as a non-modal proposition can be impossible
despite the fact that each of its singulars is possible—as is clear
in the case of 'Both of these are true', referring to two contradictory contingent propositions—so too sometimes, although
rarely, a *de modo* universal proposition can be impossible while
each of its singulars is possible. This is clear in the case of
'Both of these are necessarily true', referring to the proposition
'Socrates was in A' and 'Socrates was not in A'. The universal
proposition in question is impossible, and yet each singular is

possible. For 'This is necessarily true: "Socrates was in A" ' is possible. And, likewise, the other one is possible.[4]

Now what has been said should also be understood to apply to other modal propositions, e.g. 'Every man is known by you to be an animal'. For in order for this proposition to be true, it is required that each proposition like the following be true: 'This is known by you: "This is an animal, and that is an animal" ', and so on for each one. Therefore, 'Every man is known by you to be an animal' is false, strictly speaking, as is 'Every man is not known by you to be an animal'. And so it is with respect to many others.

11: On Propositions which, though Categorical in Form, are Equivalent to Hypotheticals

Now that categorical propositions—simple ones, as it were— have been discussed, we must treat propositions which are equivalent to hypothetical propositions.

It should be noted that every categorical proposition which implies several categorical propositions that, as it were, expound it, i.e. express what that proposition conveys in virtue of its form, can be called a proposition which is equivalent to a hypothetical proposition. As was said above,[1] exclusive, exceptive, and reduplicative propositions are of this type. Also of this type are propositions in which connotative or relative terms occur, e.g. 'Some white thing is running', 'Every white thing is a body', 'Every agent produces something', 'Every quantity is in a place', 'Every likeness is a quality', and so on. Therefore, we must first discuss these.

With respect to this matter it should be noted, as was said above,[2] that a term is properly called connotative or relative when it has a nominal definition, i.e. one definition which expresses what the name means—so that what the name means cannot be known except by having a phrase. And in such a case it always signifies something primarily and something secondarily, as is clear in the case of 'white' and 'hot'. For the nominal definition of 'white' is 'having whiteness' or 'informed by whiteness' or something of this sort. Thus, 'white' supposits for something that is its significatum or consignificatum, and it signifies or consignifies something for which, nevertheless, it does not supposit or for which it is not necessary that it supposit, even if it is distributed by a universal sign—at least not because of the distribution.[3] And so, in general, when some term connotes or consignifies something for which, nevertheless, it cannot supposit—because it is not always truly predicated of that thing—such a term is either connotative or relative. For example, the term 'white', according to one way of speaking, principally signifies whiteness. And yet it does not supposit for whiteness, just as it is not truly predicated of whiteness. For 'Whiteness is white' is false. Therefore, the term 'white' is connotative or relative. Similarly, 'being which creates' signifies or consignifies a creature, but it does not supposit for a creature. For 'A creature is a being which creates' is false. Therefore, the term 'being which creates' is connotative or relative. The same should be said of 'snubnosed', 'concave', 'quantity', and others of this type, according to Aristotle's view. For all these terms connote or introduce in some way certain things for which they do not supposit. For 'quantity' conveys that one part is distinguished in place and position from another part—and yet 'quantity' does not supposit for such a place or position. Still, if it does so supposit, this happens because each part of a quantum is quantified.

Now it will perhaps be shown in other places what the difference is, properly speaking, between a relative and a connotative name.[4]

Assuming what has just been said, it should be noted that any proposition which contains such a term is a proposition having exponents which express what is meant by such a proposition. But different propositions have different exponents because of the different connotative or relative terms. Therefore, it will suffice to talk about some of them, since one can find out how the others are expounded by comparing them with the ones to be discussed.

Hence, it should be noted that whenever there occurs in a proposition a concrete term corresponding to an abstract term that introduces a thing that informs another thing, then it is always the case that two propositions are required for the truth of such a proposition. These two propositions can be called its exponents. Moreover, one of them should be a proposition in which both extremes are in the nominative case, and the other should be a proposition in which one extreme is in an oblique case. For example, for the truth of 'Socrates is white' it is required that 'Socrates exists' be true and that 'Whiteness is in Socrates' be true. Similarly, for the truth of 'A white thing is running' these two propositions are required: 'Something is running' and 'Whiteness is in that thing'. And the same holds for the others.

Similarly, when some relative term occurs in a proposition, the truth of more than one proposition is required. For example, for the truth of 'Socrates is similar to Plato' it is required that Socrates have some quality and that Plato have a quality of the same species. Hence, in virtue of the fact that Socrates is white and Plato is white, Socrates is similar to Plato and vice versa. Similarly, if both are black or cold, then they are similar in virtue of that fact alone. Likewise, for the truth of 'A man is a quantity' it is required that a man have parts and that one part be distinguished in place and position from another.

But someone might wonder whether every universal proposition has such exponents. It seems that it does, since it has many singulars.

It should be said that a universal proposition in which the sign 'both' or the sign 'neither' occurs is, in virtue of its meaning, equivalent to a hypothetical proposition. But one in which the signs 'no' or 'every' or 'any' occur is not equivalent to a hypothetical. For although such a proposition often has many singulars, still this is not necessary. For as was claimed above,[5] 'Every phoenix exists' is true, even though there is only one phoenix.

Things analogous to those just said should be said about 'A nose is snubbed', 'A man is a likeness', 'A man is a cause'—and, in general, about propositions in which other connotative and relative terms are expressed.

The same things can also be said about collective names like 'number', 'motion', 'time', 'people', 'army', and so on. For such terms require the truth of several propositions.

Further, one thing to be noted, according to Aristotle's view, is that no such term, namely, no connotative or relative or collective or negative term, is predicated *per se* or *in quid* of a pronoun referring to something which is *per se* one thing. Still, some of these terms—or all of them—are species and *per se* in a genus, as 'number' is *per se* in the genus of quantity.

And although such terms are not, on Aristotle's view, predicated *per se* of a pronoun referring to one thing, still they are predicated *in quid* of a demonstrative pronoun taken with that common term. For example, if 'Socrates is a man' is *per se* and *in quid*, then so will 'This number is a number' be *per se* and *in quid*. And the same holds for 'This likeness is a likeness', 'This motion is a motion', and so on for the others.

Nevertheless, it should be understood that if one takes 'is predicated *per se* and *in quid*' strictly and properly, namely, as 'is predicated necessarily', then in this sense no species such as 'man', 'animal', 'number', etc., is predicated of anything *per se* and *in quid*—especially not in a present-tense non-modal proposition. The reason for this is that no proposition like the following is necessary: 'Socrates is a man', 'This donkey is a donkey', 'This number is a number', 'This motion is a motion'. But if one takes predication *in quid* and *per se* in a broad sense, namely, for a predication in which the predicate does not connote anything extrinsic to that which is connoted by the subject, then in this sense propositions like the following are *per se* and *in quid*: 'This man is a man', 'This donkey is a donkey', 'This likeness is a likeness', and so on for the others.

Therefore, it should be said that whenever a connotative or relative or collective term occurs in a proposition, it is always the case that such a proposition is equivalent to some hypothetical proposition and that it can be expounded by means of more than one exponent.

12: On Propositions in which Negative, Privative, and Infinite Terms Occur

Now not only are propositions in which connotative or relative terms occur equivalent to hypothetical propositions, but also propositions in which negative, privative, and infinite terms occur are equivalent to hyopthetical propositions. For all such terms are also really connotative, since in their nominal definitions there must occur something in the nominative case and something in an oblique case—or in the nominative case with a preceding negation.

For example, the definition of the name 'immaterial' is 'something which does not have matter'; and the definition of the term 'blind' is 'something lacking sight which by nature should have sight'; and the definition of the term 'non-man' is 'something which is not a man'; and so on for the others. And thus every such term is really connotative, although not every such term is relative. For sometimes such a term can be truly predicated of something even though an oblique term cannot truly or properly be added to it. For example, an angel is immaterial, and yet it is not proper to say that it is 'immaterial of something' or 'immaterial to something', and so on for the other oblique cases.

Now every proposition in which such a term occurs has at least two exponents, and sometimes it has more than two. This can easily be ascertained by looking at the nominal definition of the term in question. Hence, every proposition in which an infinite term occurs has two exponents. One of them is an affirmative proposition in which 'something' (in the singular or plural) or some other term equipollent to it is the subject or the predicate. Hence, 'A donkey is a non-man' is equivalent to 'A donkey is something and a donkey is not a man'.[1] Similarly, 'An angel is immaterial' is equivalent to 'An angel is something and an angel does not have matter'. And this should be understood to apply when the negative term in question signifies negatively nothing except what the opposite term signifies affirmatively. I mention this to exclude the following counterinstance: for the conjunctive proposition 'The divine essence is something and it is not generated' is not equivalent to 'The divine essence is ungenerated.'

From this it is clear that, properly speaking, 'A chimera is a non-man' should be denied, since it has one false exponent, namely, 'A chimera is something'. Similarly, if no man is white, then, strictly speaking, 'A white man is a non-man' should be denied, since the exponent 'A white man is something' is false.

Someone might claim that, according to Aristotle, one of two contradictories is said of anything. Therefore, if a chimera is not a non-man, then a chimera is a man.

It should be replied, in keeping with Aristotle's meaning, that it is not the case that one of two contradictory terms is said of any term taken significatively. For example, neither 'man' nor 'non-man' is said of the name 'chimera' taken significatively. Nevertheless, one of two contradictory terms is said of any term—suppositing significatively and not including in itself any syncategorematic element or other determination—of which 'being' or 'something' is truly predicated. Thus, if 'A chimera is something' were true, then either 'A chimera is a man' or 'A chimera is a non-man' would be true. And so it should be conceded that it is not the case that one of two contradictory terms is said of just any term taken significatively, but that, despite this fact, it is the case that any term is either truly affirmed or truly denied of such a term. This latter point is what Aristotle means when he says: "Of anything either the affirmation or the negation,"[2] and not both. So although neither 'man' nor 'non-man' is said of 'chimera', still 'man' is either truly affirmed or truly denied of 'chimera'. Hence, one of these two propositions is true: 'A chimera is a man', 'A chimera is not a man'. Similarly, one of these two propositions is true: 'A chimera is a non-man', 'A chimera is not a non-man'. The same thing holds for these two: 'A white man is a man', 'A white man is not a man'; and for these two: 'A white man is a non-man', 'A white man is not a non-man'.

However, assuming that no man is white, it can be shown that neither 'A white man is a man' nor 'A white man is a non-man' is true. For if 'A white man is a non-man' is true, then, since it is affirmative, it is necessary that the subject supposit for something. Given that, I ask: for what does it supposit? Not for a spoken word or for a concept, since it is suppositing significatively and not materially or simply. Therefore, it supposits for something else. Consequently, the term 'white man', taken significatively, would be predicated of a pronoun referring to that for which it supposits. And, as a result, 'This is a white man' would be true—which is manifestly false. For if it is true, then either a being or a non-being is being referred to. If a being, then some being would be a white man, which is contrary to what was assumed; if a non-being, then some non-being would be a white man and would, consequently, be white—which is obviously false. And so it is clear that if no man is white, then 'A white man is a non-man' is false. And similar propositions can be proven false by the same line of reasoning.

13: On Affirmative Propositions in which There Occur Privative Terms which are not Equivalent to Infinite Terms

Although propositions containing infinite terms or their equivalents have only two exponents, still affirmative propositions which contain privative terms that are not equivalent to infinite terms have more than two exponents. Hence, the proposition 'He is blind' has these exponents: 'He is something', 'By nature he should have sight', 'He will never be able to see naturally'. But it is not possible to give firm rules for such propositions, for because of the variety of such terms the propositions in which they occur have to be expounded in different ways. Hence, 'Socrates is blind' has the exponents which have been mentioned. But the proposition 'Socrates is foolish' has these exponents:

'Socrates is something' and 'Socrates does not have the wisdom which he ought to have'. Still, this is consistent with its being the case that he is able to have wisdom. Hence, the following propositions are compatible with one another: 'Socrates is foolish or stupid' and 'Socrates is able to be wise naturally'. But the following propositions are incompatible: 'Socrates is blind' and 'Socrates is able to see naturally'. And so it is clear that the two propositions have different exponents, even though a privative term occurs in each.

Now the various ways in which such propositions should be expounded can easily be seen by taking the nominal definitions of the privative terms in question and formulating the exponents from them.

14: On Propositions in which Figments, to which Nothing in Reality Corresponds, are Posited

Just as propositions containing negative and privative terms have several exponents, so too propositions in which figments are posited, i.e. which contain made-up terms to which there corresponds nothing in reality that they pretend to signify, have several exponents.

For such terms are really connotative, and nothing imaginable is signified by them except a real thing which actually exists or possibly exists or, at least, could have existed or did actually exist. Thus, negative and privative terms signify nothing except what is signified by positive terms, although the same thing which is signified by an affirmative term positively and by constructing or affirmatively is signified by a negative or privative term, not by constructing, but by destroying or negating, to use Anselm's way of speaking.[1] In the same way, by means of figment terms such as 'chimera', 'tregelaphus', 'vacuum', 'infinite', etc., nothing

is signified except what is signified by other terms, as is clear
from the nominal definitions of these terms. Still, things are not
signified in the same way by these terms and by the others.[2]
Rather, they are signified by the other terms in such a way that
those other terms can supposit for the things, whereas these figment terms cannot supposit for them, just as their nominal definitions cannot supposit for them. Hence, it should not be imag-
ined that just as there are certain beings signified by terms such
as 'man', 'animal', 'white', 'hot', 'long', 'short', and so on, so too
there are certain non-beings and impossibilia, totally distinct from
beings, which are signified by terms like 'chimera', 'goat-stag',
etc.—as if there were a world of impossibilia in the same way
that there is a world of beings. Rather, anything imaginable signified by the name 'chimera' is signified by some term of which
'being' is predicated in a non-modal proposition or in a *de possibili* proposition. Nevertheless, the name 'chimera' cannot supposit for that thing. For this reason, any affirmative proposition
in which the name 'chimera' or one just like it, taken significatively, is either the subject or the predicate is, strictly speaking,
false, since it has some false exponent. For 'A chimera is a non-
being'—and any proposition just like it—is literally false, since
each such proposition has the exponents 'A chimera is something'
and 'That thing is a non-being',[3] the first of which is false.

Now someone might ask: isn't 'A chimera is a chimera' true?
It seems that it is true, since the same thing is predicated of itself. And Boethius claims that no proposition is more true than
one in which the same thing is predicated of itself.

It should be replied that if the terms supposit significatively,
then 'A chimera is a chimera' is, strictly speaking, false, since it
implies a falsehood. And as far as Boethius is concerned, it should
be said that Boethius meant that no proposition in which something is predicated of something is more true than one in which
the same thing is predicated of itself. But since his point is a
negative one, it is consistent with its being the case that neither
proposition is true—neither the one in which the same thing is
predicated of itself nor the one in which something else is predicated of it. Still, if the proposition in which 'something' is predicated of a thing were true, then the proposition in which that

same thing is predicated of itself would be true. For example, if 'A chimera is something' were true, then 'A chimera is a chimera' would be true. And so no proposition in which something is predicated of the name 'chimera', taken significatively, can be more true than the proposition in which the name 'chimera' is predicated of itself. But this is compatible with its being the case that neither the one nor the other is true.

15: On Categorical Propositions which Contain the Pronoun 'Who'

Any proposition, categorical in form, which contains the relative pronoun 'who' should be given several exponents, since each such proposition is equivalent to a conjunctive proposition. However, such propositions must be dealt with in different ways, depending on whether they are universal, on the one hand, or particular, indefinite, or singular, on the other. For when such a proposition is particular or indefinite or singular, it is always equivalent to a conjunction of two propositions, which are composed of the antecedent and the relative pronoun 'he' (or a proper name) plus the other extreme—with no other change being made. For example, 'A man who is white is running' is equivalent to 'A man is running and he is white' or to 'A man is white and he is running'. Likewise, 'Socrates, who is running, is debating' is equivalent to 'Socrates is running and Socrates is debating'.

But if such a proposition is universal, then it is amphibolous, since it can have two senses. In one of these senses it is asserted that the predicate is said of everything that the whole phrase preceding the principal verb is said of—and nothing more is asserted. And this is called by many the sense of composition, or it is interchangeable with that sense. In the other sense it is asserted that that which follows the term 'who' is predicated universally of the antecedent and that, similarly, the predicate is predicated universally of the same antecedent. For example, by means of 'Every man who is white is running', taken in one sense, it is asserted that the predicate 'running' is said of everything that the whole phrase 'man who is white' is said of. And in that case for the truth of this proposition two propositions are required, namely 'Some man is white' and 'Each such man is running'. However, in the other sense it is asserted that these two propositions are true: 'Every man is white' and 'Every man is running'.

Nevertheless, it should be noted, as will be said below,[1] that sometimes the relation is not personal, and in such a case it is not necessary that in the corresponding conjunctive the same term has the same supposition in both parts. But sometimes the relation is personal, and in that case it should have the same supposition.

16: On Reduplicative Propositions

With respect to reduplicative propositions it should first be noted that a proposition is called reduplicative when it contains the expression 'insofar as' or some equivalent, taken reduplicatively. For, according to some, this expression can sometimes be understood reduplicatively, in which case it renders the proposition reduplicative; and it can sometimes be understood specificatively, in which case it does not render the proposition reduplicative.

Second, it should be noted that in a reduplicative proposition the reduplication itself, namely, the expression 'insofar as' or its equivalent, is sometimes affirmed, since a negation does not precede it, and sometimes denied, since a negation does precede it— as in 'It is not the case that Socrates, insofar as he is a man, is running'. Now if the reduplication is not denied, then either it occurs in an affirmative proposition such as 'Socrates, insofar as he is a man, is visible'; or it occurs in a negative proposition such as 'Socrates, insofar as he is a man, is not running'.

Thus, we must consider, first, what is required for the truth of an affirmative reduplicative proposition; second, what is required for the truth of a negative proposition in which, nevertheless, the reduplication is not negated; third, what is required for the truth of a proposition in which the reduplication is negated.

As far as the first point is concerned, it should be noted that such a proposition can be distinguished, since the reduplication can be made to express either concomitance or a cause. If the reduplication is made to express concomitance, then for the truth of the proposition four propositions, which, as it were, expound it, are required. One is a proposition in which the principal predicate is truly predicated of the principal subject. The second is a proposition in which what falls under the reduplication is predicated of the principal subject. The third is a proposition in which the principal predicate is predicated of that which falls under the reduplication, taken universally. The fourth will be a true conditional proposition in which one argues from that which falls under the reduplication to the principal predicate—in the way in which there is said to be a valid consequence from an inferior to a superior, and in the way in which it is said that one of two interchangeable propositions follows from the other. For example, for the truth of 'Socrates, insofar as he is a man, has a color' the truth of these propositions is required: 'Socrates has a color', 'Socrates is a man', 'Every man has a color', and 'If a man exists, then something which has a color exists' (or: 'If A is a man, then A has a color'). And since such a conditional is false,[1] it follows that the reduplicative proposition 'Socrates, insofar as he is a man, has a color' is likewise false—since, namely, it has a false exponent.

On the other hand, if the reduplication is made to express a cause, then for the truth of such a reduplicative, besides the four exponents just mentioned, it is required that what falls under the reduplication express the cause of what is introduced by the predicate, or that it be that in which the principal predicate inheres primarily, or that the principal predicate inhere in it prior to its inhering in a pronoun referring to that which the principal subject supposits for. For example, by means of 'An isosceles, insofar as it is a triangle, has three angles' it is asserted that an isosceles has three angles, and that an isosceles is a triangle, and that every triangle has three angles, and that if something is a triangle, then it has three angles—and, besides this, it is asserted that the predicate 'has three angles' is truly predicated of 'triangle' prior to its being truly predicated of 'isosceles', in the sense in which a logician uses 'prior' and 'posterior', namely, for relations among propositions. Similarly, by means of 'Fire, insofar as it is hot, is warmth-producing' what was just mentioned is asserted. And therefore the proposition is true. Likewise, 'A man, insofar as he has an intellective soul, is susceptible to learning' is true. For, in addition to the four exponents, an intellective soul is the cause of learning—extending the name 'cause' to the subject of some [quality]. And this is sufficient for the truth of such a reduplicative. But 'A man, insofar as he is risible, is susceptible to learning' is false, although it is true if the reduplication is made to express concomitance. The reason for this is that the four exponents alluded to above are true.

From what has been said the following rule can be inferred: there is always a formal consequence from a reduplicative proposition to its non-reduplicative counterpart. This is because its non-reduplicative counterpart is always one exponent of a reduplicative. Hence, this is formally valid: 'A man, insofar as he is an animal, is sentient; therefore a man is sentient'. Similarly, this follows: 'Fire, insofar as it is hot, is warmth-producing; therefore fire is warmth-producing'.

From these considerations it follows that many propositions which are conceded by many both in philosophy and theology are, strictly speaking, simply false. They are propositions like the following: 'A creature, insofar as it is in God, is really the divine essence', 'The Father and the Son generate [the Spirit] insofar as they are one', 'A man, insofar as he is a creature, is not a being', 'An object, insofar as it is intelligible, has diminished being', and so on. For all such propositions have some false exponent. And the same thing, *mutatis mutandis*, should be said about propositions which are just like these. And if some such propositions or ones just like them are found in the authorities—whether saints or philosophers—they should be glossed. For authorities frequently do not speak literally, as is obvious to anyone who examines their books carefully.

What has been said enables us to solve such sophisms as 'Some things, insofar as they agree, differ' and 'Some things, insofar as they differ, agree'. For if we take 'to agree' in the sense in which it is truly predicated of all things which exist in reality, and if we take 'to differ' for all things which differ in any way whatsoever, i.e. which exist and are not the same, then all such propositions and ones just like them are true, if the reduplication is made to express concomitance. For, as is manifestly clear, the four previously mentioned exponents of such propositions are true. On the other hand, if the reduplication is made to express a cause, then in that case they are false. For 'to agree' neither agrees with nor is said of differing things prior to its being said of things which agree. Nor does it designate the cause of their differing. Therefore, the propositions are false if taken in this sense.

However, the same does not hold for these propositions: 'Some things, insofar as they are dissimilar, are similar'. For neither the following consequence nor its converse is valid: 'These things are similar; therefore they are dissimilar'. Nor does this follow: 'They agree in the predicable "dissimilar"; therefore they are similar'. For in order for them to be similar it is required that they have qualities of the same lowest level species.

Another rule is that it is a valid consequence when one argues from an inferior to a superior, without distribution, on the part of the principal subject. Hence, this is a good consequence: 'Socrates, insofar as he is a man, is risible; therefore an animal, insofar as he is a man, is risible'. For it is impossible for the exponents of the antecedent to be true unless the exponents of the consequent are true. And this holds whether the reduplication is made to express concomitance or to express a cause.

Similarly, it is a valid consequence when one argues in the same way with respect to the principal predicate. However, when one argues from that which falls under the reduplication to its superior, there is a fallacy of consequent, as in the following: 'Socrates, insofar as he is a man, is risible; therefore Socrates, insofar as he is an animal, is risible'. For if that consequence were valid, then it would follow that this consequence is valid: 'Every man is risible; therefore every animal is risible'. It would follow in accord with this rule: 'When a reduplicative entails a reduplicative, the exponents of the antecedent entail the exponents of the consequent'.

Nevertheless, it should be noted that someone could use these propositions in some other sense and not in their literal sense. In that case such consequences could be denied. And this is the way in which one would have to respond to authorities if they were found to say the opposite of some of the things said here.

The second principal task is to discuss a negative reduplicative, in which, nevertheless, the reduplication is not denied. A proposition of this sort is 'A man, insofar as he is rational, is not a donkey'.

And it should be noted that such a reduplicative proposition, if the reduplication is made to express concomitance, has four exponents: two negative, one affirmative, and one conditional. The affirmative exponent is a proposition in which what falls under the reduplication is truly affirmed of the principal subject. One of the negative exponents is the non-reduplicative counterpart of the reduplicative proposition in question, namely, it is a proposition in which the principal predicate is denied of the principal subject. The other negative exponent is a proposition in which the principal predicate is denied of that which falls under the reduplication, taken universally. The conditional is a proposition in which the negation of the principal prediate follows from the positing of that which falls under the redpulication. For example, 'A man, insofar as he is risible, is not a donkey' has these exponents: 'A man is risible', 'A man is not a donkey', 'No risible thing is a donkey', 'If something is risible, then it is not a donkey'.

Because of this, propositions such as the following are literally false: 'A logician, insofar as he is a logician, differs from a grammarian', since the exponent 'Every logician differs from a grammarian' is false; 'A white thing, insofar as it is white, differs from a sweet thing'; and others just like them. Similarly, propositions such as the following are false: 'An intellect, insofar as it is an intellect, does not will', 'A soul, insofar as it is an intellect, does not will', 'A soul, insofar as it is active, is not passive', 'A soul, insofar as it is passive, does not act', 'Fire, insofar as it is hot, is not dry', 'A body, insofar as it is altered, does not undergo local motion', and so on for many others. For all such propositions have some false exponent.

On the other hand, if the reduplication is made to express a cause, then it is required that the principal predicate be denied of what falls under the reduplication primarily or prior to its being denied of a pronoun referring to what the principal subject supposits for—always assuming that the proposition has the four exponents mentioned above. For this reason, if the reduplication is taken in the sense in question, then 'A man, insofar as he is risible, is not a donkey' is false.

Similarly, it should be understood, just as before, that there is always a formal consequence from a reduplicative proposition to its non-reduplicative counterpart. Therefore, this consequence is formal: 'A logician, insofar as he is a logician, differs from a grammarian; therefore a logician differs from a grammarian'—from which it follows that a logician is not a grammarian.

Third, we must deal with a proposition in which the reduplication is negated. And it should be noted that such a proposition is the contradictory of a reduplicative proposition in which the reduplication is affirmed. And, therefore, the opposite of any exponent of its contradictory reduplicative is sufficient for the truth of such a proposition. For it is a general rule that when a proposition is the contradictory of some proposition which has several exponents, then the truth of the opposite of any exponent is sufficient for the truth of the proposition in question. Hence, for the truth of 'It is not the case that Socrates is a man insofar as he is white' it is sufficient that any of the following be true: 'Socrates is not a man', 'Socrates is not white', 'Some white thing is not a man', 'It is not the case that if it is white, then it is a man'.

It should also be noted that the expressions 'since it is . . .', 'qua', 'by reason of its being . . .', etc., are equivalent to the expression 'insofar as', and so they render propositions reduplicative. And the propositions in which they occur should be treated in the same way that propositions in which 'insofar as' occurs have already been treated.

On the other hand, if such an expression is understood specificatively rather than reduplicatively, then it is not required that that to which such an expression is added be the subject with respect to the principal predicate in a universal proposition. Rather, it is required that what falls under the reduplication designate that in virtue of which the principal predicate belongs to the primary subject. For example, if in the proposition 'Fire, insofar as it is hot, is warmth-producing' the expression 'insofar as' is taken specificatively rather than reduplicatively, then it is not required that 'Every hot thing is warmth-producing' be true. Rather, it is required that the name 'hot' convey the heat in virtue of which fire produces warmth. For to produce warmth belongs to heat prior to and more *per se* than its belonging to fire. Or at least 'hot' must convey that heat is a principle of producing warmth. Thus, for the truth of such a proposition it is required that the principal predicate be predicated of the principal subject and of that to which the reduplicative expression is added, and that the latter be predicated of the principal subject. But it is not required that the principal predicate be predicated universally of that to which the reduplicative expression is added. Rather, it is required that the latter designate that by reason of which the principal predicate truly agrees, through predication, with the principal subject. And in this way propositions like the following are verified: 'Socrates, insofar as he is white, dilates vision',[2] 'Socrates, insofar as he has a free will, sins', 'A being, insofar as it is a being, is the subject of metaphysics', and so on. But one should not be concerned with the examples.

It is also necessary to point out that the expression 'insofar as' and, likewise, the expressions 'since it is . . .', 'by reason of its being . . .', etc., are in some propositions equivalent to a temporal adverb. For example, one sense of the proposition ' "Dog", insofar as it signifies an animal which can bark, makes this proposition true: "Every dog is an animal" ' is this: 'The proposition "Every dog is an animal" is true only when "dog" stands for an animal which can bark'. And, similarly, we say that the following proposition is true: 'This image is a man, since "man" is being used in an improper sense'. That is, the proposition is true when 'man' is being used in an improper sense. Thus, the expression 'insofar as' can also be used in various senses and equivocally.

17: On Exclusive Propositions

With respect to exclusive propositions we must note, first, what makes a proposition exclusive; second, what is required for the truth of an exclusive proposition; third, how the terms supposit in exclusive propositions; fourth, certain rules which must be given.

Concerning the first point it should be noted that the expressions 'only' and 'alone' render propositions exclusive. However, it should be noted that the expression 'alone' is sometimes understood syncategorematically, in which case it is an exclusive expression, and it is sometimes understood categorematically, in which case it is not an exclusive expression. Rather, in the latter case it conveys that what is designated by the term added to it is all by itself. For example, we say 'He is alone', i.e. all by himself, since no one else is with him in that particular place. Similarly, if someone says 'Socrates is running alone', then if 'alone' is understood categorematically, this signifies that Socrates, who is all by himself, is running. And this can be true even if many others are running. However, if it is understood syncategorematically, then it is asserted that no one other than Socrates is running.

Second, it should be noted that when the two expressions 'only' and 'alone' can be added to the same term, then it does not matter whether the one or the other is added—as long as 'alone' is understood syncategorematically. For such propositions are equivalent. For example, these propositions are equivalent: 'Only a man is running' and 'A man alone is running'.

Concerning the second point it should be noted that an exclusive expression is sometimes added to the subject, sometimes to the predicate, and sometimes to the composition, so that it is a determination of the composition. And so first we should deal with the cases in which it is added to the subject.

It should first be noted that sometimes a categorematic expression signifies one thing in its primary use and something else in a transferred or secondary use. For example, 'man' primarily signifies the same thing as 'composed of a body and intellective soul', while it secondarily signifies a statue or image of such a composite. The same thing holds for an exclusive expression and other syncategorematic expressions. Sometimes it signifies or has one role in its primary use and another in a secondary use—and so it is with an exclusive expression. And so we should deal first with its primary use and then with its secondary use.

With respect to the former it should be noted that whenever an exclusive expression is taken in its primary sense and is added to the subject, it is always asserted that the predicate is truly predicated of the subject and that it is denied of everything of which its subject is not truly predicated—this is so if the proposition is affirmative. Thus, every exclusive proposition has two exponents: one affirmative and the other negative. For example, 'Only a man is an animal' has these exponents: 'A man is an animal' and 'Nothing other than a man is an animal'. On the other hand, if the proposition is negative, then it is asserted that the predicate is truly denied of the subject and that it inheres in everything of which the subject is truly denied. And so it has two exponents, namely, its corresponding non-exclusive negative proposition and an affirmative proposition. For example, 'Only a man is not a donkey' has these two exponents: 'A man is not a donkey' and 'Everything other than a man is a donkey'.

From what has been said it is clear that if one takes the exclusive expression in its primary sense, then all propositions such as the following are false and include a contradiction: 'Only a man is white', 'Only air is here inside', 'Only an animal exists', 'Only a father exists', 'Only an individual exists', and so on. For from these propositions it follows that the predicates are truly predicated of the parts, of which parts, nonetheless, the whole or names of the wholes are denied. And so all such propositions include a contradiction.

Similarly, such propositions as the following are false: 'The Father alone is God', 'The Father alone generates the Holy Spirit', 'The Father alone is good', and others of this type. Similarly, propositions such as 'Only every man is rational' and 'Only every animal is sentient' are false, since their exponents cannot both be true at the same time if there is more than one man and more than one animal. This is the case with the exponents 'Every man is rational' and 'Nothing other than every man is rational'. For if nothing other than every man is rational, and if this man is other than every man, then it follows that this man is not rational—which is incompatible with 'Every man is rational'. The same thing holds for 'Only every animal is sentient'.

Second, we must examine the exclusive expression in its secondary use. And it should be noted that there can be three such uses: first, when it just excludes the predicate from every individual of which the subject is not predicated; second, when it just excludes those things which are neither designated by the subject nor parts of things so designated; third, when it just excludes a greater number of things than that expressed by the subject.

Accordingly, three rules will be given. One is that when the exclusive expression is added to a distributed common term, then either there can be an exclusion properly speaking, in which case what is excluded is everything that the term to which the exclusive expression is added is not truly predicated of; or there can be an exclusion improperly speaking, in which case it is asserted that the predicate is denied of every other common term, taken with a particular sign, of which the subject is not truly predicated. This can be called the exclusion of an incompatible common term taken with a particular sign.

Hence, 'Only every man is running' must be distinguished as equivocal in the second mode. For either 'only' can be understood properly, in which case the proposition has these exponents: 'Every man is running' and 'Nothing other than every man is running'; or 'only' can be taken improperly, so that there is an exclusion of any incompatible common term taken with a particular sign. In this case the proposition has these exponents: 'Every man is running' and 'Some ox is not running' and 'Some donkey is not running' and 'Some she-goat is not running', and so on for each common term. Thus, by means of such an exclusive proposition—as long as the exclusive expression is taken improperly—it is asserted that the predicate is truly predicated of the common term which occurs in the proposition with a universal sign and that it is not truly predicated of any other common term taken universally. Now this distinction never applies except when the exclusive expression is added to a common term taken universally.

With respect to the second improper sense of the exclusive

expression there is another rule. It is this: when the exclusive expression is added to a term designating something which has several parts, then the proposition in question has to be distinguished. For either there can be an exclusion properly speaking, in which case it is asserted that the predicate belongs to the subject and is denied of everything of which the subject is denied; or there can be an exclusion speaking improperly, in which case what is excluded is anything of which neither the subject nor a term designating a part of the subject is truly predicated. This can be called the exclusion of any term which designates something extrinsic. Accordingly, the proposition 'Only Socrates is is white' must be distinguished. For the exclusive expression can be taken properly, in which case the proposition includes a contradiction. For in that case its exponents are 'Socrates is white' and 'Nothing other than Socrates is white'—which are incompatible with one another, since they entail incompatible propositions. For this follows: 'Socrates is white; therefore some part of Socrates' body is white'. And this follows: 'Nothing other than Socrates is white; every part of Socrates is other than Socrates; therefore no part of Socrates' body is white'. The two conclusions are incompatible with one another. On the other hand, if the exclusive expression is taken improperly, so that there is an exclusion just of any term designating only something extrinsic to Socrates, then 'Only Socrates is white' is possible. For in that case nothing is asserted except that Socrates is white and that nothing extrinsic to Socrates is white. But these two assertions are compatible with one another, and they correspond to 'Socrates is white' and 'Nothing extrinsic to Socrates is white', which are the exponents of the proposition in question. Now this distinction never applies except when the exclusive expression is added to a term which designates some whole which has several parts—whether it is a whole properly speaking or in an extended sense.

Now someone might object that if this were so, then on both of these interpretations propositions such as the following would, without qualification, include a contradiction: 'Only a body is white', 'Only a man is white', 'Only fire produces warmth', 'Only a man is here inside' 'Only a quantum is in a place', and others of this sort. For the surface is excluded by the first example, since it is not something intrinsic to a body because it is not a part of it. For the same reason the surface would be excluded by the second example. Heat would be excluded by the third example, all accidents by the fourth example, and points by the last example.

It should be responded that everything just said about the above examples—with the exception of the third—proceeds in Aristotle's opinion from a false conception, namely, that surfaces, lines, and points are things really distinct from bodies and substances. I have shown that this conception is contrary to Aristotle's view in the *Categories.*[1] As far as the third example is concerned, if one assumes that fire cannot produce warmth except by means of heat, then a different response must be given. For it should be maintained that, whether the exclusive expression is taken properly or in the improper sense under discussion, the proposition 'Only fire produces warmth' includes a contradiction. Hence, if this proposition ought to be salvaged, then the exclusive expression must be taken in some sense other than its proper sense or the three improper senses mentioned above. Specifically, in this new sense the exclusive expression would exclude just those terms which designate neither something intrinsic nor a formally inhering accident.[2] Given this interpretation, it can be conceded that 'Only fire produces warmth' is possible. For in that case heat is not excluded, since it formally inheres in fire.

With respect to the third improper sense of the exclusive expression a third rule can be given: when the exclusive expression is added to a numerical term or its equivalent, or to a term connoting a number or unity, then the proposition in question has to be distinguished, since there can be either an exclusion properly speaking or an exclusion improperly speaking. In the first sense what is excluded is everything of which the subject is not truly predicated. In the second sense what is excluded is a plurality greater than that to which it is asserted that the predicate belongs. This can be called the exclusion of a greater number. Accordingly, the proposition 'Only four men are here inside' has to be distinguished. For assume that there are four men—and no

more than four—here inside. In that case, if one makes the exclusion by taking the exclusive expression in its proper sense,
then it is asserted that four men are here inside and that nothing
other than four men is here inside. Consequently, it is asserted
that no stones are here inside, and that no horses are here inside,
and no donkeys. And it is also asserted that it is not the case that
two men are here inside, since two men are other than four men.
On the other hand, if an exclusion of a greater number is being
made, then it is asserted that four men are here inside and no
more than four. In that case the exponents of the proposition
are these: 'Four men are here inside' and 'It is not the case that
there are more than four men here inside'. And this is true in the
circumstances assumed above.

In this way one can solve the sophism 'Only one exists'. For
if the exclusive expression is taken properly, then 'Only (what is)
one exists' is true. For both of its exponents, namely, '(What is)
one exists' and 'Nothing other than (what is) one exists', are
true. The same holds for 'Only (what is) one animal is a man'.
On the other hand, if the exclusive expression is understood improperly in such a way that there is an exclusion of a greater
number, then the proposition is false. For in that case its exponents are 'One thing exists' and 'It is not the case that more
than one thing exists'. In the same way 'Only one animal is a
man' has, in that case, the following exponents: 'One animal is
a man' and 'It is not the case that more than one animal is a
man'. The same holds for 'Only one of these exists', referring to
two beings. For if the exclusive expression is taken properly, then
the proposition is true. For in that case both exponents are true
if there are not more than two beings, say God and an angel.
However, if the exclusive expression is taken improperly, then
the proposition is false. For in that case it is asserted that one
of the two things exists, but not both of them.

These are the senses, then, in which the exclusive expression
can be taken improperly. And perhaps there are still other senses
in which it can be taken improperly. But since they are not as
widely used as the ones we have dealt with, I will leave them
to the specialists.

Now that we have discussed the exclusive expression insofar

as it is added to the subject, we should discuss it insofar as it is added to the predicate.

It should first be noted that in such a case it is also possible to understand the exclusive expression either properly or improperly. If it is taken properly, then it is asserted that the predicate is said of the subject and that everything of which the predicate is not truly predicated is denied of the subject. For example, by means of 'A man is only an animal' it is asserted that a man is an animal and that a man is not other than an animal. However, when the exclusive expression is taken improperly and in a transferred sense, then it is added to the verb, in which case it excludes from the subject every other verb which designates a distinct action or passion. For example, by means of 'A man only sees' it is asserted that a man is seeing and that he is not hearing or stamping his feet, etc. Thus, the proposition 'A man is only a running thing' must be distinguished as equivocal in the second mode. For the exclusive expression can be taken properly, in which case the two exponents are 'A man is a running thing' and 'A man is not other than a running thing'—and this is compatible with its being the case that a man is seeing and stamping his feet, and so on for the others. But if the exclusive expression is taken improperly, then the proposition is false. For in that case it is asserted that a man is running and not hearing and not seeing, etc.

A distinction just like this one can be drawn with respect to the following: 'A man is only white', 'Milk is only sweet', 'Fire is only hot', 'Earth is only cold', and so on. For if the exclusive expression is taken properly, then each of them is true. For in that case these are the exponents: 'A man is white' and 'A man is not other than a white thing'; 'Milk is sweet' and 'Milk is not other than something sweet'; and so on for the others. On the other hand, if the exclusive expression is taken improperly, then all predicables are excluded which designate accidents distinct from that accident which is designated by the predicate. For example, by means of 'A man is only white' it is asserted that a man is white and that no predicable which designates an accident distinct from whiteness is predicated of a man.[3] Thus, it is asserted that a man is not hot or humid or thirsty or cold or lucid, etc. And what has been said of this proposition should be uniformly said of the others.

With respect to the third principal point, namely, how the terms supposit in exclusive propositions, it should be noted that when the exclusive expression is added to the subject and that subject is taken without distribution, then if the subject is a common term, it has merely confused supposition. For as was said above,[4] merely confused supposition occurs when it is not possible to descend to the inferiors either by a disjunctive proposition or by a conjunctive proposition. But this does not follow: 'Only a man is running; therefore only this man is running or only that man is running', and so on for every other man. Nor does this follow: 'Only a man is running; therefore only this man is running and only that man is running', and so on for each man. And so the subject term in such a proposition has merely confused supposition. But the predicate has confused and distributive supposition, since it is possible to descend to the inferiors by means of a conjunctive proposition. Hence, this is valid: 'Only a man is running; therefore only a man is this running thing', referring to any running thing whatsoever. For this follows: 'Only a man is running; therefore nothing other than a man is running', and further, 'therefore no running thing is other than a man', and further, 'therefore this running thing is not other than a man'. And it is clear that if it is running, then it is something; therefore it is a man. Consequently, a man is this running thing; therefore only a man is this running thing. For when the predicate is a demonstrative pronoun or some equivalent, then there is a valid consequence from an indefinite proposition to an exclusive proposition with respect to that predicate.

Indeed, no matter what sort of term the predicate is, there is a valid consequence from an indefinite or particular proposition to an exclusive proposition. For this is a valid consequence: 'A man alone is risible; therefore only an animal is risible'. For this holds by reason of the following rule: 'There is a valid consequence from an inferior to a superior without distribution— whether that superior has merely confused or determinate supposition'. For example, this follows: 'Every man is a man; therefore every man is an animal'.

Second, it should be noted that when an exclusive proposition is negative, then the subject supposits just as it does in an affirmative exclusive—and the same holds for the predicate. For this follows: 'Only a substance is not an accident, therefore only a substance is not this accident'.[5]

Third, we must deal with the supposition of the terms in an exclusive proposition in which the exclusive expression is added to the predicate. It should be said that the subject in such a proposition supposits just as it does in that proposition's non-exclusive counterpart. And the same holds for the predicate. The reason for this is that the same thing cannot be both truly affirmed and truly denied of the same thing. Therefore, an exclusive proposition always follows from its non-exclusive counterpart when the exclusive expression is added to the predicate. This should be understood to apply when both extremes of the proposition are in the nominative case—it is not universally true when one of the extremes is in an oblique case. In fact, if one of the extremes of the proposition is in an oblique case and if the exclusive expression is a determination of the predicate and not a determination of the composition, then the predicate has merely confused supposition. For assume that Socrates is seen by many men and by no animal other than a man. In that case the proposition 'Socrates is seen by a man alone' is true, since its exponents are true, namely, 'Socrates is seen by a man' and 'Socrates is seen by nothing other than a man'. And yet this does not follow: 'Socrates is seen by a man alone; therefore Socrates is seen by this man alone or by that man alone'. In fact, this does not even follow: 'Socrates is seen by a man alone; therefore Socrates is seen by that man'. And so the predicate has merely confused, rather than confused and distributive or determinate, supposition.

However, if the exclusive expression is a determination of the composition, then the predicate supposits just as it does in the proposition's non-exclusive counterpart. For example, in 'A man is only seen by a man', if 'only' is a determination of the composition, then the proposition has these exponents: 'A man is seen by a man' and 'A man is not other than a thing seen by a man'. From this it is clear that the terms do not supposit in the exclusive proposition in a way different from the way they supposit in its non-exclusive counterpart. For this sort of exclusive proposition and its non-exclusive counterpart are always interchangeable. However, if the subject of an exclusive proposition in which the exclusive expression is added to the subject is taken with distribution, then the subject has confused and distributive supposition. For such a proposition, whether it is affirmative or negative, includes contradictories. Thus, I will say no more about this case at present.

Furthermore, it should be noted that all that has just been said should be understood to apply when the exclusive expression is taken properly. For when it is taken improperly, then not all the things just said are true. But which of those things do hold true and which do not will be clear with no difficulty to one who examines them carefully with the improper significations of the exclusive expression in mind. And I have already talked about these improper senses.

Finally, we should look at some rules dealing with exclusive expressions. One is that there is a valid consequence from an exclusive proposition to a universal proposition with the terms transposed, and conversely. For an exclusive proposition and the corresponding universal proposition with the terms transposed are always interchangeable. This rule should be understood to apply when both the non-exclusive counterpart of the proposition in question and the universal proposition with the terms transposed are convertible propositions, i.e. when each can be properly converted. Or, if the non-exclusive counterpart is a proposition which can always be converted—either with no change in the terms except for the transposition alone or with some other change as well—then the universal proposition just like it should be taken as the one with which the exclusive proposition in question is interchangeable. In what follows we will deal with these conversions and modes of converting.[6]

From these remarks and those which will be made later about conversions, it is clear that a consequence such as the following is not valid: 'Only what is necessary is necessarily true; therefore everything which is true is necessarily necessary'—even though this consequence is valid: 'Only what is necesary is true; therefore everything true is necessary'. Similarly, this does not follow:

'Only a man was white; therefore every white thing was a man'.
And the same holds for similar propositions, which will be dealt
with in their proper place below.

Another rule is that every exclusive proposition has two exponents: one affirmative and the other negative. Therefore, the
opposite of an exclusive proposition has two causes of truth, since
the opposite of either exponent is a cause of the truth of the negation of the exclusive proposition in question.

Another rule is that when the dictum of an exclusive proposition occurs with some mode which renders a proposition modal,
then the exclusive proposition in question has to be distinguished.
For example, the proposition 'Only a man is Socrates is true' has
to be distinguished.[7] For 'only' can be uttered either continuously
with the whole dictum '. . . a man is Socrates' or not continously
with it. If it is not uttered continuously with it, i.e. if one says,
'Only "A man is Socrates" is true', then the proposition is false.
For in that case it has the following sense: 'Only this proposition
is true', referring to 'A man is Socrates'. On the other hand, if
'only' is uttered continuously with the whole dictum '. . . a man
is Socrates', and if the parts of the dictum are connected,[8] then
the proposition has this sense: 'That only a man is Socrates is
true'—and this is equivalent to: 'This is true: "Only a man is
Socrates"'. Now if the parts of the dictum are not connected,
then it is not asserted that 'Only a man is Socrates' is true.
Rather, it is asserted that 'Socrates', taken with the exclusive
expression, is truly predicated of something contained under
'man'. Hence, the case is similar with respect both to these propositions and to others taken without an exclusive expression. (There
is a variation, however, depending on whether or not the predicate
is a singular term.) Hence, if 'only' is continuous with the whole
dictum and if the parts of the dictum are disconnected, then 'Only
a white thing is running is possible' is false.[9] For it is possible
that something other than a white thing is running. If, on the
other hand, the parts of the dictum are connected, then the proposition is true. For in that case it is asserted that this proposition is
possible: 'Only a white thing is running'. But by means of the
other proposition it was asserted that no proposition is possible
in which 'running' is predicated of a pronoun referring to something which is not white—which is not true.

As far as exceptive propositions are concerned we must examine, first, which propositions are exceptive; second, what is required for the truth of exceptive propositions; third, the supposition of the terms in exceptive propositions; fourth, certain
rules which should be given for exceptive propositions.

On the first point it should be noted that such syncategorematic expressions as 'except' and 'unless' make the propositions
in which they occur exceptive propositions.

But it should first be understood that sometimes 'unless' is
used as a conjunction, in which case it renders the proposition
hypothetical, as is clear from the proposition 'Socrates cannot
run unless he has feet'. Sometimes, however, it is used exceptively, in which case it does not make the proposition hypothetical, as is clear from the proposition 'No man is running unless
Socrates'. In such a case the expression 'unless' has the same
function as the expression 'except', when the latter is taken
exceptively.

Moreover, it should also be noted that the expression 'except'
is sometimes used exceptively and sometimes diminutively. It is
used exceptively, for instance, in 'Every man except Socrates is
running'. It is used diminutively, for example, in 'Ten except five
is five'.

With respect to the second principal point it should be noted
that for the truth of an exceptive proposition it is required that
the predicate be denied of the excepted thing and that it inhere
in everything else contained under the subject—if the proposition
is affirmative. If the proposition is negative, then the converse is
required. Thus, every exceptive proposition has two exponents,
namely, one affirmative and one negative. For example, 'Every
man except Socrates is running' has these exponents: 'Socrates
is not running' and 'Every man other than Socrates is running'.
And the proposition 'No man except Socrates is running' has
these exponents: 'Socrates is running' and 'No man other than
Socrates is running'. Thus it is impossible for an exceptive proposition to be true unless each of its exponents is true. Therefore,

the falsity of the exceptive follows from the falsity of a given exponent, but not conversely.

With respect to the third principal point it should be noted that the predicate in an affirmative exceptive proposition has merely confused supposition, since it is not possible to descend to the inferiors by either a disjunctive or a conjunctive proposition. The subject, however, has confused and distributive supposition.

Still, a distinction must be made with regard to confused and distributive supposition. For sometimes it is absolute, namely, when the term is equally distributed over each of the things contained under it in such a way that it is distributed over one no more than over another. Now the subject in an exceptive proposition does not have this sort of confused and distributive supposition. The other sort is, as it were, limited and circumscribed, namely, when the term is distributed over some of the things contained under it but, in virtue of something added to it, is not distributed over others of them. This does not happen except when the categorical proposition in question is equivalent to a conjunctive proposition composed of one affirmative part and one negative part. This is the case with an exceptive proposition, as has been pointed out.

Now if an exceptive proposition is negative, then both the subject and the predicate have confused and distributive supposition of the limited type.

From what has been said it is clear that rules such as the following are not universally true: 'There is a valid consequence from a distributed superior to its inferior' and 'There is a valid consequence from a universal proposition to its singular'. Rather, it must be added that the inferior in question is not an excepted term or that the universal proposition in question is not equivalent to a conjunctive proposition composed of one affirmative part and one negative part.

With respect to the fourth point it should be noted that many rules are given for exceptive propositions. One is that if the non-exceptive counterpart of an exceptive proposition is true, then the exceptive is false. This is clear from what has been said.

Another rule is that an exceptive proposition is never properly formed unless its non-exceptive counterpart is a universal proposition. Hence, 'A man except Socrates is running' is not properly formed. Thus, such a piece of discourse is neither true nor false.

From this another rule follows, namely, that there is not always a valid consequence from a universal to its corresponding indefinite or particular. Hence, this does not follow: 'Every man except Socrates is running; therefore some man except Socrates is running'—or 'therefore a man except Socrates is running'.

Another rule which follows from this is that not every universal proposition has a corresponding indefinite or particular proposition as its contradictory. For these are not contradictories: 'Every man except Socrates is running' and 'Some man except Socrates is not running'. Nor are the following contradictories: 'No man except Socrates is running' and 'Some man except Socrates is running'.

From this rule follows another, namely, that it is not always the case that the expression 'some . . . not' may be used in place of 'not every'. For the following propositions are not equivalent: 'Not every man except Socrates is running' and 'Some man except Socrates is not running'. The reason is that the one is not properly formed and thus is neither true nor false, while the other is properly formed and is either true or false.

Another rule which follows is that some universal propositions are contraries, even though they do not have as subcontraries categorical propositions which are indefinite or particular and which have subjects determined by particular signs. This is obvious from what has been said already.

Another rule is that it is always the case that that which is excepted in an exceptive proposition should be something contained under the subject. Therefore, any proposition such as the following is not properly formed: 'Every man except an animal is running', 'Every animal except a substance has a soul'.

Another rule is that when that which falls under the exception is a common term, then for the truth of such an exceptive proposition it is not required that the predicate universally inhere in that which falls under the exception, if the proposition is negative, or that it be denied of it universally, if the proposition is affirmative.

It should also be noted that 'except' is never taken diminutively unless it is added to a numerical term or to a term which designates some whole. However, when it is taken diminutively and added to a numerical term, then it is asserted not that the predicate is denied of that to which the expression 'except' is added, but rather that it is denied of the subject. For example, by means of 'Ten except five is five' it is asserted not that five is removed from five but that five is removed from ten. Similarly, by means of such a proposition it is not asserted that the predicate inheres in that to which the expression 'except' is added. For example, by means of 'Ten except four is six' it is not asserted that four is six, but rather that six is left after four is taken away. And the same holds for other such cases. These remarks about exceptive propositions should suffice for the present.

19: On Propositions in which the Verbs 'Begin' and 'Cease' Occur

Every proposition in which either of the verbs 'begin' or 'cease' occurs has two exponents, since each such proposition is equivalent to a conjunctive proposition. Now some writers assign exponents in different ways with respect to different kinds of things. Hence, they claim that such propositions should be expounded in one way with respect to successive entities and in another way with respect to enduring entities.[1]

But although this could be so insofar as the intentions of those who use these terms are concerned, still it does not seem very reasonable.

Therefore, I claim that the propositions in question have the same exponents with respect to any kind of entity, but that the exponents of a proposition in which 'begin' occurs are different from the exponents of a proposition in which 'cease' occurs. Hence, a proposition in which 'begin' occurs has two exponents, one of which is a present-tense affirmative and the other of which is a past-tense negative. For example, the exponents of 'Socrates begins to be white' are 'Socrates is white' and 'Socrates was not white immediately before this'. Now the past-tense negative exponent of the proposition in question is not 'Socrates was not white', since the proposition in which 'begin' occurs can be true even if this latter past-tense negative proposition is false. For example, if Socrates is first white and afterwards black and after that becomes white, then at some instant 'Socrates begins to be white' is true even though 'Socrates was not white' is false. For it was assumed that he was white at a previous time. In the same way we also say that this tree is now beginning to blossom, even though it blossomed last year.

Nevertheless, it should be noted that the verb 'begin' can be understood in two ways. If it is taken strictly and properly, then it is expounded as above. But it can also be taken loosely and improperly, in which case it is expounded in this way: 'It is such-and-such, and it has not been such-and-such for long before this'. For example, we say that this tree is beginning to blossom when it is now blossoming and has not been blossoming for very long this year, even though it was blossoming yesterday. In the same way we ordinarily say 'He is beginning the Mass', even though he has already recited the Introit. The distinction in question is similar to the one which the Philosopher makes in *Physics* IV[2] with respect to the word 'now'. He says that 'now' can be taken for an individual (point of time) and it can be taken for a short duration of time surrounding the present.

It should also be understood that although such a proposition, strictly speaking, has exponents such as those mentioned above, still sometimes, in virtue of the use made of it by speakers, it does not have such exponents. Rather, it is used in place of another proposition—one which lacks such exponents. In that case such a proposition has to be distinguished as amphibolous.

With this in mind one can discern what should be said about propositions such as the following: 'God begins to beatify every blessed man whom he beatifies'; 'God begins to punish every

man whom he punishes'; 'God begins to beatify them', referring
to two men, one of whom he has beatified before and the other
of whom he has not beatified before. For the truth of such propositions can be conceded strictly speaking, i.e. in accord with the
general rules by which these propositions and ones just like them
should be judged. For example, the proposition 'God begins to
beatify them' can be conceded, since both of the following are
true: 'God is beatifying them' and 'God has not beatified them
immediately before this'. Still, the proposition can have another
sense, so that its exponents are the following: 'God beatifies
them' and 'He had previously beatified neither of them'—and
on this reading the proposition is false. Similarly, one sense of
'God begins to beatify everyone whom he now beatifies' is this:
'God beatifies everyone whom he now beatifies and God did not
immediately before this beatify everyone whom he now beatifies'—
and in this sense the proposition is true. The other sense is this:
'God beatifies everyone whom he now beatifies and he did not
immediately before this beatify anyone whom he now beatifies'—
and in this sense the proposition is false. Exactly the same can
be said of the proposition 'God begins to punish everyone whom
he now punishes'. Propositions such as the following should be
treated in a similar way: 'Peter begins to be like Paul in a certain
respect', assuming that each is first an unbeliever and later becomes a believer.[3] In that case 'Peter begins to be like Paul in a
certain respect' can be conceded without qualification, since he
is now for the first time like Paul in a certain respect and before
this he was not like Paul in that respect. Nevertheless, 'Peter begins to be similar to Paul' is, strictly speaking, false, since he was
similar to Paul before this. Still, this proposition can be understood improperly to have this sense: 'Peter is similar to Paul, and
he was not similar to Paul with respect to a certain quality, with
respect to which he is now similar to him'.

And so it is clear that a proposition in which the verb 'begin'
occurs has two exponents and, as a result, is equivalent to a conjunctive proposition.

In the same way, a proposition in which the verb 'cease' occurs
has two exponents. One exponent is a present-tense affirmative
proposition and the other is a future-tense negative proposition—

not just any one, but one in which the phrase 'will not be such-and-such immediately after this' is added. For example, 'Socrates ceases to be white' has these exponents: 'Socrates is white' and 'Immediately after this he will not be white'. And just as it was said, with respect to propositions in which the verb 'begin' occurs, that sometimes such propositions can be distinguished as amphibolous, since they can be taken either properly or improperly, so too many propositions in which the verb 'cease' occurs can be distinguished as amphibolous, since they can be taken either properly or improperly.

With regard to the supposition of the terms in such propositions it should be noted that the subject of such a proposition supposits in the same way that it does in the corresponding proposition which does not contain 'begin' or 'cease'. However, there is a difficulty with respect to the supposition of the predicate.

It should be claimed that the predicate in a universal affirmative proposition of this type has merely confused supposition, since it is not possible to descend either conjunctively or disjunctively. For this does not follow: 'Every man ceases to be white; therefore every man ceases to be this white thing or every man ceases to be that white thing'. Nor, consequently, is it possible to descend conjunctively. Similarly, in a universal negative proposition of this type the predicate has confused and distributive supposition, while in a non-universal proposition it has determinate supposition.

Still, two things must be taken into account at this point. The first is that both determinate supposition and confused and distributive supposition are of two types. One type occurs when it is possible to descend to the things for which the term supposits—or is able to supposit—by means of demonstrative pronouns alone. For example, in the proposition 'A man is running' the term 'man' supposits for this man and that one, and so on for the others. And this follows correctly: 'A man is running; therefore this is running', referring to this man, 'or that is running', referring to that man, and so on for the others. However, sometimes it is possible to descend not by means of demonstrative pronouns alone but only by means of demonstrative pronouns taken with the common term under which the descensus is supposed to occur.

Now the predicate of a proposition in which 'begin' or 'cease' occurs does not have determinate supposition of the first type. For this does not follow: 'Socrates begins to be white; therefore Socrates begins to be this or begins to be that', no matter what is referred to. For if Socrates changes from being black to being white, then 'Socrates begins to be white' is true, even though, no matter what is referred to, the proposition 'Socrates begins to be this' is false. For the second of the following propositions is false: 'Socrates is this' and 'Socrates was not this before'. Rather, the predicate supposits determinately in the second way. For this is valid: 'Socrates begins to be white; therefore he begins to be this white thing or he begins to be that white thing', and so on for the others. Hence, 'Socrates begins to be this white thing', referring to Socrates, is true, since Socrates is now this white thing and he was never previously this white thing.

But this is not valid: 'Socrates begins to be this white thing; therefore he begins to be this', always referring to the same thing. Rather, this is a fallacy of a figure of speech, committed by confusing *'quale quid'* with *'hoc aliquid'*.[4] For there is frequently a fallacy of a figure of speech in such cases when one argues from some connotative term—whether it is the whole predicate or is taken with a demonstrative pronoun—to a demonstrative pronoun taken by itself.

Now someone might object that 'this' and 'this white thing', referring to the same thing, are interchangeable and that, therefore, an inference from one to the other is valid. It should be replied that the rule 'There is a valid consequence from one of two interchangeable terms to the other' has many counterinstances, specifically, when the terms do not supposit personally, and also sometimes when some syncategorematic expression is added to the verb. For example, this does not follow: 'A man is *per se* in the second mode risible; therefore a man is *per se* in the second mode a man'.[5] It is especially true, however, that the rule does not hold with respect to many past-tense and future-tense propositions when the interchangeable terms in question are interchangeable at present but not interchangeable without qualification. This is the case with the two terms 'this' and 'this white thing', for when the thing in question is not white, the two terms are not interchangeable.

Second, it should be noted that sometimes determinate sup-position is such that it is possible to descend to the inferiors and, conversely, it is possible to ascend from the inferiors—but some-times this is not so. Hence, this follows: 'A man is running; there-fore this man is running or that man is running', and so on for the others. And, conversely, this follows: 'This man is running; therefore a man is running'. But this is not always the case with a term suppositing determinately in the predicate position in a proposition containing 'begin' or 'cease'. Hence, this is valid: 'Socrates begins to be this colored thing; therefore he begins to be white or black', and so on for the others. But the converse does not follow. For this does not follow: 'Socrates begins to be white; therefore he begins to be colored'. The reason for this is that the negative exponent of the antecedent does not entail the negative exponent of the consequent. For this does not fol-low: 'Socrates was not white; therefore Socrates was not colored'. And it is a general rule that when the antecedent and consequent have exponents, then if an exponent of the consequent does not follow from some exponent of the antecedent, the inference in-volving the antecedent and consequent is not valid.

From what has been said one can gather that the consequence from an inferior to a superior with respect to the verb 'begin' or 'cease' is not valid, just as this is not valid: 'Socrates begins to be white; therefore Socrates begins to be colored'. Similarly, this does not follow: 'The Son of God begins to be a man; therefore the Son of God begins to be some thing'. Nor is an argument such as this valid: 'Every man is some thing; the Son of God begins to be a man; therefore the Son of God begins to be some thing'. Rather, this is a fallacy of accident. For just as there is always a fallacy of accident when in the first figure the major premise is affirmative and the minor negative, so too there is always a fal-lacy of accident when in the first figure the major premise is af-firmative and the minor premise has some negative exponent. For example, this is invalid: 'Every man is an animal; only what is risible is a man; therefore only what is risible is an animal'. But this is the case with the argument proposed above, for the minor premise, 'The Son of God begins to be a man', has this negative exponent: 'The Son of God was not a man immediately before this'. Therefore, in such an argument there is a fallacy of accident.

Similarly, it may be clear to the diligent reader that the following consequence is not valid: 'The Son of God begins to be a man; therefore some man begins to be the Son of God'.

Nevertheless, it should be noted that sometimes the saints concede such a proposition, taking it not in its strict and literal sense, but rather in the true sense which they had in mind.

Despite what I have just said, however, it should be noted that whenever two or more incompossible inferiors cannot be truly predicated successively of a thing while the superior remains truly predicable of that thing, then there is always a valid consequence when one argues from such an inferior to such a superior. For example, this follows: 'Socrates begins to be a man; therefore he begins to be an animal'. The reason for this is that it is impossible for anything, while remaining an animal, to be first a man and afterwards not a man, or vice versa. Similarly, in Aristotle's opinion the following is a valid inference: 'Socrates begins to be rational; therefore Socrates begins to be sentient'. In the same way this follows: 'A donkey begins to be a man; therefore it begins to be an animal'. And yet this does not follow: 'A donkey begins to be black; therefore it begins to be colored'.

20: On Propositions in which the Verb 'Become' Occurs

Now just as a proposition containing one of the verbs just discussed has two exponents, so too propositions containing the verb 'become' or some equivalent, such as the expression 'came to be' or 'was made', etc., have two exponents—one present-tense and one past- or future-tense. For example, the proposition 'Socrates becomes white' has these exponents: 'Socrates is white' and 'He was not always white'. Similarly, the proposition 'Socrates will become white' has these exponents: 'Socrates is not white and will not be white for some time' and 'Socrates will be white'. The same holds for such propositions as 'Socrates became a man', 'Socrates came to be colored', and so on for propositions just like them.

Now just as a proposition containing the verb 'begin' or 'cease' is not converted by a mere transposition of the terms which precede and follow the verb, so it is with the propositions in question here. And, therefore, strictly speaking, this consequence should be denied: 'The Son of God became a man; therefore a man became the Son of God'—although the saints sometimes concede such propositions with a true meaning in mind. Similarly, this does not follow: 'The Son of God becomes a man; therefore a man becomes the Son of God'. The reason is that the second exponent is not converted in this way. For this does not follow: 'The Son of God was not always a man; therefore it is not the case that a man was always the Son of God'. Hence, in accord with the proper use of the terms it should be conceded that a man was always the Son of God. This is why Christ said: "Before Abraham came to be, I am."

Likewise, with respect to such propositions a consequence from an inferior to a superior on the part of the predicate does not hold. Hence, this does not follow: 'Socrates becomes white; therefore Socrates becomes colored'. Likewise, this does not follow, properly speaking: 'The Son of God comes to be a man; therefore the Son of God comes to be an existing being'—nor does 'therefore he comes to be something' follow, properly speaking.

Now someone might object that the Son of God becomes (or became) a man, therefore he becomes either something or nothing; and he does not become something; therefore he becomes nothing. It should be replied that this does not follow: 'The Son of God becomes a man; therefore the Son of God becomes something or the Son of God becomes nothing'—just as this does not follow: 'Socrates begins to be white; therefore Socrates begins to be a being or he begins to be nothing'. And thus both parts of such disjunctive propositions should be denied.

Nevertheless, it should be noted that one finds in the writings of the saints many propositions like 'A man became God', just as one finds propositions like 'A man begins to be God'. Such propositions are not true, properly speaking, but are true as the saints understood them.

Similarly, just as an argument such as the following is not valid: 'Every white thing is colored; Socrates begins to be white; therefore Socrates begins to be colored'—so too an argument such as this is invalid: 'Every man is some thing; the Son of God became a man; therefore the Son of God became some thing'. The reason is the same in both cases.

These remarks about categorical propositions which are equivalent to hypothetical propositions are sufficient for now—although there remain many things which should be said. I will discuss them in different places.

21: On the Conversion of
Non-Modal Present-Tense Propositions

Now that we have discussed what is required for the truth of categorical propositions, what remains is to talk about conversions. The conversion of non-modal propositions should be treated first, and then the conversion of modal propositions.

With respect to non-modal propositions, the conversion of present-tense propositions should be treated first, and then the conversion of past-tense and future-tense propositions.

Now it should first be noted that a conversion occurs when the predicate is formed from the subject and vice versa. Sometimes such a conversion is accomplished without any other change in the words, while sometimes a change in the words over and beyond the transposition of the terms is made.

Second, it should be noted that sometimes the extremes of a present-tense non-modal proposition are both in the nominative case, while sometimes one of the extremes is in an oblique case.

Third, it should be noted that there are three kinds of conversion, namely, simple, accidental, and contrapositional. A conversion is simple when the quality and quantity of both propositions remain the same. However, simple conversion can be taken more loosely in such a way that a conversion is called simple when it is mutual, so that just as, in virtue of the propositions involved, the proposition which is converted implies the proposition into which it is converted, so too the converse holds. And this frequently happens even when the antecedent and the consequent do not have the same quantity—as when a singular proposition is converted into a particular proposition, and vice versa.

A conversion is called accidental when the quantity of the antecedent and the consequent does not remain the same. However, a conversion can be called accidental in another sense, namely, when the conversion is not mutual. For example, this follows: 'Every man is white; therefore some white thing is a man'—but the converse does not follow.

A conversion is called contrapositional when finite terms are changed into infinite terms.

Fourth, it should be noted that a universal negative proposition with both extremes in the nominative case is converted simply, if one takes simple conversion in the loose sense. And this involves no change in the words other than the transposition of the terms—except perhaps for a change involving the grammatical gender of a word. However, if one takes simple conversion in the strict sense, then such a proposition is not always converted simply. For example, this does not follow: 'No donkey is Socrates; therefore no Socrates is a donkey'. Rather, what follows is this: 'therefore Socrates is not a donkey'.

Similarly, a singular affirmative proposition is converted simply into a particular and an indefinite proposition, or into a singular proposition. For example, this follows: 'Socrates is a man; therefore a man is Socrates', and 'therefore some man is Socrates'— and conversely. Likewise, this follows: 'Socrates is Plato; therefore Plato is Socrates'—and conversely.

A singular negative proposition is converted simply into either a universal negative or a singular negative. For example, this follows: 'Socrates is not white; therefore no white thing is Socrates', and conversely. Likewise, this follows: 'Socrates is not Plato;

therefore Plato is not Socrates', and conversely. Thus, a singular proposition is converted by a simple conversion into different types of propositions depending on whether its predicate is a common term or a singular term.

Similarly, both an indefinite affirmative and a particular affirmative are converted either into both an indefinite proposition and a particular proposition or into a singular proposition, depending on whether the proposition to be converted has as its predicate a common term or a singular term. For example, this follows: 'A man is white; therefore some white thing is a man', and 'therefore a white thing is a man'. And this follows: 'Some man is white; therefore some white thing is a man', and 'therefore a white thing is a man'. Likewise, this follows: 'A man is Socrates; therefore some man is Socrates; therefore Socrates is a man'—and conversely.

Similarly, a universal affirmative proposition is only converted accidentally, since the conversion is not mutual in such a case. And this is so when the predicate term is a common term. In that case the proposition is converted accidentally into both a particular proposition and an indefinite proposition. For example, this follows: 'Every man is white; therefore some white thing is a man', and 'therefore a white thing is a man'—but not conversely. However, when the predicate is a singular term, then such a proposition is converted, again accidentally, into a singular proposition. For this is valid: 'Every man is Socrates; therefore Socrates is a man'—but not conversely.

A particular negative proposition is not converted either simply or accidentally. For this does not follow: 'Some animal is not a man; therefore some man is not an animal'; nor does this follow: 'therefore no man is an animal'. In the same way, an indefinite negative proposition is not converted, since a particular proposition and an indefinite proposition are always interchangeable. This is at least true when the subjects of both propositions supposit personally.

In *Prior Analytics* I[1] the Philosopher proves some of the conversions discussed above. I have decided to omit these proofs, since the conversions are obvious and do not require extensive proof.

Now it might be objected to certain things said above that, according to both Porphyry[2] and the Philosopher,[3] a species is not predicated of its genus, and an inferior is not predicated of its superior, and a singular or individual is predicated only of one thing alone. Therefore, conversions such as this and others like it are not valid: 'Every man is an animal; therefore some animal is a man'.

It should be responded that Porphyry and the Philosopher mean that an inferior is not predicated by a true predication of a superior which is actually common to more things than the inferior is, when that superior is taken universally. Hence, they mean nothing more than that no proposition like the following is true: 'Every animal is a man', 'Every man is Socrates', and so on for the others. But they do not deny that the corresponding particular and indefinite propositions are true.

What has been said so far applies to propositions in which both extremes are in the nominative case. However, propositions with one extreme in an oblique case cannot in all instances be treated in the same way. Rather, in such propositions it is frequently necessary to make some change in the words besides the mere transposition of the terms. And often one does this by adding to the predicate the participle of the main verb, as when one argues in this way: 'No man is in the house; therefore nothing existing in the house is a man'. The same holds when one argues like this: 'No man sees a donkey; therefore nothing seeing a donkey is a man'. Now this is true when the oblique case occurs in the predicate position, since such a change is not necessary when the oblique case occurs in the subject position. Hence, the proposition 'All men a donkey sees' should be converted into 'therefore a donkey sees a man'. Similarly, 'It is the Son the Father generates; therefore the Father generates the Son'.

With respect to what has been said it should be noted that when a present-tense non-modal proposition contains an adverbial determination or some equivalent thereof, then in the proposition into which it is converted that determination should not be a determination of the verb—rather, it should be a determination of the participle of the same verb. Thus, in such a case—whether or not both of the extremes of the proposition to be converted are in the nominative case—it is necessary to resolve the verb into its participle and the verb 'is'. And so it is necessary to make some change in the words over and above the transposition of the terms. Thus, the proposition 'An altered thing is running quickly' should not be converted into 'therefore a running thing is altered quickly'. For assume that the same thing is altered slowly and is running quickly. In that case the antecedent is true and the consequent false. Rather, it should be converted into 'therefore a thing running quickly is an altered thing'—so that 'quickly' is a determination of the participle 'running' and not of the verb 'is'. Similarly, the proposition 'A being which creates is always God' should not be converted into 'therefore God is always a being which creates'. Rather, it should be converted into 'therefore something which is always God is a being which creates'.

22: On the Conversion of Past-Tense and Future-Tense Non-Modal Propositions

With respect to the conversion of past-tense and future-tense propositions it should first be noted that every past-tense or future tense proposition in which the subject is a common term must be distinguished as equivocal in the third mode. For if the proposition is past-tense, then the subject can supposit for that which is such-and-such or for that which was such-and-such. That is, such a proposition is equivocal because the subject can supposit for that of which the subject is truly predicated by means of a present-tense verb, or it can supposit for that of which the subject is truly predicated by means of a past-tense verb. For example, the proposition 'A white thing was Socrates' must be distinguished, since 'white thing' can supposit either for that which is white or for that which was white. On the other hand, if the proposition is future-tense, then it should be distinguished because the subject can supposit for that which is such-and-such or for that which will be such-and-such. That is, it can supposit for that of which the subject is truly predicated by means of a present-tense verb, or it can supposit for that of which the subject is truly predicated by means of a future-tense verb. This rule should be understood to apply when the subject supposits personally, i.e. significatively.

Second, it should be noted that when the subject of such a proposition supposits for that which is such-and-such, then the proposition in question should be converted not into a past-tense proposition, but rather into a present-tense proposition in which the subject is taken with the verb 'was' and the pronoun 'which'. Hence, this consequence is not valid, if the subject of the antecedent is taken for what is white: 'No white thing was a man; therefore no man was white'. For suppose that many men, both living and dead, were white, and that many other things were white and are now white, and that no man is now white. In that case the antecedent is true and the consequent false. For 'Nothing which is white was a man' is true, since each of its singulars is true in the assumed case. But 'No man was white' is false no matter how the subject is taken. Therefore, the proposition in question should not be converted in the way proposed above. Rather, it should be converted as follows: 'No white thing was a man; therefore nothing which was a man is white'. And in the same way the converse follows: 'Nothing which was a man is white; therefore no white thing was a man'—where the subject of the consequent supposits for those things which are white and not for those things which were white. If, on the other hand, the subject in such a proposition is taken for that which was such-and-such, then the proposition is converted simply into a past-tense proposition and not into a present-tense proposition. For if the subject of the antecedent is taken for what was white, then this follows: 'No white thing was a man; therefore no man was white'—this is so as long as the subject of the consequent is taken for that which was a man. For it is impossible that some man was white and yet that nothing which was white was a man.

Now if such a past-tense proposition is a singular proposition in which the subject is a demonstrative pronoun standing alone or a proper name, then the proposition is converted either into a singular proposition, a universal proposition, or a particular or indefinite proposition—with the subject of the consequent being taken for that which was such-and-such. Hence, this is valid: 'Socrates was not white; therefore nothing which was white was Socrates'. But if the subject of the consequent is taken for that which is white, then the consequence is not valid. For this does not follow: 'Socrates was not white; therefore nothing which is white was Socrates'; nor does the corresponding present-tense proposition follow, namely, 'No white thing is Socrates'. For suppose that Socrates is now white for the first time. In that case 'Socrates was not white' is true, while both of the proposed consequents are false.

It should also be noted that just as such a proposition is distinguished when the subject is a common term, so also it can be distinguished when the subject is a demonstrative pronoun with a common term. Thus, the proposition 'This white thing was Socrates' should be distinguished, since either the implied clause has a present-tense verb, in which case the proposition has this sense: 'This thing, which is white, was Socrates'; or the implied clause has a past-tense verb, in which case the proposition has this sense: 'This thing, which was white, was Socrates'. And such a proposition is converted just like a past-tense proposition in which the subject is a common term.

As far as the distinction just noted is concerned, what was said of a past-tense proposition should be applied, *mutatis mutandis,* to a future-tense proposition.

It should also be noted that, as was pointed out above,[1] in present-tense propositions an adverbial determination should, in the consequent, be added not to the main verb, but to the participle of the antecedent's verb. The same thing should be done in these past-tense and future-tense propositions.

From what has been said it is clear that consequences such as the following are not valid: 'God was not always a being which creates; therefore a being which creates was not always God'. For the antecedent, namely, 'God was not always a being which creates', is true, since he was not creating before the creation of the world; but the proposition 'A being which creates was not always God' is false, since this being which creates was always God.[2] For just as 'A white thing was black' is true even though 'A white thing is black' was never true, so also 'A being which creates was always God' is true even though 'A being which creates is God' was not always true. And thus the consequence alluded to above is not valid. Rather, the proposition in question should be converted as follows: 'God was not always a being which creates; therefore nothing which was always a being which creates is God', or 'therefore nothing which was always a being which creates was God'. And the consequent is true, since it has two causes of truth: either nothing was always creating, or something was always creating and yet is not God. The first cause is true, although the second is false. Similarly, this consequence is not valid, if the subject of the antecedent is taken for that which is with sight: 'No one with sight was blind; therefore no one blind was with sight'. Rather, the antecedent should be converted into 'No one who was blind is with sight'. And so when the subject is taken for that which is such-and-such, a past-tense proposition is converted into a present-tense proposition in the way noted above. In the same way, when the subject is taken for that which was such-and-such, such a proposition is converted into a past-tense proposition, the subject of which is taken for that which was such-and-such.

The same holds for propositions such as 'Nothing impossible will be true'. If the subject is taken for that which is impossible, then the proposition is converted into a present-tense proposition in the following way: 'Nothing impossible will be true; therefore nothing which will be true is impossible'. If the subject is taken for that which will be impossible, then the proposition is converted into 'therefore nothing true will be impossible'—with the subject of the consequent being taken for that which will be true.

It should also be noted that if the subject of such a past- or future-tense proposition is a common term or includes a common term with a demonstrative pronoun, and if the predicate is a demonstrative pronoun standing alone or a proper name, then if the subject is taken for that which is such-and-such, the proposition is converted into a present-tense proposition without any other change. For example, this follows: 'A white thing will be Socrates; therefore Socrates is white'. But the converse does not follow if it is possible to assign a last moment of existence to an enduring entity.[3] Similarly, if the subject of the antecedent is taken for that which is white, then this is valid: 'Some white thing was Socrates; therefore Socrates is white'. But the converse is not valid if it is possible to assign a first moment of existence to an enduring entity. On the other hand, if the subject is taken for that which will be or was such-and-such, then such a proposition is converted without qualification into a past-tense or present-tense proposition—and such a conversion is mutual.

23: On the Conversion of Propositions which are not Simply Categorical, e.g. Exclusives, Reduplicatives, Exceptives, etc.

What has been said in the two preceding chapters can in some way clarify the conversion of reduplicative propositions, exclusive propositions, exceptive propositions, and those propositions in which the verb 'begin' or the verb 'cease' occurs. For a proposition which has exponents is converted in the same way that its exponents are converted, and if all the exponents are converted in the same way, then the expounded proposition is converted in that same way. On the other hand, if one exponent is converted in one way and another in another way, namely, one simply and the other accidentally, then the expounded proposition will have the same kind of conversion that the one exponent has, but not the same kind that the other has.

Still, we should deal more specifically with these propositions. Hence, it should be noted that a reduplicative proposition is not converted into a reduplicative proposition. Rather, it is converted into a non-reduplicative proposition, the subject of which will have one part consisting of the predicate of the antecedent, the reduplicative expression, and the term which falls under the reduplication. This part will be joined to the rest by the pronoun 'which'. For example, 'An animal, insofar as it is a man, is risible' is converted into 'Something, which insofar as it is a man is risible, is an animal'. It is not converted into 'A risible thing, insofar as it is a man, is an animal'. The following is a clear counterinstance: 'Socrates, insofar as he is a man, is risible, therefore a risible thing, insofar as it is a man, is Socrates'. For the antecedent is true and the consequent false. Similarly, 'Nothing active, insofar as it is passive, is active' is converted into 'therefore nothing, which is active insofar as it is passive, is active'.

Similarly, what has been said here and in the preceding chapter should be applied, *mutatis mutandis*, to the conversion of past-tense and future-tense reduplicative propositions.

As far as the conversion of exclusive propositions is concerned, it should be noted that an exclusive proposition is not converted into an exclusive proposition. For this does not follow: 'Only an animal is a man; therefore only a man is an animal'. Rather, an exclusive proposition is converted into a universal proposition. For example, this follows: 'Only an animal is a man; therefore every man is an animal'. Similarly, this follows: 'Only a man is not running; therefore everything which is not running is a man'.

And what was said about the conversion of past-tense and future-tense propositions also applies to the conversion of past-tense and future-tense exclusive propositions. Hence, this does not follow, if the subject of the antecedent is taken for what is white: 'Every white thing was Socrates; therefore only Socrates was white'. For suppose that nothing except Socrates is now white, and that many other things were white. In that case the antecedent is true and the consequent false. Therefore, the proposition in question is not coverted in the way proposed above. Rather, it is converted as follows: 'Every white thing was Socrates; therefore only Socrates is white'. But this conversion is not mutual. And what was said in the previous chapter should be applied, *mutatis mutandis,* to other exclusives in the way in which it has been applied to the one under discussion here.

With respect to the conversion of exceptive propositions it should be noted that an exceptive proposition is not converted into an exceptive proposition. For this does not follow: 'Every man except Socrates is running; therefore some running thing except Socrates is a man'—for the consequent is not properly formed. Rather, an exceptive proposition is converted into a non-exceptive proposition, the subject of which will consist of the predicate of the exceptive proposition and the excepted term, joined by the phrase 'which is not', as follows: 'Every man except Socrates is running; therefore some running thing which is not Socrates is a man'. And the proposition 'No man except Socrates is running' is converted into 'No running thing which is not Socrates is a man'.

Concerning the conversion of propositions in which the verbs 'begin' and 'cease' occur, it should be noted that they are not converted into propositions of the same type. For this does not follow: 'Some man begins to be white; therefore some white thing begins to be a man'. Rather, such propositions should be converted in the following way: 'Some man begins to be white; therefore something which begins to be white is a man'. And the same holds for the others.

From what has been said one can determine the modes of conversion of any non-modal proposition, whether it is present-, past- or future-tense, and whether it is a categorical proposition which is not equivalent to a hypothetical proposition or a categorical proposition which is equivalent to a hypothetical.

24: On the Conversion of *de necessario* Propositions

Now that we have seen how non-modal propositions are converted, we should look into the conversion of modal propositions— and first of all into the conversion of *de necessario* propositions.

Now it should first be noted that, as was pointed out before,[1] when a mode occurs with a dictum, then the proposition in question must be distinguished with respect to composition and division. Therefore, we should first treat the conversion of such propositions in the sense of composition and of propositions equivalent to them; and, second, we should treat the conversion of such propositions in the sense of division and of propositions equivalent to them.

With respect to the former it should be noted, in brief, that such propositions are converted just as their non-modal counterparts are, since in the conversion of such propositions one always argues in accord with the following rule: 'If one of two interchangeable propositions is necessary, the other is necessary'—or in accord with this rule: 'If the antecedent is necessary, the consequent is necessary'. Hence, in a simple conversion, taken loosely, one argues in accord with the first rule, while in an accidental conversion one argues in accord with the second rule. For example, one argues in accord with the first rule when he argues like this: 'That no man is a donkey is necessary; therefore that no donkey is a man is necessary'. Because, as was pointed out above,[2] the propositions 'No man is a donkey' and 'No donkey is a man' are interchangeable, if 'No man is a donkey' is necessary, then it must be the case that 'No donkey is a man' is necessary. And what has been said about these propositions should be said of others like them. And this is universally true of all such propositions, whether they are reduplicative or exclusive or exceptive, or categorical propositions of any other kind.

It should also be noted that in *Prior Analytics* I[3] the Philosopher proves only that *de necessario* propositions in the sense of composition and their equivalents are converted—and not that the others are converted. For neither proof holds for the others, as is obvious from the text. Hence, the proposition 'If one of two interchangeable propositions is possible, then the other is possible' is valid only for *de possibili* propositions taken in the sense of composition. The same holds for this rule: 'If a necessity is incompatible with some actuality, then that necessity is incompatible with the possibility of that actuality'— that is, if a *de necessario* proposition is incompatible with some non-modal proposition, then that same *de necessario* proposition is incompatible with the *de possibili* proposition corresponding to that non-modal proposition. Hence, if the propositions 'Some man is running' and 'It is necessary that no animal is running' are incompatible, then the following propositions will be incompatible: 'It is possible that some man is running' and 'It is necessary that no animal is running'. This rule is always true when both of the modal propositions are taken in the sense of composition or are equivalent to propositions so taken. For if one were taken in the sense of division, then the rule would not be valid—since in that case there are many counterinstances. For example, 'Something true is impossible' and 'It is necessary that nothing true is impossible' are incompatible. And yet 'Something true is possibly impossible' and 'It is necessary that nothing true is impossible' are compatible, when the *de necessario* proposition is taken in the sense of composition. For both of them are true. And so in the *Prior Analytics* the Philosopher does not talk about the conversion of *de necessario* propositions except insofar as they are taken in the sense of composition or in an equivalent sense.

With respect to the conversion of *de necessario* propositions taken in the sense of division and of their equivalents, it should be noted that such propositions are not converted without some change or variation in the words over and beyond the transposition of the terms. For this does not follow in virtue of the nature of conversion: 'No man is necessarily a donkey; therefore no donkey is necessarily a man'. For it does not follow in the sense of division when other propositions are used. Hence, this does not follow: 'Nothing impossible is necessarily true; therefore nothing true is necessarily impossible'. For the antecedent is true and the consequent false. For nothing impossible is possibly true, and yet something true is possibly impossible. For 'I have not been to Rome' is now true, and yet it is possibly impossible. For if I go to Rome, then it will be impossible afterwards.[4]

Similarly, this does not follow: 'A being which creates is necessarily God; therefore God is necessarily a being which creates'. For the antecedent is true and the consequent false. Likewise, this does not follow: 'A man is necessarily understood by God; therefore something understood by God is necessarily a man'. For the antecedent is true and the consequent false. Again, this does not follow: 'A white man is necessarily a man; therefore a man is necessarily a white man'.

Therefore, such propositions cannot be converted in the way indicated above. Rather, the mode of necessity along with the phrase 'something which is' must be added to the subject of the consequent (which was the predicate of the antecedent). For example, 'Everything impossible is necessarily not true' should be converted into 'therefore something which is necessarily not true is impossible'. Similarly, the proposition 'A being which creates is necessarily God' should be converted into 'therefore something which is necessarily God is a being which creates'. And the proposition 'A man is necessarily understood by God' is converted into 'therefore something which is necessarily understood by God is a man'; and so on for the others.

From these remarks it is clear that if one construes 'modal proposition' and 'non-modal proposition' in the strict sense, then a *de necessario* proposition, taken in the sense of division, or the equivalent of such a proposition is converted into a non-modal proposition rather than into a *de necessario* proposition.[5]

It is also clear from what has been said that a consequence such as the following is not valid: 'Only what is necessary is necessarily true; therefore everything true is necessarily necessary'. For this latter universal proposition is not interchangeable with the exclusive proposition in question. Rather, this universal proposition is interchangeable with it: 'Everything which is necessarily true is necessary'. For it is always the case that propositions having exponents are converted in different ways insofar as their exponents are converted in different ways. Thus, insofar as the exponents of one exclusive proposition are converted differently from the way in which the exponents of another exclusive proposition are converted, the one exclusive will be converted in a way which differs from the way in which the other exclusive is converted. Again, this does not follow: 'Only a being which creates is necessarily God; therefore every being which is God is necessarily a being which creates'. Rather, the antecedent is converted into 'therefore every being which is necessarily God is a being which creates'.

Now the reason why in the foregoing consequences the antecedent is true and the consequent false was stated before[6] when it was explained how the predicate names its form in a way different from the subject. Therefore, what was said there should be absolutely impressed upon the memory, so that one might know what is required for the truth of past-tense and future-tense propositions and for the truth of modal propositions and their equivalents.

25: On the Conversion of *de possibili* Propositions

With respect to the conversion of *de possibili* propositions it should first be noted that in this chapter 'possible' is always being construed in such a way that it is common both to what is necessary and to what is contingent and not necessary. Thus, 'possible' means the same as 'a proposition which is not impossible'. And if one takes 'possible' in this way, then it should be conceded that God is possibly God and that a man is possibly an animal.

Now, taking 'possible' in this sense, it should be noted that the same rules which were given for the conversion of *de necessario* propositions should be applied to the conversion of *de possibili* propositions. For a *de possibili* proposition taken in the sense of composition—or an equivalent proposition—should be converted in the same way that its non-modal counterpart is converted. For in all such conversions one argues in accord with the rule 'If one of two interchangeable propositions is possible, the other is possible', or in accord with the rule 'If the antecedent is possible, the consequent is possible'. And these rules are always true.

However, if such propositions are taken in the sense of division or are equivalent to propositions so taken, then they are not converted in the same way. Hence, this does not follow: 'God is possibly a being which does not create; therefore a being which does not create is possibly God'—where the subject of the consequent is taken for that which is actually a being which does not create. Similarly, this does not follow: 'A person who is living on earth is possibly damned; therefore someone who is damned is possibly living on earth'. Rather, this consequent follows: 'therefore someone who is possibly damned is living on earth'.

Nevertheless, in order to make it clearer how such *de possibili* propositions should be converted, it should be noted that when the subject of a *de possibili* proposition is a common term or includes a common term, then the proposition must be distinguished. For the subject can supposit either for that which is actually such-and-such or for that which is possibly such-and-such. This rule should be understood as analogous to what was said above about past-tense and future-tense propositions. Now if the subject of the antecedent is taken for those things which are actually such-and-such, then the proposition in question is converted into a *de possibili* proposition, the subject of which is taken for those things which are possibly such-and-such—and not for those things which are actually such-and-such. Hence, this is valid: 'Someone who is living on earth is possibly damned; therefore someone who is possibly damned is possibly living on earth'. Similarly, this follows: 'God is possibly not a being which creates; therefore a being which is possibly not a creator is possibly God'. (And not only does this *de possibili* proposition follow, but the corresponding non-modal proposition, with the addition 'which is possibly . . .', also follows. For example, this follows: 'God is possibly not a being which creates; therefore a being which is possibly not a being which creates is God'.) On the other hand, if the subject of the antecedent is taken for those things which are possibly such-and-such, then that antecedent is converted into a *de possibili* proposition, the subject of which is taken for those things which are possibly such-and-such—and it is not converted into a non-modal proposition. However, if the predicate of the antecedent is a singular term or a demonstrative pronoun standing alone, then that antecedent is converted without qualification into a *de possibili* proposition. For example, this follows: 'A being which creates is possibly God; therefore God is possibly a being which creates'. This holds whether the subject of the antecedent is taken for those things which are actually creators or for those things which are possibly creators.

From what has been said it is clear that consequences such as the following are not valid: 'A being with sight is possibly blind; therefore a blind being is possibly with sight'; 'Something true is possibly impossible; therefore something impossible is possibly true'; 'Nothing necessary is possibly false; therefore nothing false is possibly necessary'. They are invalid, that is, if the subject of the consequent is taken for those things which are actually such-and-such. Otherwise these consequences are valid.

26: On the Conversion of *de impossibili* Propositions

As far as the conversion of *de impossibili* propositions is concerned, it should be noted that *de impossibili* propositions, taken in the sense of composition, are converted just as their non-modal counterparts are converted, as long as those non-modal counterparts are converted simply. For in such cases one argues in accord with the rule 'If one of two interchangeable propositions is impossible, the other is impossible'. This rule is true. However, when its non-modal counterpart is converted only accidentally and not simply, then a *de impossibili* proposition in the sense of composition is not converted—nor is any proposition equivalent to such a proposition converted. The reason is that such a conversion could not hold except in accord with the following rule: 'If the antecedent is impossible, the consequent is impossible'. But this rule is false, for sometimes the antecedent is impossible and the consequent is necessary.

Thus, consequences such as the following are valid: 'That no man is an animal is impossible; therefore that no animal is a man is impossible'; 'That some man is a donkey is impossible; therefore that some donkey is a man is impossible'; 'That God is a corporeal being is impossible; therefore that a corporeal being is God is impossible'. However, consequences such as the following are not valid: 'That every animal is a man is impossible; therefore that some man is an animal is impossible'; 'That every being in act or in potency is God is impossible; therefore that God is a being in act or in potency is impossible'; and so on.

On the other hand, if such a *de impossibili* proposition is taken in the sense of division or is equivalent to a proposition so taken, then it is converted just as its *de necessario* counterpart is converted. Hence, this consequence is not valid: 'Some white thing is not possibly a man; therefore some man is not possibly white'. For the antecedent is true and the consequent false. Rather, the antecedent should be converted into 'therefore something which is not possibly a man is white'. (Similarly, the proposition 'No white thing is possibly a man' is not converted into 'therefore no man is possibly white'. Rather, it is converted into 'therefore something which is not possibly a man is white'.)

[*Ockham himself crossed out the following.*]

Now it should be noted that when a negation precedes the mode, it changes the mode in such a way that the proposition should not be called one of that mode. Therefore, the proposition 'No man is possibly white' is a *de impossibili* proposition rather than a *de possibili* proposition. In the same way, the proposition 'No man is necessarily white' is not, properly and strictly speaking, a *de necessario* proposition. Rather, it is a *de possibili* proposition, since it is equivalent to 'Every man is possibly not white'. Thus, since propositions in which the modes are negated are equivalent to affirmative propositions of other modes, such propositions are converted only accidentally and not simply. Hence, the proposition 'No being necessarily creates' is not converted into 'therefore no being which creates is necessarily a being'. For the latter is false, since its contradictory, namely, 'Some being which creates is necessarily a being', is true. For this being which creates, referring to God, is necessarily a being. Nor is the proposition in question converted into 'Nothing which does not necessarily create is a being'. This does not follow, since the antecedent is true and the consequent false. Rather, the proposition in question is converted into 'therefore something which does not necessarily create is a being'.

27: On the Conversion of *de contingenti* Propositions

Next we must look into the conversion of *de contingenti* propositions. And it should first be noted that in this chapter 'contingent' should always be taken for what is contingent with respect to truth and falsity. Thus, only a proposition which is neither necessary nor impossible is called contingent. Now since such a proposition has two sorts of conversion, one in the terms and one through opposite qualities, we should deal first with the former and then with the latter.

Now it should first be noted that *de contingenti* propositions, taken in the sense of composition, and propositions equivalent to those so taken are converted just as their non-modal counterparts are converted, as long as those non-modal counterparts are converted simply. The reason for this is that such a conversion holds in accord with the following rule: 'If one of two interchangeable propositions is contingent, the other is contingent'. This rule is always true. Therefore, this is valid: 'That a man is white is contingent; therefore that a white thing is a man is contingent'. Similarly, this follows: 'That God creates is contingent; therefore that a being which creates is God is contingent'. And so a particular affirmative as well as a universal negative *de contingenti* proposition, taken in the sense of composition, is converted simply. Similarly, this is valid: 'This is contingent: "No man is white"; therefore this is contingent: "No white thing is a man"', and so on for the others.

However, when its non-modal counterpart is converted only accidentally and not simply, then a *de contingenti* proposition in the sense of composition is not converted in the terms. For such a conversion can hold only in accord with this mediating proposition: 'If the antecedent is contingent, the consequent is contingent'. But this is simply false, since what is necessary follows from what is contingent. Therefore, this does not follow: 'That every man is white is contingent; therefore that some white thing is a man is contingent'—just as this does not follow: 'That every actually existing substance is God is contingent; therefore that God is an actually existing substance is contingent'. For in this latter case the antecedent is true and the consequent false. For the proposition 'Every actually existing substance is God' is contingent, since it can be true and it can be false. And yet the proposition 'God is an actually existing substance' is necessary.

On the other hand, if a *de contingenti* proposition is taken in the sense of division or is equivalent to a proposition so taken, then if that proposition has for its subject a common term or something which includes a common term (e.g. 'this white thing', 'this man', 'this donkey'), or if it has for its subject a participle or some equivalent thereof, then the proposition must be distinguished. For the subject can supposit either for those things which are such-and-such or for those things which are contingently such-and-such. If the subject of such a proposition is taken in the first way, then even if the subject is a proper name or demonstrative pronoun, the proposition is not converted into the same type of *de contingenti* proposition. Rather, it is converted into a non-modal proposition and into a *de possibili* proposition, where the subject of the consequent is taken with the additional phrase 'which is contingently . . .'.

The first point is obvious, namely, that it is not converted into the same type of *de contingenti* proposition. For this does not follow: 'God is contingently a being which creates; therefore a being which creates is contingently God'; nor does this follow: 'therefore something which is contingently a creator is contingently God'. For this latter proposition is incompatible with the following true proposition: 'Something which contingently creates is necessarily God'—and, consequently, it is not contingently God.

The second point, namely, that such a proposition is converted into a non-modal proposition in the way indicated above, is clear. For this is valid: 'God is contingently a being which creates; therefore something which is contingently a being which creates is God'.

This conversion can be proven. For if 'God is contingently a being which creates' is true, then it is obvious that both of these propositions are true: 'This is God', referring to that for which the subject of the *de contingenti* proposition supposits, and 'This is contingently a being which creates'. But then this follows by means of an expository syllogism: 'This is God; this is contingently a being which creates; therefore something which is contingently a being which creates is God'. Consequently, the proposition 'God is contingently a being which creates' is not compatible with the opposite of the proposition 'Something which is contingently a being which creates is God'. And, consequently, the latter follows from the former. And so this conversion is proven by means of an expository syllogism. And just as this one is proven by means of an expository syllogism, so too many of the previous conversions, the proofs of which were omitted, are proven in the same way.

Now such a proof is sufficient, since an expository syllogism is evident in itself and does not require any further proof. Thus, those who deny such a syllogism no matter what its material element is commit a serious mistake, unless they can show that there is in such a syllogism a fallacy of equivocation, or of amphiboly, or of composition and division, or of accent, or of figure of speech, or of relative and absolute, or that there is an *ignoratio elenchi* or a *petitio principii.* But there cannot be, as many claim, a fallacy of accident in such a syllogism.

And since expository syllogisms, which are evident in themselves, are frequently denied by modern theologians—and so one should not argue with such people, since they deny what is known in itself—I will digress somewhat from what I proposed to do and offer some examples in which a syllogism is not expository even though it seems to be.

Hence, this is not an expository syllogism: 'This animal is a dog (*canis*); this animal is not a celestial constellation; therefore a celestial constellation is not Canis'. The reason is that both the major premise and the conclusion must be distinguished as equivocal.

Similarly, this is not an expository syllogism: 'Iste vellet se accipere pugnantes; iste vellet vincere; igitur qui vellet vincere, vellet se accipere pugnantes'. The reason is that the major premise must be distinguished as amphibolous, as is made clear in other places.[1]

Again, this is not an expository syllogism: 'This is false: "You are a donkey"; this is true if it is necessary: "You are a donkey"; therefore something true, if it is necessary, is false'. For the minor premise and the conclusion have to be distinguished with respect to composition and division.

Again, this is not an expository syllogism: 'Iste vult pendere; iste non vult pendere; igitur qui vult pendere, non vult pendere'. For the propositions must be distinguished with respect to accent.[2]

Similarly, this is not an expository syllogism: 'Sortes est albus; Sortes est animal; igitur animal est albus'. Rather, in this case there is a fallacy of a figure of speech. For the same reason this is not an expository syllogism: 'Iste homo est sanus; iste homo est substantia; igitur aliqua substantia est sanus'.[3]

Similarly, this is not an expository syllogism: 'Socrates is not the son of Plato; Socrates is a father; therefore some father is not a son'. Instead, there is an *ignoratio elenchi* in this case.

Likewise, this is not an expository syllogism: 'Socrates is white with respect to his teeth; Socrates is black; therefore something black is white'. Here there is a fallacy of relative and absolute.

Nor is this a probative expository syllogism: 'Socrates is hot; Socrates is productive of heat; therefore a thing productive of heat is hot'. For in this case there is a *petitio principii*. And so the argument does not prove the conclusion, even though its form is valid.[4]

And just as these examples, which appear to be expository syllogisms and are not, contain some obvious defect other than a fallacy of accident, so it is with others.

Hence, it should be noted that it is a general rule that when the propositions involved are just present-tense non-modal propositions, and when they are arranged in a syllogistic figure without any addition or subtraction on the part of the subject and the predicate, then there is never a fallacy of accident in such an argument—just as there is never a fallacy of accident in an argument arranged in the first mode of the first figure. This will be shown below.[5] In the same way, when an argument can be reduced to such an expository syllogism—either by conversion or *per impossibile* or by using equivalent propositions—then there is no fallacy of accident.[6]

It should be noted, however, that for a syllogism to be expository it is not sufficient that one argue by using a demonstrative pronoun or the proper name of some singular thing as the middle term. Rather, besides this it is necessary that the thing referred to or designated by such a proper name is not really more than one distinct thing. For this reason the following is not an expository syllogism: 'This essence (referring to the divine essence) is the Father; this essence is the Son; therefore the Son is the Father'. The reason is that the essence in question is more than one distinct thing. Thus, in such a paralogism there is a fallacy of consequent, although there is also a fallacy of accident in this case.

Now no defect can be pointed to in this syllogism: 'This is God; this is contingently a being which creates; therefore a being which is contingently a being which creates is God'. Therefore, it is clear that it is an evident expository syllogism. Consequently, it has been sufficiently proven that 'God contingently creates' is converted into 'Something which contingently creates is God'. From this it is also clear that the proposition in question is converted into the following *de possibili* proposition: 'Something which contingently creates is possibly God'. For a non-modal proposition always formally entails its *de possibili* counterpart.

Now if the subject of such a *de contingenti* proposition is a demonstrative pronoun or a proper name, then the proposition is converted just as before, namely, into a non-modal proposition and into a *de possibili* proposition. However, if the subject of such a *de contingenti* proposition is taken for those things which are contingently such-and-such, then the proposition is converted into the same type of *de contingenti* proposition, where the subject of the consequent is taken for what is contingently such-and-such. Hence, this is valid: 'Some man is contingently running; therefore some running thing is contingently a man'—as long as the subject of each proposition is taken for that which is contingently such-and-such. For then the consequent has this sense: 'Something which is contingently running is contingently a man'. The conversion is valid, since the opposite of the consequent is incompatible with the antecedent, namely, this is not compatible with the antecedent: 'Nothing which is contingently running is contingently a man'. For if 'Something which is contingently a man is contingently running' is true, then let that thing be A. In that case both of the following are true: 'A is contingently a man' and 'A is contingently running'. From these propositions I argue as follows: '*A* is contingently a man; *A* is contingently running; therefore something which is contingently running is contingently a man'. This conclusion is the contradictory of the proposition noted above. Therefore, that proposition cannot stand. And so this clearly follows: 'Something which is contingently a man is contingently running; therefore something which is contingently running is contingently a man'. And so this consequence is valid: 'Some man is contingently running; therefore some running thing is contingently a man'—as long as the subject of each proposition is taken for that which is contingently such-and-such.

Now someone might object that if this were so, then the following would be valid: 'God contingently creates; therefore something which creates is contingently God'. For this follows: '*A* is contingently God; *A* contingently creates; therefore something which contingently creates is contingently God'—just as it was argued in the above example.

It should be replied that this last syllogism is valid, but that it still does not prove the conversion in question. The reason is that the proposition 'God contingently creates' does not yield the propositions '*A* is contingently God' and '*A* contingently creates'. For these two propositions are not required for the truth of the proposition in question in the way that two such propositions are required for the truth of 'Some man is contingently running', when the subject is taken for those things which are contingently men. Therefore, the one conversion is proved by the one expository syllogism and yet the other conversion is not proved by the other syllogism. Hence, if the subject of a *de contingenti* proposition is a demonstrative pronoun or a proper name, then the proposition is not converted into the same type of *de contingenti* proposition. Nor can its subject be taken in that way, namely, for what is contingently such-and-such.

It should be noted, however, that the above distinction with respect to *de contingenti, de possibili,* past-tense and future-tense propositions should be understood in this way: either the subject is taken for what is such-and-such, etc., or it is asserted that it is taken for what is such-and-such or for what is contingently such-and-such or for what was such-and-such, etc. Hence, if nothing is white, then in the proposition 'A white thing is possibly a man' the subject cannot be taken for what is white, since nothing is white. But it can still be asserted that it is taken for what is white. Therefore, if nothing is white, then the proposition is false, since something false is asserted by means of it. For by means of that proposition it is asserted, in the sense in question, that something is white, even though nothing is white.

28: On the Conversion of *de contingenti* Propositions through Opposite Qualities

Next we will look into the conversion of *de contingenti* propositions through opposite qualities. It should be noted that every proposition, which contains the mode of contingency with respect to truth and falsity, is converted through opposite qualities if it is taken in the sense of division. That is, an affirmative proposition is converted into a negative proposition, and vice versa. For example, this follows: '*B* is contingently *A*; therefore *B* is contingently not *A*'. Likewise, this follows: 'Every man contingently runs; therefore every man contingently does not run'.

It should be noted that when a proposition, which contains the mode of contingency with respect to truth and falsity, is converted through opposite qualities, then in both propositions the mode should be affirmed and not denied. Therefore, this does not follow: 'Every man contingently runs; therefore no man contingently runs'. Nor does this follow: 'No man contingently runs; therefore every man contingently runs'. Rather this follows: 'Every man contingently runs; therefore every man contingently does not run'. Similarly, this follows: 'Every man contingently does not run; therefore every man contingently runs'.

The conversion just mentioned is obvious. For this follows formally: 'A man contingently runs; therefore a man possibly runs'.

Likewise, this follows: 'Every man contingently runs; therefore it is not necessary that every man run'—from which this follows: 'Some man possibly does not run'. But then from the two propositions 'Some man possibly does not run' and 'He possibly runs' it follows that some man contingently does not run. Therefore, this last proposition follows from the first one alluded to above in accord with the rule: 'Whatever follows from the consequent follows from the antecedent'. This rule is always true.

Now for the sake of certain perverse people it should be noted that whenever I use a proposition like 'A man contingently runs' or 'A man contingently does not run' I mean the following: 'It is contingent that a man runs' and 'It is contingent that a man does not run'.[1] I mention this lest someone impudently argue against me by claiming that the following is valid: 'A man contingently runs; therefore a man runs'.

Thus, it is manifestly clear how such a *de contingenti* proposition in the sense of division or an equivalent proposition is converted through opposite qualities. But such a proposition in the sense of composition is not converted through opposite qualities. For in such a case one would be arguing in accord with one of the following rules: 'One of two contrary propositions is contingent; therefore the other is contingent', or 'One of two subcontrary propositions is contingent; therefore the other is contingent'. But these rules are false. And thus this does not follow: 'That no existing being is a man is contingent; therefore that every existing being is a man is contingent'. Nor does this follow: 'That every existing being is God is contingent; therefore that no existing being is God is contingent'. Similarly, this does not follow: 'That some existing being is a man is contingent; therefore that some existing being is not a man is contingent'. For in all these examples the antecedent is true and the consequent false, if all the propositions are taken in the sense of composition.

29: On the Conversion of Modal Propositions which are not Conceded by Everyone to be Modal

Now that we have treated the conversion of those modal propositions which are conceded by everyone to be modal, what remains is to talk about the conversion of those modal propositions which are not conceded by everyone to be modal—even though they are really modal propositions, as was claimed above.[1] Since such propositions are, as it were, innumerable, I do not intend to treat all of them specifically. Rather, I want to give some general rules.

Now it should be noted that when a given modal term can be truly predicated of one of two interchangeable propositions without being truly predicated of the other, then such a modal proposition, taken in the sense of composition, or an equivalent of such a proposition is not converted simply—even though its non-modal counterpart might be converted simply. Again, if such a mode can be truly predicated of the antecedent without being truly predicated of the consequent, then such a proposition, taken in the sense of composition, or one equivalent to it is converted neither simply nor accidentally—even though its non-modal counterpart might be converted accidentally. On the other hand, if such a mode cannot belong to one of two interchangeable propositions unless it agrees with the other, then such a proposition in the sense of composition or one equivalent to it is always converted simply if its non-modal counterpart is converted simply—in short, it is converted in the same way that its non-modal counterpart is converted. Again, if such a mode cannot belong to the antecedent unless it belongs to the consequent, then the proposition in question is converted accidentally in the same way that its non-modal counterpart is.

From this rule it is clear that the following conversion is valid: 'That a man is running is true; therefore that a running thing is a man is true'. The same holds for this one: 'That every man is running is true; therefore that some running thing is a man is true'. For the first conversion holds in accord with this rule: 'If one of two interchangeable propositions is true, the other is true'; and the second conversion holds in accord with this rule: 'If the antecedent is true, the consequent is true'. Both of these rules are true. Similarly, the following conversion is valid: 'That no man is running is false; therefore that no running thing is a man is false'. For it holds in accord with the rule 'If one of two interchangeable propositions is false, the other is false'. But the following conversion is not valid: 'That every man is running is false; therefore that some running thing is a man is false'. For it proceeds in accord with the rule 'If the antecedent is false, the consequent is false'—which is false.

From these remarks it is clear that when a universal affirmative proposition of this type is not converted accidentally, the corresponding particular affirmative and particular negative are frequently converted accidentally in accord with the rule 'The consequent is false, therefore the antecedent is false'.

From what has been said it is also clear that a consequence such as the following is not valid: 'That no man is running is known; therefore that no running thing is a man is known'. For the following rule is not always true: 'One of two interchangeable propositions is known; therefore the other is known'. For one of two interchangeable propositions can be known, even though the other is not known—in fact, even though the other is not thought. Similarly, consequences such as the following are not valid: 'That every man is an animal is *per se* in the first mode; therefore that some animal is a man is *per se* in the first mode'. For this does not follow: 'The antecedent is *per se* in the first mode; therefore the consequent is *per se* in the first mode'. Nor is this valid: 'That every man is risible is *per se* in the second mode; therefore that some risible thing is a man is *per se* in the second mode'. And so in such cases one must always carefully examine propositions of the following forms: 'One of two interchangeable propositions is such-and-such; therefore the other is such-and-such'; and 'The antecedent is such-and-such; therefore the consequent is such-and-such'. By means of these propositions one can determine which propositions in the sense of composition and their equivalents are converted as their non-modal counterparts are, and which such propositions are not so converted.

On the other hand, with respect to the conversion of such propositions in the sense of division and their equivalents, it should be noted that they are always or frequently converted just like some of the modal propositions which have already been treated specifically. For example, 'A white thing is known to be a man' is not converted into 'therefore some man is known to be white'. For assume that I know that Socrates is a man, and assume that he is white but that I do not know it. In that case 'Some white thing is known by me to be a man' is true. For the following expository syllogism is valid: 'Socrates is known by me to be a man; Socrates is white; therefore some white thing is known by me to be a man'. And yet 'Some man is known by me to be white' is false—let it be assumed that I do not know that some man is white. Therefore, the first proposition is converted into 'therefore something which is known to be a man is white'. Similarly, this conversion is not valid: 'God, who is three and one, is known by philosophers to be immortal; therefore something which is immortal is known by philosophers to be the God who is three and one'. Rather, the antecedent is converted into 'therefore something which is known by philosophers to be immortal is the God who is three and one'.

Now someone might claim that 'God, who is three and one, is known by philosophers to be immortal' is false. For it is impossible for philosophers to know the following proposition naturally: 'God, who is three and one, is immortal'. Therefore, this is not true: 'God, who is three and one, is known by philosophers to be immortal'.

It should be replied that 'God, who is three and one, is known by philosophers to be immortal' is true—and yet they do not know that proposition. Indeed, they would deny it and claim that it is false. For they would claim that it implies something false, namely, that God is three and one. Nevertheless, that proposition is true, since by means of it no more is asserted than that, with respect to that being which is three and one—although it is not known that he is three and one—it is known by philosophers that he is immortal. Hence, by means of 'God, who is three and one, is known by philosophers to be immortal' nothing is asserted except this conjunctive proposition: 'God is three and one, and with respect to him it is known by philosophers that he is immortal'. And this is true, since both parts of this conjunctive proposition are true.

Similarly, that the consequent is true is clear. That is, the proposition 'Something which is known by philosophers to be immortal is the God who is three and one' is true. For God, who is known by philosophers to be immortal, is the God who is three and one. But if this is so, then I argue by means of an expository syllogism: 'God is the God who is three and one; God is something which is known by philosophers to be immortal; therefore something which is known by philosophers to be immortal is the God who is three and one'. The premises are true; therefore the conclusion is true. Further, this also follows: 'God is known by philosophers to be immortal; God is three and one; therefore the God who is three and one is known by philosophers to be immortal'. Thus, in this way both the truth of the proposition under discussion and the validity of the conversion are patently obvious.

Likewise, 'An intellect is known to be an intellective soul' is not converted into 'therefore an intellective soul is known to be an intellect'. Rather, it is converted into 'therefore something which is known to be an intellective soul is an intellect'.

Similarly, the proposition 'Someone who is coming is known by you to be Coriscus' is not converted into 'therefore Coriscus is known by you to be coming'. Rather, it is converted into 'Someone who is known by you to be Coriscus is coming'.

Similarly, 'Some man is *per se* an animal' is not converted into 'Some animal is *per se* a man'. Rather, it is converted into 'Something which is *per se* an animal is a man'. Again, the proposition 'A white thing is *per se* building' is converted into 'Something which is *per se* building is white'.

Again, the proposition 'God is *per accidens* a being which creates' is not converted into 'Something which creates is *per accidens* God'. Rather, it is converted into 'Something which is *per accidens* a being which creates is God'.

And just as it has been said with respect to these propositions, so it should be said with respect to the others that such a proposition is converted just like a *de necessario* proposition or a *de possibili* or a *de impossibili* or a *de contingenti* proposition.

And perhaps the reason why the Philosopher did not devote a special tract to such propositions and their propoerties and conversions was this: from what should be known about *de necessario, de contingenti, de possibili,* and *de impossibili* propositions—and a few others—one can easily discern what should be said of other modal propositions and their properties. Still, ignorance of these things, just like ignorance of other propositions and their properties, leads many modern thinkers to make mistakes and to be caught up in confusions in theology and in the other particular sciences, both speculative and practical.

Moreover, in order to clarify the conversion of all modal propositions, it should be noted that modal propositions in the sense of division and their equivalents are commonly converted just like non-modal propositions in which some adverbial determination is added to the verb. For in these latter propositions the adverbial determination or its equivalent should not be added to the composition in the same way in the proposition to be converted and in the proposition into which it is converted. Rather, in the consequent such a determination should be placed only in the subject position, as has been pointed out.[2] In the same way, in the consequent the mode should be placed totally in the subject position, as has been illustrated by the examples.

30: On Hypothetical Propositions and their Properties

Now that categorical propositions and their properties have been briefly treated, a few things should be said about hypothetical propositions and their properties.

It should first be noted that a proposition is called hypothetical when it is composed of two or more categorical propositions joined by some adverb or conjunction. Not only is it possible for a single adverb or a single conjunction to join the categorical propositions and form a hypothetical proposition, but it is also possible for several conjunctions and adverbs to do so—and sometimes one or more adverbs plus one or more conjunctions can combine to form a hypothetical proposition. Hence, the following is a hypothetical proposition: 'Socrates is running or Plato or John'. And so is this: 'If a man is running an animal is running, and Plato is debating'. Accordingly, some hypothetical propositions are composed of more than two categorical propositions.

However, it could simply be stipulated that a proposition is not hypothetical when it contains both an adverb and a conjunction—or two conjunctions—which normally form hypothetical propositions of different types. And the same can be said about adverbs.

Second, it should be noted that hypothetical propositions are assigned to five species, namely, conditional, conjunctive, disjunctive, causal, and temporal.

But it seems that there are other hypothetical propositions besides these. For every proposition, true or false, which is composed of two categoricals, is a hypothetical proposition. But there are many propositions of this sort besides those named above. Therefore, etc. The major premise is sufficiently obvious. The minor is clear, for the following proposition is of the requisite form: 'Socrates is running where Plato is debating'.

However, it should be noted that although there are many hypothetical propositions besides the ones named above, still there are many which seem to be different from those named above but which should be reduced to the latter. For example, 'Socrates philosophizes, lest he be ignorant' is a causal proposition. For it is equivalent to this: 'Since Socrates does not want to be ignorant, Socrates philosophizes'. And so it is with many other propositions.

31: On the Conditional Proposition

Next we will look at these propositions specifically. However, since a conditional proposition is equivalent to a consequence—so that a conditional proposition is true when the antecedent entails the consequent and not otherwise—this discussion will be deferred until the tract on consequences.[1]

Nevertheless, it should be noted that a hypothetical proposition is called conditional when it is composed of two categoricals joined by the conjunction 'if' or some equivalent. For this reason it should be said that this is a conditional proposition: 'Socrates does not teach unless he is an instructor'. For it is equivalent to: 'If Socrates is not an instructor, Socrates does not teach'. And it is always the case that when two propositions are joined by some conjunction and the whole is equivalent to a conditional proposition, then the proposition in question will be called hypothetical and conditional.

It should also be noted that neither the truth of the antecedent nor the truth of the consequent is required for the truth of a conditional proposition. In fact, sometimes a conditional proposition is necessary even though each of its parts is impossible, as in 'If Socrates is a donkey, Socrates is able to bray'.

32: On the Conjunctive Proposition

A conjunctive proposition is one which is composed of two or more categoricals joined by the conjunction 'and' or by some particle equivalent to such a conjunction. For example, this is a conjunctive proposition: 'Socrates is running and Plato is debating'. Similarly, this proposition is conjunctive: 'Socrates is neither white nor black'; and so is this: 'Socrates is both white and hot'. For the first is equivalent to 'Socrates is not white and Socrates is not black', while the second is equivalent to 'Socrates is white and Socrates is hot'.

Now for the truth of a conjunctive proposition it is required that both parts be true. Therefore, if any part of a conjunctive proposition is false, then the conjunctive proposition itself is false. Similarly, in order for a conjunctive proposition to be necessary it is required that each of its parts be necessary. And for it to be possible it is required that both parts be possible. However, in order for it to be impossible it is not required that both parts be impossible. For this is impossible: 'Socrates is sitting and not sitting'. And yet each part is possible. Rather, for a conjunctive proposition to be impossible it is required either that one part be impossible or that one part be incompossible with the other. For example, 'Socrates is white and Socrates is a donkey' is impossible, since 'Socrates is a donkey' is impossible. And 'Socrates is sitting and not sitting' is impossible, since the two parts are not compossible.

It should also be noted that the contradictory opposite of a conjunctive proposition is a disjunctive proposition composed of the contradictories of the parts of the conjunctive. Thus, the same thing that is necessary and sufficient for the truth of the opposite of a conjunctive proposition is necessary and sufficient for the truth of a disjunctive proposition. Hence, the following are not contradictories: 'Socrates is white and Plato is black' and 'Socrates is not white and Plato is not black'. Rather, the contradictory of the first conjunctive is this: 'Socrates is not white or Plato is not black'.

Now it is necessary to note that there is always a valid consequence from a conjunctive proposition to either of its parts. For example, this follows: 'Socrates is not running and Plato is debating, therefore Plato is debating'. But the converse commits a fallacy of consequent. Still, it should be noted that sometimes, in virtue of the material element, there can be a valid consequence from one part of a conjunctive proposition to that conjunctive. For example, if one part of a conjunctive proposition entails the other part, then there is a valid consequence from that part to the whole conjunctive proposition.

A disjunctive proposition is one composed of two or more categoricals joined by the conjunction 'or' or by some equivalent. For example, this is a disjunctive proposition: 'You are a man or a donkey'. Likewise, this is a disjunctive proposition: 'You are a man or Socrates is debating'.

Now for the truth of a disjunctive proposition it is required that some part be true. And this should be understood to apply when the propositions are present-tense and not future-tense or equivalent to future-tense propositions. This is what the Philosopher would say.[1] However, the fact of the matter is that for the truth of a disjunctive proposition it is required that one of the parts be true. For, in fact, a future-tense proposition is either true or false, though not in a deterministic way.

But in order for a disjunctive proposition to be necessary it is not required that one of its parts be necessary. For example, in order for 'Socrates is sitting or not sitting' to be necessary, it is not required that either part be necessary. Rather, for a disjunctive proposition to be necessary it is required either that one part be necessary or that the parts contradict each other—or that they be equivalent to contradictories or that they be interchangeable with contradictories. Hence, this is necessary: 'Socrates is running or God exists'. For the second part is necessary. On the other hand, 'God creates or does not create' is necessary because the parts contradict each other.

Now for a disjunctive proposition to be possible it is sufficient that one of its parts be possible. But for a disjunctive proposition to be impossible it is required that both parts be impossible.

It should also be noted that the contradictory opposite of a disjunctive proposition is a conjunctive proposition composed of the contradictories of the parts of that disjunctive proposition. Thus, the same thing that is necessary and sufficient for the truth of the opposite of a disjunctive proposition is necessary and sufficient for the truth of a conjunctive proposition.

It should also be noted that it is valid to argue from one part of a disjunctive to the whole disjunctive proposition. But the converse commits a fallacy of consequent—except that sometimes there is some special reason that blocks the fallacy of consequent.

Similarly, it is valid to argue from a disjunctive proposition along with the negation of one of its parts to the other part. For example, this follows: 'Socrates is a man or a donkey; Socrates is not a donkey; therefore Socrates is a man'.

34: On the Causal Proposition

A causal proposition is one which is composed of two or more categoricals joined by the conjunction 'since' or by some equivalent. Hence, this is a causal proposition: 'Since Socrates is a man, Socrates is an animal'. This is also a causal proposition: 'Socrates is working, in order that he might be healthy'. For it is equivalent to 'Socrates is working, since he wants to be healthy'. Likewise, this is a causal proposition: 'Socrates takes a walk after dinner, lest he become ill'. For it is equivalent to 'Since Socrates does not want to become ill, he takes a walk after dinner'. Similarly, this is a causal proposition: 'Socrates becomes warm insofar as he moves'. For it is equivalent to: 'Since Socrates moves, he becomes warm'.

Now for the truth of a causal proposition it is required that each part be true and, besides this, that the antecedent be the cause of the consequent. Therefore, the proposition 'Socrates is white, since Plato is white' is not true. For although each of its parts is true, still the following is not true: 'Socrates is white in virtue of the fact that Plato is white'. Therefore, the proposition in question is false.

It should be noted that 'cause' is being used here in a loose sense and not in the strict sense. For it is not required for the truth of a causal proposition that the one proposition be the cause of the other proposition's coming into being. Rather, it is sufficient that it express a cause which is required for the other proposition's being true, as in 'The wood becomes hot, since fire is present in it'. For by means of that antecedent, 'Fire is present in it', there is expressed a cause without which 'The wood becomes hot' would not be true. Therefore, the causal proposition in question is true. Or else it is required that the one proposition be prior to the other in such a way that the predicate of the antecedent is predicated of its subject prior to the predicate of its subject. Accordingly, this can be true: 'An isosceles has three etc., since a triangle has three, etc.'.

It should be noted that 'cause' is being used loosely here for a *per se* cause or a *per accidens* cause, or for a voluntary cause or a natural cause.

From these remarks it is clear that all propositions such as the following are false: 'A donkey is risible, since it is a man', 'Every man sins, since he has a free will', etc.

Hence, in order for a causal proposition to be necessary it is required that both parts be necessary. But for a causal proposition to be impossible neither the impossibility nor the falsity of one of the parts is required. Rather, it is sufficient that the antecedent cannot be the cause of the consequent—taking 'cause' in the way noted above.

And it should be noted that 'antecedent' here does not designate what comes first in word order. Rather, the antecedent is the proposition which immediately follows the conjunction 'since'.

Similarly, in order for a causal proposition to be possible it is required that each part be possible. But this is not sufficient, just as the necessity of each part is not sufficient in order for such a proposition to be necessary.

From what has been said it is clear that there is a valid consequence from a causal proposition to one of its parts—but not conversely. Similarly, there is a valid consequence from a causal proposition to a conjunctive proposition—but not conversely. Hence, this is valid: 'Every man sins, since he has a free will; therefore every man sins and every man has a free will'. But the converse is not valid.

A temporal proposition is one which is composed of two or more categoricals joined by some adverb of time. For example, this is a temporal proposition: 'Socrates is running while Plato is debating'. And so are these: 'Socrates was white when Plato was black' and 'Socrates was white when Plato was not running'.

Now for the truth of a temporal proposition it is required that both parts be true for the same time or for different times. Thus, there are some adverbs which convey that the propositions which they join are true for the same time, and others which convey that they are true for different times. Hence, for the truth of 'God acts when a creature acts' it is required that both of the parts be true and at the same time. Similarly, for the truth of 'The apostles were preaching while Christ preached' it is required that both parts be true and that they were true at the same time, if they were formed. But for the truth of 'Paul was converted after Christ had suffered' it is required that the propositions were true for different times. Likewise, for the truth of 'Christ preached before he suffered' it is required that both parts were true for different times.

Still, it should be noted that in order for a temporal proposition to be true, it is not required that the parts were never true for the same time or that they were never true for different times. Rather, it is required that they were sometime true for the same time or for different times. Hence, the following two propositions are compatible: 'The apostles preached while Christ preached' and 'The apostles preached after Christ preached'.

Likewise, in order for a temporal proposition to be necessary it is required that each part be necessary. Hence, no proposition such as the following is necessary: 'Wood becomes warm when fire is brought near it', 'A creature is created when God creates', 'A donkey is risible when it is a man'. Now if such propositions are found in some author and he asserts that they are necessary, then they should be glossed. For the author is not speaking literally. Rather, he is taking a temporal proposition as a conditional, so that a proposition like 'A creature is created when God creates' means this: 'If God creates, a creature is created'.

Hence, the proposition 'Socrates exists while he exists' or 'Socrates is moving while he is running' is not necessary, but can be false. Nevertheless, some take such temporal propositions as conditional propositions—and those conditional propositions are true.

Similarly, for a temporal proposition to be impossible it is not required that some part be impossible. Rather, it is sufficient that the parts be incompossible. Thus, this is impossible: 'God creates while he does not create'. For the parts are incompossible. However, if the temporal proposition in question signifies that the propositions are true for different times, then in order for it to be impossible it is sufficient that the parts be interchangeable—so that one cannot be true without the other being true, and vice versa.

From what has been said it is clear what is required in order for a temporal proposition to be possible or contingent. It is also clear from what has been said that there is a valid consequence from a temporal proposition to one of its parts—but not conversely. Similarly, a conjunctive proposition follows from a temporal proposition—but not conversely. For this does not follow: 'Adam existed and Noah existed; therefore Adam existed when Noah existed'. Nor does this follow: 'Jacob existed and Esau existed; therefore Jacob existed when Esau existed'.

36: On the Local Proposition

A hypothetical proposition can be called a local proposition when it is composed of two or more categoricals joined by an adverb of place or some equivalent—as in 'An accident is where its subject is' and 'Christ suffered where he preached'.

For the truth of such a hypothetical proposition it is required that each part be true for the same place or for different places. In this regard it differs from a temporal proposition. For in order for a temporal proposition to be true it is required that both parts be true either for the same time or for different times, while in order for a local proposition to be true it is required that both parts be true for the same place or for different places.[1]

However it should be noted that 'time' is being taken loosely for time properly speaking and for eternity or the negation of time. It has been explained in other places how this should be understood, namely, in the commentaries on *Physics* IV and *Sentences* II.[2] I mention this because of propositions like 'God existed before the world existed', etc.

From what has been said about the temporal proposition it is clear what should be said about the local proposition. For everything—or almost everything—said of the temporal proposition can, *mutatis mutandis,* be said of the local proposition.

Also, from what has been said about the hypothetical propositions specified above one can easily ascertain what should be said about other hypothetical propositions, if there are any others. Perhaps the following propositions belong to this group: 'Whiteness is in Socrates, in whom there is no blackness', 'God exists, from whom all things are', and so on. However, such propositions can be reduced to a conjunctive proposition.

37: On Propositions in which Conjunctions or Adverbs are Placed between Two Terms

To what has already been said it should be added that when one of the conjunctions or adverbs mentioned above is placed between two terms—so that the categorical propositions are not expressed completely—then the proposition in question must be distinguished with respect to composition and division. For it can be either a categorical proposition or a hypothetical proposition. Or else it must be distinguished as amphibolous, since it can be either categorical or hypothetical. And perhaps this latter distinction is clearer and more proper. Still, whether such a proposition is distinguished with respect to composition and division or with respect to amphiboly, the point remains the same. Hence, when the conjunction 'or' occurs in such a proposition, the proposition must be distinguished, since it can be either a disjunctive proposition or a proposition with a disjunctive extreme. For example, the proposition 'Every man will be saved or damned' should be distinguished, since either it can be a disjunctive proposition, in which case it is equivalent to 'Every man will be saved or every man will be damned'—which is false; or it can be a proposition with a disjunctive extreme, in which case it is equivalent to 'The whole phrase "will be saved or damned" is truly predicated of everything contained under "man"'—this is true and so the original is true.

It should be noted that when such a proposition is singular, then the disjunctive proposition and the proposition with a disjunctive predicate are equipollent. But this is not the case when the proposition in question is universal, as is clear from the above example.

Similarly, when the conjunction 'and' occurs in such a proposition, that proposition has to be distinguished. For it can be either a conjunctive proposition or a proposition with a conjunctive extreme. For example, the proposition 'Three and two are five' has to be distinguished. If it is a proposition with a conjunctive subject, it is true. If it is a conjunctive proposition, it is false.

The same holds for such a proposition when it contains the conjunction 'if'. Such a proposition must be distinguished, since it can be either a conditional proposition or a proposition with a conditional extreme. For example, the proposition 'Everything possible, if it is necessary, is true' must be distinguished. For it can be a conditional proposition, in which case it has this sense: 'If everything possible is necessary, then everything possible is true'—which is true. If it is a proposition with a conditional subject, then it is equivalent to this: 'The predicate "true" is truly predicated of everything of which the whole phrase "possible, if it is necessary" is truly predicated'. And this is false. For the whole phrase 'possible, if it is necessary' is truly predicated of the proposition 'A donkey is a man'. For this is true: 'That you are a donkey is possible, if it is necessary'—whether it is a conditional proposition or a proposition with a conditional subject. And yet 'That you are a donkey is true' is not true.

The same holds for a causal conjunction. A proposition in which it occurs must be distinguished. For it can be either a causal proposition or a proposition with a causal extreme. For example, the proposition 'Every man is receptive to God since he has a rational soul' must be distinguished, since it can be either a causal proposition or a proposition with a causal predicate. However, these two senses are always or frequently interchangeable.

Similarly, when a temporal adverb occurs, the proposition in question must be distinguished. For it can be either a temporal proposition or a proposition with a temporal extreme. For example, the proposition 'Everyone damned, while he was on earth, sinned' must be distinguished, since it can be either a temporal proposition or a proposition with a temporal predicate. If it is a temporal proposition, then it is equivalent to 'While everyone damned was on earth, everyone damned sinned'—which is false, since the two parts have never been true at the same time. If it is a proposition with a temporal extreme, then it is equivalent to this: 'The whole phrase "sinned while he was on earth" is truly predicated of everyone who is damned'. And this is true, since each of its singulars is true.

The same thing holds for an adverb of place. This is clear from the proposition 'Every man was running where he was debating'. For assume that every man was running in the same place in which he was debating, but that different men were in different places. Then it is obvious that the proposition in question is true if it is a proposition with a local predicate and false if it is a local proposition.

It should also be noted that the distinction in question is not only applicable in the cases just mentioned. Rather, exactly the same distinction can also be posited when the pronouns 'who' and 'which' are placed between two terms. For example, the distinction applies to the proposition 'Every man, who is white, is running'. For in the sense of division it is equivalent to a conjunctive proposition, namely, 'Every man is running and he is white'. In the sense of composition it is asserted that the predicate 'running' is truly predicated of everything of which the whole phrase 'man who is white' is truly predicated.

These remarks about propositions should be sufficient for the time being.

NOTES

1: On the Classification of Propositions in General

1. A *de inesse* proposition is in general a proposition without a mode or modal term. However, this characterization is somewhat inexact, since in order for a proposition to be modal, the mode in question must, as Ockham indicates below, be asserted to be true of a whole proposition. In *Summa Logicae* (hereafter: *SL*) III–1, chap. 41, Ockham gives the following more precise characterization of a modal proposition: ". . . it should be noted that not every proposition which contains such a mode is a modal proposition. Rather, in order for a proposition to be modal two things are required. First, it is required that the mode not be just a part of one extreme. For this reason propositions such as the following are not modal: 'That which is known by me to be an animal is white', 'That which *per se* builds is hot', 'That which is possibly running is a man who is sitting', 'Something which is possibly impossible is true'. The other requirement is this: in virtue of the form of the proposition the mode is asserted to belong to some non-modal (*de inesse*) proposition, although it is not always asserted that it belongs to the non-modal counterpart of the modal proposition in question. For example, by means of 'A white thing is possibly black' it is asserted that some proposition is possible in which 'black' is predicated of something which is white—although it is not asserted that the proposition 'A white thing is black' is possible." Thus, a *de inesse* proposition is one which is not modal according to the above account of modal propositions. Literally, such a proposition is one in which a predicate other than a mode is asserted to be (or not to be) in a subject which is other than a proposition—in the sense of 'be in' or 'inhere in' explicated by Ockham in *SL* I, chap. 32. (The first part of the *Summa Logicae* is found in English translation in Michael J. Loux, trans., *Ockham's Theory of Terms: Part I of the Summa Logicae* (Notre Dame, Ind., 1974).) Another common translation of the Latin 'de inesse' is 'assertoric'.

2. Aristotle, *Prior Analytics* I, chaps, 2–3, 25a1–25b25.

3. See below, chap. 29.

4. See *SL* I, chap. 5. A concrete term in the first mode is normally a term that primarily signifies a subject in which there inheres the accident or form primarily signified by that term's abstract counterpart. Thus, on Ockham's view 'white' is a concrete term in the first mode, since it signifies white things, i.e. things in which whiteness inheres. However, this relation may be reversed. That is, a concrete term in the first mode may primarily signify an accident which inheres in the thing which is primarily signified by that term's abstract counterpart. Ockham gives the term 'fiery' as an example of this sort of concrete term in the first mode. For 'fiery' signifies an accident of that which is signified by its abstract counterpart, namely, 'fire'.

5. The Latin term 'isti', translated here by 'they', is a demonstrative pronoun in this context. Like 'they', it can also be used as a relative pronoun, as in (3) below.

6. Perhaps the best English translation of this sentence is 'A man a donkey sees'. But this sentence, unlike its Latin counterpart, is syntactically ambiguous. This ambiguity disappears when the subject and predicate differ in grammatical number, as in 'The men a donkey sees'.

7. An alternate translation of this sentence is 'A donkey is a man's', which preserves the copula found in the Latin but is somewhat awkward.

2: What is Required for the Truth of a Singular Non-Modal Proposition

1. See Ockham, *Scriptum in Librum I Sententiarum: Ordinatio*, dist. II–III, ed. Stephen Brown and Gedeon Gál (St. Bonaventure, N.Y., 1970), dist. II, ques. 6. The book just cited constitutes the second volume of the critical edition of Ockham's theological works. Also, see Ockham, *Expositio in Librum Porphyrii de Praedicalibus*, chap. 1, and Ockham, *Expositio in Librum Praedicamentorum Aristotelis*, chap. 8. Both of these works appear in the second volume of the critical edition of Ockham's philosophical works (St. Bonaventure, N.Y., 1978). The first of these works is edited by Ernest A. Moody and the second by Gedeon Gál.

2. See Ockham, *Scriptum in Librum I Sententiarum: Ordinatio*, dist. II, ques. 1 and 6.

3: What is Required for the Truth of an Indefinite Proposition and of a Particular Proposition

1. The opinion referred to here is the one according to which propositions which have the term 'God' as subject are indefinite rather than singular.

2. Literally '. . . with something which pertains to a sign'. But Ockham frequently uses the term 'signum' ('sign') to refer to quantifiers rather than to signs in general.

4: On Universal Propositions

1. See below, chap. 6.

2. See *SL* I, chap. 69.

3. Ockham apparently has in mind here the work of William of Sherwood, namely, his *Introductiones in Logicam*, the section on appellation, and his *Syncategoremata*, the chapter on the term 'omnis' ('every'). Both of these works have been translated by Norman Kretzmann, the first in *William of Sherwood's Introduction to Logic* (Minneapolis, 1966) and the second in *William of Sherwood's Treatise on Syncategorematic Words* (Minneapolis, 1968).

4. This solution is alluded to by Peter of Spain in his *Summulae Logicales*, tract XII.

5. See *SL* I, chaps. 63 and 72.

6. The reference here is again to William of Sherwood.

7. The case alluded to is one in which the only animals are men.

8. See above, chap. 1.

6: On Universal Propositions in which the Sign Distributes over Integral Parts, e.g. the Sign 'Whole'

1. Although 'whole' will be used here to translate the Latin term 'totus', no single English expression seems to have both the categorematic and syncategorematic functions of 'totus'. 'Whole' captures the former, while 'each part of' captures the latter.

2. In this example and the ones which follow, the Latin sentence containing a syncategorematic use of the term 'totus' will be left untranslated. The English meaning of the sentence in question will in each case be captured by the translation of the sentence which Ockham claims to be equivalent to it.

3. The subjective parts of a given whole are such that the name of the whole (e.g. 'man') is truly predicable of each of them. This is not necessarily the case with integral parts (e.g. feet, hands, etc.). For more on this distinction and reference to some medieval texts in which it is discussed, see Alfred J. Freddoso, "Abailard on Collective Realism," *Journal of Philosophy* 75 (1978), pp. 527–538.

7: On Past-Tense and Future-Tense Propositions

1. See *SL* I, chap. 72. Ockham emphasizes the importance of this point below, in chap. 24. Again, in *SL* III–1, chap. 43, he characterizes this notion in the following way: "The predicate names its form, the subject does not. That is, . . . for the truth of a modal proposition in the sense of division it is required that the expressed mode agree with a proposition in which that predicate—or another signifying exactly the same thing—is predicated of a pronoun referring to that for which the subject supposits. However, it is not required that such a mode agree via predication with a proposition in which that subject—or another signifying exactly the same thing—is the subject with respect to the predicate or with respect to a pronoun referring to that for which the predicate supposits. . . . In short, then, this is the difference between a term occurring in the subject position and a term occurring in the predicate position: if the proposition is modal, then for the truth of such a proposition it is required that such a mode agree with some proposition in which the very same predicate, or some other signifying exactly the same thing—I mention this because of certain trivial objections which can be made against some of the things I previously said—is predicated. But it is not required that such a mode agree with any proposition in which the very same subject—or another signifying exactly the same thing—is the subject." Ockham then notes that similar considerations apply to past-tense and future-tense propositions.

9: What is Required for the Truth of Modal Propositions

1. See note 1, chap. 1. In what follows modal propositions containing the modes 'necessary', 'possible', 'impossible', and 'contingent' will be re-

ferred to, respectively, as *de necessario, de possibili, de impossibili,* and *de contingenti* propositions. Thus, 'A being which creates is necessarily God' is a *de necessario* proposition, even though it is only contingently true. On the other hand, 'God exists' is necessarily true, but it is not a *de necessario* proposition. Thus, the classification of a proposition as non-modal or as a modal proposition of a given type is independent of its being a necessary or possible or impossible contingent proposition.

2. In English the dictum of a proposition is normally formed by prefixing 'that' to the proposition in question. Hence, 'that every man is an animal' is the dictum corresponding to 'Every man is an animal'. However, in some cases the best English translation of a Latin dictum is by means of a phrase equiform with the translation of the corresponding Latin proposition itself. See, e.g., below, note 7, chap. 17.

3. An alternate reading is used here. The text has 'false' rather than 'future' contingent propositions. But the former does not preserve Ockham's point, since no contradiction is engendered by the assertion that all false propositions are false. On the other hand, since at least one future contingent proposition has another future-tense contingent proposition as its contradictory, a contradiction is entailed by the assertion that all future contingent propositions are false.

4. See *SL* III-3, chap. 33.

5. The subordinate clause alluded to here is the dictum. Ockham makes this point in Latin by distinguishing the subject of the indicative verb from the subject of the infinitive.

6. See *SL* III-1, chaps. 30, 51, and 64.

10: On Modal Propositions without a Dictum

1. In *Posterior Analytics* I, chap. 15, 34b 16–17, Aristotle appears to affirm the assertion that a man is necessarily an animal. Ockham himself denies the truth of both 'It is necessary that every man is an animal' and 'Every man is necessarily an animal'. For the dictum of the former was false before God created human beings, even though the conditional 'If a man exists, an animal exists' was true. Moreover, on Ockham's view 'Every man is necessarily an animal' is true only if 'This is an animal' is necessary, no matter which presently existing man is indicated by 'this'. But no such proposition is necessary, since every man only contingently exists and hence is only contingently a man and only contingently an animal. See below, chap. 11 and *SL* III-2, chap. 5.

2. See below, chap. 7.

3. Here an alternate reading is used. The text has ". . . each such proposition is true. . . ." But it is clear that 'necessary' is more appropriate than 'true' in this context.

4. The necessity involved here is the necessity of the past. See footnote 4 of chapter 24 below.

11: On Propositions which, though Categorical in Form, are Equivalent to Hypotheticals

1. See above, chap. 1.

2. See *SL* I, chap. 10.

3. It is not entirely clear what Ockham meant by the qualification which occurs at the end of this sentence. Perhaps it has something to do with the case of the connotative term 'quantity' which is discussed at the end of this paragraph.

4. See *SL* I, chap. 44.

5. See *SL* II, chap. 4.

12: On Propositions in which Negative, Privative, and Infinite Terms Occur

1. The second part of this conjunctive proposition does not imply that any donkeys exist, since it is a negative proposition. See above, chap. 3.

2. Aristotle, *Topics* VI, chap. 6, 143b 15–16. See *SL* III-3, chap. 9, for more on this point.

14: On Affirmative Propositions in which There Occur Privative Terms which are not Equivalent to Infinite Terms

1. Anselm, *De Casu Diaboli*, chap. 11. This work is found in English translation in Jasper Hopkins and Herbert Richardson, trans., *Anselm of Canterbury*, vol. II (Toronto, 1976), pp. 127–177.

2. The 'other' terms referred to here are positive terms, e.g. 'man', 'animal', 'white', etc., which might occur in the nominal definition of a figment term.

3. Taking as paradigmatic the exponential analysis given in chapter 12 for the proposition 'A donkey is a non-man', it appears that the second exponent of 'A chimera is a non-being' should be 'That thing is not a being' rather than the affirmative proposition 'That thing is a non-being'.

15: On Categorical Propositions which Contain the Pronoun 'Who'

1. See *SL* III-4, chap. 7. The relation in question is not personal when the antecedent (or relative) pertains to signs while its counterpart pertains to things which are not signs. For example, if 'A white man is a man and it differs conceptually from man' is to be true, then, according to Ockham, 'white man' in the first conjunct supposits personally, while 'it' in the second conjunct refers back to 'white man' taken materially or simply. For the second conjunct is equivalent to 'The term "white man" is distinct from the term "man"'.

16: On Reduplicative Propositions

1. According to the editors of the critical edition, a reader of one of the manuscripts suggested in a marginal note that Ockham denied the truth of the conditional proposition in question because by the power of God a certain man, namely, Christ, can exist without a color (in the Eucharist).

2. According to the physical theory which Ockham has in mind here, whiteness is a color which dilates or extends one's vision, whereas blackness is a color which contracts or constricts vision.

17: On Exclusive Propositions

1. See *SL* I, chaps. 44–45, and *Expositio in Librum Praedicamentorum Aristotelis,* chap. 10.

2. Here 'intrinsic' has been used instead of 'extrinsic', which appears in the text, since the former seems to accord better with the point Ockham is making. In one manuscript 'exclude' is changed to 'include'. But this does not help, since in that case terms designating formally inhering accidents would be excluded—just the opposite of what Ockham intends.

3. This should be taken to mean that what is asserted is that there is some man who is white and such that no accident distinct from whiteness is truly predicable of him.

4. See *SL* I, chap. 70.

5. The editors of the critical edition note that this dubious sounding inference is valid on the assumption that there is only one accident. They also note that one of the transcribers wrote in the margin of his manuscript that 'This does not follow' would have been more correct than 'This follows'.

6. See below, chaps. 21–29.

7. This translation is somewhat awkward. However, it has the advantage of preserving the ambiguity which Ockham is discussing. This is one case in which the dictum of a proposition is best rendered in English without the use of the term 'that'.

8. When the parts of the dictum are disconnected, then the modal proposition in question is being taken in the sense of division. When the parts are connected, then the proposition is being taken in the sense of composition.

9. The proposition in question is being taken in the sense of division and has the following sense: 'Only a white thing is possibly running'. This proposition is false for the reason which Ockham gives below.

19: On Propositions in which the Verbs 'Begin' and 'Cease' Occur

1. See Norman Kretzmann, *William of Sherwood's Treatise on Syncategorematic Terms,* chapter on 'begins' and 'ceases'; and Philotheus Boehner, ed., *Walter Burleigh: De Puritate Artis Logicae, Tractatus Longior* (St. Bonaventure, N.Y., 1955), III, II, chap. 4. Successive entities (*entia successiva*) are those whose parts do not all exist at the same time, e.g. days, years, etc., while enduring entities (*entia permanentia*) are those whose parts all exist at the same time, e.g. animals, human beings, etc.

2. Aristotle, *Physics* IV, chap. 13, 222a 10–12.

3. The Latin sentence here is "Petrus incipit esse talis, qualis Paulus est." Ockham is here contrasting the strict sense of the Latin expressions 'talis . . . qualis' and 'similis'.

4. A designator 'hoc aliquid' is generally a term from the category of substance, or a proper name or demonstrative pronoun referring to an individual substance, e.g. 'man', 'Socrates', 'this (man)'. Such designators signify a thing at all the times at which it exists. A designator 'quale quid', on the other hand, is a descriptive phrase involving a term from one of the accidental categories, e.g. 'this white thing'. Some such designators may signify an individual at some of the times at which it exists and not at others. It seems, moreover, that Ockham would extend the notion of a

designator 'hoc aliquid' to substantival terms from the categories other than substance, e.g. 'number', 'motion', etc. See above, chap. 11.

5. The properties of a thing, i.e. those of its essential characteristics which are not part of its definition in the strict sense (see *SL* III-2, chaps. 32–33), are predicated of it *per se* in the second mode. On the other hand, the parts of a thing's definition (whether these parts are explicit or implicit) are predicated of it *per se* in the first mode. Thus, a man is *per se* in the second mode risible, while he is *per se* in the first mode rational and an animal and sentient, etc. For a more precise characterization of this distinction, see *SL* III-2, chap. 7.

21: On the Conversion of Non-Modal Present-Tense Propositions

1. Aristotle, *Prior Analytics* I, chap. 2, 25a 1–26.
2. Porphyry, *Isagogue,* chapter on the properties of genera and species. An English translation of this work is found in O. F. Owen, ed. and trans., *Aristotle's Works,* vol. II (London, 1902), pp. 609–633.
3. Aristotle, *Categories*, chap. 5, 2b 20–21.

22: On the Conversion of Past-Tense and Future-Tense Non-Modal Propositions

1. See above, chap. 21.
2. The indefinite proposition in question here is proven false by citing the truth of this singular proposition apparently because, as Ockham hints below, the term 'being which creates' supposits in a present-tense non-modal proposition for just one thing, namely, God.
3. Whether it is possible to assign a first and/or last moment of existence to an enduring entity is, of course, a disputed metaphysical question. Aristotle discusses it in *Physics* VIII, chap. 8, 263b 9ff.

24: On the Conversion of *de necessario* Propositions

1. See above, chap. 9.
2. See above, chap. 21.
3. Aristotle, *Prior Analytics* I, chap. 3, 25a 27–36.
4. Once I go to Rome, no one can afterwards bring it about that the proposition 'I have been to Rome' is false. Hence, this proposition, though logically contingent, is in some sense necessary. This type of necessity is sometimes called *per accidens* necessity. But given that 'I have been to Rome' is *per accidens* necessary, its negation, 'I have not been to Rome', is *per accidens* impossible. So before I go to Rome, the proposition 'I have not been to Rome' is true, but after I go to Rome it becomes *per accidens* impossible. But granted this, it is still not clear how this example proves that the conversion under discussion is not valid. For its consequent is false only if there is some true proposition which is necessarily impossible. But 'I have not been to Rome', before I actually go to Rome, is only possibly impossible and not necessarily impossible. It seems clear that the conversion which Ockham has in mind here is: 'Nothing impossible

is possibly true; therefore nothing true is possibly impossible'. But it is hard to see how one can correctly translate the antecedent and consequent that he actually gives—whether they are taken in the sense of composition or the sense of division—in such a way that the resulting inference is equivalent to the one just mentioned.

5. See note 1, chap. 1.

6. See above, chap 7, and *SL* I, chap. 72.

27: On the Conversion of *de contingenti* Propositions

1. See *SL* III-1, chaps. 4 and 16. The major premise of this syllogism may be translated as either 'He should want to capture the warriors' or 'He should want to be captured by the warriors'. The ambiguity in the Latin is syntactic. The minor premise is translated as 'He should want to be victorious'. The conclusion, then, means either 'therefore he who should want to be victorious should want to capture the warriors' or 'therefore he who should want to be victorious should want to be captured by the warriors'. If the major premise is understood in the first way and the conclusion in the second way, then the argument is invalid. Likewise, if the major premise is understood in the second way and the conclusion in the first way, the argument is invalid.

2. 'Pendere', accent on the first syllable, means 'to value or esteem', while 'pendere', accent on the second syllable, means 'to hang'. The syllogism is translated as follows, where the blanks are to be filled by the translation of 'pendere': 'He wants to _____ ; he does not want to _____ ; therefore he who wants to _____ does not want to _____'. If 'pendere' is used in two different senses in the premises but in the same sense in both of its occurrences in the conclusion, then the argument is invalid.

3. The English translations of these two syllogisms express valid arguments. The first is: 'Socrates is white; Socrates is an animal; therefore an animal is white'. The second is: 'This man is healthy; this man is a substance; therefore some substance is healthy'. However, in the Latin there is a disagreement in grammatical gender in each of the conclusions. In the conclusion of the first argument 'animal' (neuter) is matched with 'sanus' (masculine). In the conclusion of the second argument 'substantia' (feminine) is matched with 'sanus' (masculine).

4. For more on the fallacy *petitio principii* see *SL* III-2, chap. 12. The problem here is that it is impossible that someone know the premises and not know the conclusion. So the syllogism is not probative, i.e. does not constitute a proof of the conclusion, since the premises cannot be epistemically prior to the conclusion. This is so even though the syllogism is valid.

5. See *SL* III-1, chap. 4.

6. These reductions are illustrated in *SL* III-1, chap. 11.

28: On the Conversion of *de contingenti* Propositions through Opposite Qualities

1. Ockham here uses 'Contingit . . .' to mark the sense of division, whereas he had earlier used '. . . est contingens' to mark the sense of

composition. This difference is difficult to capture in translation, since both locutions are used with an infinitive plus accusative construction.

29: On the Conversion of Modal Propositions which are not Conceded by Everyone to be Modal

1. See above, chap. 9.
2. See above, chap. 21.

31: On the Conditional Proposition

1. *SL* III–3 constitutes Ockham's treatise on consequence or inference.

33: On the Disjunctive Proposition

1. Aristotle, *De Interpretatione,* chap. 9, 18a28–19b4.

36: On the Local Proposition

1. There is some confusion about what Ockham means here. In some manuscripts "for the same place or for different places" is replaced by "for the same place and not for different places," thus making the contrast between temporal and local propositions more pronounced. The editors of the critical edition claim that if a local proposition is negative, then it is required that each part be true for a different place. But this seems mistaken, since this condition is at best sufficient. For 'It is not the case that Socrates is sleeping where Plato is debating' is also true if either of the parts is false. On the other hand, if one or both of the parts is a negative proposition and the whole proposition is affirmative, then it is still required that each part be true for the same place. For example, in order for 'Socrates is not sleeping where Plato is debating' to be true, 'Socrates is not sleeping' must, it seems, be true for the same place at which Plato is debating.

2. See Ockham, *Expositio in Physicam Aristotelis* IV, and *Scriptum in Libros Sententiarum: Reportatio,* II, ques. 10. Neither of these works is as yet available in a critical edition.

Index

207